Return to Oneness with Shiva

Why I meditate on Hanuman ji

with You Hold the Healing Codes

Who and what you meditate on, you become.

By Ricardo B Serrano, R.Ac.

Return to Oneness with Shiva

Why I meditate on Hanuman ji

Who and what you meditate on, you become.

© Ricardo B Serrano, R.Ac.

ISBN 978-0-9880502-1-1

August 27, 2012

Published by Holisticwebs.com

Disclaimer: The Hanuman Qigong and Hanuman mantras are not intended to replace expert medical care. Consult with your physician or licensed health care practitioner regarding the treatment of any medical condition. The author is not held responsible for any negative effects of the meditation practices.

DEDICATION

This book is dedicated to all the people whose life challenge is battling their monkey-mind (ego) which I believe is the cause of suffering and can be conquered by becoming like Hanuman whose love and devotion to his Sadguru is shown by the application of Hanuman Qigong and Hunaman ji's mantras and self-realization teachings of Kashmir Shaivism contained in this book.

Above Photo: Turbulent, noisy and negative thoughts and emotions of the monkey-mind (ego) within the energy bubble (aura) of a human being.

May you apply the time-honored and tested meditations and healing codes contained in this book for healing, quieting the monkey-mind (ego) and spiritual awakening (*ascension*). With thanks and acknowledgemens to all my meditation and Qigong teachers especially to my Sheng Zhen Gong teacher *Li Junfeng*, Siddha teachers *Swami Lakshmanjoo*, *Baba Muktananda*, and *Bhagawan Sadguru Nityananda*, Baba Hari Dass and especially to *Master Djwhal Khul* and my Arhatic yoga and pranic healing teachers *Master Choa Kok Sui* and *Mang Mike Nator* for their grace, teachings and inspirational contributions to my spiritual awakening (*ascension*) and to the completion of this book. Lastly, with thanks to my Kundalini Yoga teacher Raja Choudhury.

The Shiva in me salutes the Shiva in you. Namaste!

The five books *Return to Oneness with Shiva, Meditation and Qigong Mastery, Return to Oneness with the Tao, Return to Oneness with Spirit*, and *Keys to Healing and Self-Mastery* comprise all together my *Master Pranic Healer* thesis for the *Integral Studies of Inner Sciences*.
– Ricardo B Serrano, R.Ac.

TABLE OF CONTENTS

Preface ... 5

Introduction ... 6

Why I meditate on Hanuman ji ... 7

Hanuman Qigong for integrating the Heart and Spirit ... 9

Why Hanuman is Shown Tearing Open his Own Chest ... 10

The Spiritual Significance of Hanuman and The Enduring Relevance of Hanuman ... 11

Hanuman Quotes from Ramayana ... 12

Lord Hanuman Gayatri ... 13

Hanuman's Birth and Education ... 15

Hanuman as Yogachara, The First to Teach Pranayama and the Inventor of the Surya Namaskar ... 16

Benefits of Monkey Mind Meditation ... 16 Shri Hanuman Chalisa ... 17

How I quiet my mind ... 24 Baba Hanuman ... 25

Epilogue ... 27 How people tame their monkey mind ... 27

Quotations from Siddha Scriptures ... 28 Awakening your Kundalini ... 31

Why a Guru is Necessary ... 32 Ego, Desire and Attachment ... 33

Hanuman, Shri Rama, Sita and Lakshmana Photos ... 34

Shiva and Parvati with Ganesha Photos ... 35

Shiva Lingam and Bhagawan Nityananda with Baba Muktananda Photos ... 35

Nataraj, the Dancing form of Lord Shiva with Shiva Sutras ... 36

Pancha Kosha Meditation ... 37 Talks on Discipline ... 39

The guru is the means, and Talks on Practice ... 40 Pancha Kosha ... 43

Notable Quotations from Meditation Masters ... 44 What is Raja Yoga? ... 47

Invocations for Divine Blessing ... 48 The Five Agreements ... 49

References and Acknowledgements ... 50 *and* Buddha's Four Noble Truths ... 51

You Hold the Healing Codes ... 52 Dedication ... 53

Introduction ... 54 Theory ... 55 Quotes from Vibrational Medicine ... 56

Hologram of Love ... 60 Healing Conscious Mind Encodements ... 62

You Hold the Keys to Healing ... 65 Enlightenment Qigong Forms ... 66

Invocation to the Unified Chakra ... 69 Divine Light Invocation ... 74 Conclusion ... 75

Supplementary Material on Gugu Yoga ... 76 Guru Rinpoche ... 80 Master Choa Kok Sui ... 81

Lady Kuan Yin ... 82 Om Mani Padme Hum ... 83

Gurukripa Yoga ... 85 Shaktipat Meditation ... 86

What is Guru? ... 88 Shiva Sutra 1.1 ... 89 Shiva Sutra 1.12 ... 90

Sananda, the Cosmic Christ and Taoist Immortals ... 91 and Djwhal Khul ... 93

Photos of Ascended Masters ... 94 Shiva Sutra 3.25 ... 95 Shaktipat Initiation and Nityananda Lineage ... 96 Quotes from Kashmir Shaivism ... 98 Cannabis and Acupuncture ...100

A Healer's Oath ... 101 Twelve Steps of Recovery ... 103 8 Limbs of Ashtanga Yoga ...104

Universal Prayer ... 105 Prayer of St. Francis of Assisi ... 106 Meditation on Twin Hearts ... 107

Triangles Work ... 108 Pranic Healing ... 110 Inner Smile ... 111 Epilogue ... 113

Book References ... 116 Mang Mike Nator ... 117 Origin of SUFI-ISIS ... 119

Introduction to Unicorn Meditation ... 122 ISIS Prerequisites ... 124 The Great Invocation ... 125

Death, Dying and Spiritual Liberation ... 127 What is Pranic Healing? ... 129

What is Distance Healing? ... 131 Tonic Herbs and Three Treasures ... 132 Three Dantians ... 133

Qigong is the Pillar of Chinese Medicine ... 136 Hand Mudras ... 139 What is Ascension? ... 140

Shamballa Temple of Love ... 141 Ascended Masters of the Shamballa Temple of Love ... 142

Thyroid connection to healing and ascension ... 143 Thyroid Gland ... 144 Chakras ... 150

Ain Soph Aur and the 12th Sephirah ... 152 Microcosmic Orbit ... 153 Conclusion ... 155

Healing and Returning to Oneness ... 157 Techniques of a Master ... 159 About the Author ... 161

PREFACE

Do people have to suffer greatly making major human mistakes in life decisions creating negative karma in the process such as physical, mental or emotional imbalances, hitting rock bottom from addictions or other self-inflicted diseases, before waking up to the truth or realization of what is most important in life or what they really are looking for or who they really are or where they are going?

The above enlightened philosophical questions need an innovative explanation from an eastern philosophical perspective that will end or lighten most people's suffering rooted especially from the *monkey-mind* or *ego*'s unsatiable worldy attachments and desires for its self-interest and short-lived self-gratification. What is the connection of the subject of Qigong or meditation with these questions? One answer is found through understanding the reason in practicing Hanuman Qigong and meditation in this book where we will realize, know or experience the inner peace and loving blissful sensation of *Self* which liberates us from suffering and frees us from the hold of *ego*'s attachments and desires.

It has also been repeatedly said in the scriptures elaborated by enlightened *Siddha* masters (*gurus*) *Swami Muktananda* and *Swami Lakshmanjoo* and exemplified by *Hanuman ji* that the only hindrance to enlightenment or *Self-realization* is the limited *ego* with its attachments and desires for its self-interest.

What does true love have to do with our path to freedom from suffering? Because blissful love is our very own spiritual nature, and everyone instinctively wants and needs to love and be loved. There are many ways to experience and express romantic and true love. Poets hint of love in their poems. Singers sing of love in their songs. Romance writers romanticize love in their stories. Artists express love and presence of nature through their artwork such as paintings, sculpture or other creative designs. Movie writers get their creativity and energy to write fictional and non-fictional movie creations by connecting with *The All There Is*. Musicians express or evoke love of harmony through their music. Pranic healers heal their clients through the power of universal love passing through them. *Siddha* masters *Baba Muktananda* and *Swami Lakshmanjoo* in this book awaken and share inner love (*bhakti*) through *shaktipat* or spiritual empowerment, *Sadguru Nityananda* devotion and teaching *Siddha* meditation *practices* with five *niyamas* (disciplines) and five *yamas* (moral prescriptions) to their students to quiet the ego-mind. The meditation masters teach that the true source of true love is within our inner hearts which is also the unlimited source of healing, wisdom and inspiration for Qigong meditation masters, musicians, writers, artists, songwriters, philosophers, psychologists, scientists, healers and poets.

Lord Buddha's quotation will shed light on his reason for following his meditation path to freedom and self-realization which have been giving his devotees their own path to salvation from internal suffering which everyone of us shares no matter what station in life anybody is in. Lord Buddha said, *"A life without knowledge is painful."* Old age and death are miserable when one lacks *knowledge* of the *Self*. In fact, without this knowledge, all of life – from one corner to the other, from east to west, from north to south, above and below – is filled with anguish. *Who and what you meditate on, you become*.

With thanks and acknowledgements to Nitin Kumar, author of *The Mystery of Hanuman - Inspiring Tales from Art and Mythology*; Baba Muktananda, author of *Where Are You Going?, Play of Consciousness,* and *the Perfect Relationship*; Swami Chidvilasananda, author of *Kindle my Heart*; Krishna Das for *Hanuman Chalisa* and *Baba Hanuman* mantras; Master Li Jun Feng, author of *Hanuman Qigong*; Acharya Kedar for his article "*Why a Guru is necessary*"; Subhamoy Das About.com, Hinduism for the article *Nataraj, Dancing Shiva*; Swami Lakshmanjoo for his *Self Realization in Kashmir Shaivism* and *Shiva Sutras*; don Miguel Ruiz and don Jose Ruiz, author of the *Five Agreements*; Baba Hari Dass for his Ego, Desire and Attachment and Ashtanga Yoga with Fire Without Fuel: The Aphorisms; and Master Choa Kok Sui for his *Pranic Psychotherapy* and *Inner Teachings of Hinduism Revealed*.

INTRODUCTION

I believe that the problem – monkey-mind, and the solution – meditation to quiet the mind, is best described by the brief quotation below by Baba *Muktananda*. This book will elaborate about Hanuman's way to quiet the mind through Hanuman Qigong and Hanuman mantras – love, devotion or reverence to the Sadguru to open the heart – such as Hanuman Gayatri, Shri Hanuman Chalisa and Baba Hanuman.

According to Siddha Guru Baba *Muktananda*, "There is one great obstacle that keeps us from knowing the Self, and that is the mind. The mind veils the inner Self and hides it from us. It makes us feel that God is far away and that happiness must be found outside. Yet the same mind that separates us from the Self also helps us to reunite with it. That is why the ancient sages, who were true psychologists, concluded that the mind is the source of both bondage and liberation, the source of both sorrow and joy, our worst enemy as well as our greatest friend. That is why, if there is anything worth knowing in this world, it is the mind.

The sages of the Upanishads said that the mind is the body of the Self (Consciousness). The Self shines through the mind and makes it function. But although the Self is so close to the mind, the mind does not know it. The mind is always moving outside, focusing on external objects, and as a result it has become very dull. It has lost the capacity to reflect the radiance of the Self, just as a lake whose waters are filled with silt loses its capacity to reflect the sun. However, when we practice meditation, the mind goes deeper and deeper within, and becomes more and more quiet. When it is truly still, we begin to drink the nectar of the Self. That is why yoga and meditation came into existence: to quiet the mind, to make it free of thoughts, and to enable it to touch its own source...

True psychology is born of meditation. The scriptures of meditation are the greatest works of psychology. Psychology is not just talking, talking, talking. Real psychology is yoga. There was a great sage called Maharishi Patanjali whose Yoga Sutras are the authoritative text on yoga. Patanjali said that through yoga one can still the movements of the mind. That is true psychology. One cannot cure the troubles of the mind by talking, nor can one steady the mind by using herbs or drugs. Drugs may calm the mind for a while, but once the effect of the drugs fade away, the mind will return to its former state. One can straighten out the mind only by making it still, by calming the thoughts and feelings that cause it to become agitated. If psychotherapists truly understood what the mind is and improved their own minds with meditation, they would be be able to practice great therapy...

In our yoga scriptures, the mind is represented as the horse that pulls a chariot. The reins are in your hands. If you let the horse go where it wishes, it will take you into a pit. You should not be defeated by your own mind. You should still the mind, purify the mind, discipline the mind. You should bring it under control with your intellect..."

As a Siddha yogi of *Sadguru Bhagawan Nityananda* lineage, the Hanuman Qigong and especially the intonation of the Hanuman mantras in Sanskrit by Hanuman devotees (*bhakta*) opens the heart, expand their energy bubble and experience divine oneness through reverence to the Sadguru which increases the internal conductivity and receptivity to the Shakti of the Sadguru. May the joined application of the *meditation on the gap*, Hanuman Qigong / mantras and *Five Agreements* quiet the monkey-mind (ego).

Why I meditate on Hanuman ji

Who you meditate on, you become.

I find experientially that meditating on Hanuman through his mantras *Chalisa*, *Gayatri* and *Baba Hanuman* during stressful situations have been healing and opening my heart to the unconditional love of the universe, and have been cleansing and clearing my meridians in the process. I believe that the main reason for the physical, mental, emotional and spiritual benefits derived by chanting the mantras is because as the palpable personification as *Sankata Mochan* (reliever of suffering) and as Lord of Breath, *Pranadeva* Hanuman infuses the meditator devotee (*bhakta*) with the essential love energy which is the greatest force in the universe. Jai Hanuman Jai Hanuman.

With Hanuman Qigong as one of the Enlightenment Qigong forms, its potential for the self-realization or enlightenment of its meditation and Qigong practitioners is made possible when his heart is integrated with spirit, one's thoughts gradually melt from the mind, merging with the purest qi and the most sincere love in the universe.

According to popular tradition, Hanuman is not only the greatest devotee in terms of loving Rama, but also the greatest in worshipping him, particularly in the devotional chanting known as kirtan that calls upon sacred pranic energies which serve to quiet the mind, remove obstacles, open and heal the heart, and bring us back to the center of our being. According to popular belief, Hanuman is present wherever Rama's name is sung, since taking part in this is his highest bliss. See Baba Hanuman.

Tulsidas' most famous and wisely read poem of 40 verses (Chalisa) was written in praise of Lord Hanuman. Many recite it as a prayer on a regular basis (daily or weekly on Tuesdays and Saturdays). It is said to provide inner-strength and deliverance from ones troubles.

Maharaj-ji said, "Hanuman is the breath of Ram," the breath of God. God is not far away from us but as close as our breath. Symbolically Hanuman represents the breath, our constant companion and aid along the spiritual path. He is the son of the wind, (*Vayu*) the very essence of *prana* (vital energy) itself. Whenever we need increased power and vitality Hanuman is there for us, we need only remember him. Our breath is interrelated with prana for it is breath that serves the divine within us all.

Therefore, Hanuman is also called *Pranadeva*, or the God of Breath or Life.

Hanuman Gayatri is for those who want to develop amazing stamina, the power of selfless love, great physical strength and the power to heal wounds promptly. Hanuman is the embodiment of strength, stamina, wit, loyalty and unwavering devotion. Hanuman is also fearless and never hesitating. Hanuman gayatri is an extraordinary gayatri mantra for those who want to develop qualities like Hanuman. If you are ever in need of strength Hanuman Gayatri is for you. And the strength is both physical as well as inner strength. You can get rid of your fears with Hanuman Gayatri and get rid of doubts too. Your loyalty and devotion will increase manifold and you will also be blessed with clarity of mind to see through things. For where there is clarity of mind, doubts and hesitation will be pushed out of the back door.

Conclusion:

Most people are the wrong type of Hanuman. Instead of meditating on Lord Rama or their Sadguru, they regularly meditate on the wrong type of role models such as actors, actresses, singers and rock stars. If you meditate on them, you do not get spiritual empowerment. This is using the wrong model. Who you meditate on, you become.

Hanuman is the ultimate bhakti yogi because he is constantly looking at the Sadguru, not just physically, but also internally, and always listening to his instructions. You can say to your Sadguru, "I am your disciple, but spiritually we are one," only if you become a Hanuman.

Hanuman personifies the grace of Lord Rama and Lord Shiva.

He has the distinctive power of Rudra (Shiva).

Hanuman with Sri Rama, Sita and Lakshmana

This is how I quiet my monkey mind – I become aware of my breath and my monkey mind quiets down. Calling on Hanuman will help tame the monkey mind. – Acharya Ricardo B Serrano

Hanuman Qigong for integrating the Heart and Spirit

When I think of myself as a body, I am your servant;

when I think of myself as an individual soul, I am part of you;

but when I realize I am atman, you and I become one.

- Valmiki Ramayana

Integrating Heart and Spirit

The basic idea for this qigong is to integrate qi with Heaven, to integrate the heart with the spirit in dance-like movements. The spirit we refer to here means both the human being's soul and also the soul of the Universe. This qigong is beneficial to health when the practitioner reaches a state of integrating himself and heaven. In comparison with other Sheng Zhen Wuji Yuan Gong, this qigong practice may not be as effective in treating disease because the health benefits will only occur when the practitioner has reached a very high level of practice. So this form is recommended for those who have practiced Sheng Zhen Wuji Yuan Gong for more than three years. Beginners are not encouraged to study.

In this qigong practice when the qi is integrated, dancing is the state of gong. When the practice integrates Heaven's qi, dancing becomes expressed in a state of wholeness. The whole body dances as it joins in the movements. This helps qi and blood to move, too. With these dancing movements, one's thoughts gradually melt from the mind, merging with the purest qi and the most sincere love in the universe. At this moment, the practitioner becomes integrated with nature, his heart is integrated with spirit, Heaven is integrated with Earth, and everything in this world returns to its most original state. This is the state we are trying to reach in this qigong practice.

Hanuman qigong practice includes 24 movements with every three movements considered a session, making eight sessions in all:

The First Session

(1) Wind, (2) Rain, (3) Sign (Climate) of the times

The Second Session

(4) Sun, (5) Moon, (6) Star

The Third Session

(7) Consciousness (Yi), (8) Thought (Nian),

(9) Awakening (Xing)

The Fourth Session

(10) Heaven (Tian), (11) Earth (Di), (12) Humanity (Ren)

The Fifth Session

(13) Fullness (Bao), (14) Emptiness (Xu),

(15) Roundness (Yuan)

The Sixth Session

(16) Light (Guang), (17) Qi, (18) Essence (Jing)

The Seventh Session

(19) Tao, (20) Dharma (Fa), (21) Love (Ai)

The Eighth Session

(22) Origin, (23) Nothingness, (24) Oneness

Prerequisite: To take this course, you must know, and practice well, at least one Sheng Zhen standing form taught by *Master Li Junfeng*, originator of *Sheng Zhen Wuji Yuan Gong*. With thanks to teacher Li.

The name *Hanuman* gives a clue to his character. It is a combination of two Sanskrit words, *hanan* (annihilation) and *man* (mind), thus indicating *one who has conquered his ego*.

Why Hanuman is Shown Tearing Open his Own Chest

Once Sita gave Hanuman a necklace of pearls. After a while, the residents of the city observed him breaking the necklace and inspecting each pearl minutely. Intrigued they asked him the reason. "I am looking for Rama and Sita," replied Hanuman. Laughing at his apparent naivety the spectators pointed out to him that the royal couple was at the moment seated on the imperial throne. "But Rama and Sita are everywhere, including my heart" wondered aloud the true bhakta. Not understanding the depth of his devotion, they further teased him: "So Rama and Sita live in your heart, can you show them to us?" Unhesitatingly, Hanuman stood up and with his sharp talons tore open his chest. There, within his throbbing heart, the astonished audience were taken aback to find enshrined an image of Rama and Sita. Never again did anyone make fun of Hanuman's devotion.

The Spiritual Significance of Hanuman

The goal of all mystical yearning is union of the individual soul with the universal soul. In the Adhyatma ('spiritual') Ramayana, a Sanskrit text dating from the fourteenth or fifteenth century, *Sita* represents the individual (*jiva-atma*), which has separated from the universal (*param-atma*) symbolized by *Rama*. In a beautiful interpretation, *Hanuman here is said to personify bhakti, which annihilates the 'ahankara' or ego (Ravana), and re-unites the two.*

The Enduring Relevance of Hanuman

In Hindu symbolism, a monkey signifies the human mind, which is ever restless and never still. This *monkey-mind* happens to be the only thing over which man has absolute control. We cannot control the world around us but we can control and tame our mind by ardent discipline. We cannot choose our life but we can choose the way we respond to it. Hanuman, when he was a child, was tempted by the sun and he rushed towards it thinking it to be a delectable fruit. On his way however, he was distracted by the planet Rahu and changed his path. Thus Hanuman is the temperamental human intellect, which is unquiet and excitable. It is only by diverting it to the path of pure bhakti (*devotion*), that it can be made aware of its profound and silent essence.

According to the Hindu point of view, there is no objective world 'out there.' The whole manifested world is a subjective phenomenon created by our own selves. We - as humans - have the unique ability to condition our minds. In other words, we have the power to change the way we perceive life. And by changing our perceptions of life, we have the power of changing our world. When Hanuman enters Rama's life, he changes Rama's world. He transforms a crisis (the loss of Sita) into an opportunity (rid the world of Ravana). He transforms a victim into a hero.

Thus, Hanuman is no ordinary monkey. While embarking on the search for Sita, the monkeys were confronted by the vast ocean lying between them and Lanka. They wondered how they would make their way across this mighty obstacle. Someone suggested that Hanuman jump and cross over the sea. But Hanuman was doubtful, "I cannot do that," he said. At that moment, one of his companions reminded Hanuman of the awesome powers lying dormant within him. Instantly Hanuman regained memory of his divine strength and he successfully leaped across the ocean. Thus our mind too needs to be reminded of its divine potential and of the fact that it can achieve phenomenal heights provided it believes in its ability to perform the task in question. Truly *Hanuman is symbolic of the perfect mind, and embodies the highest potential it can achieve*.

Source: The Mystery of Hanuman - Inspiring Tales from Art and Mythology by Nitin Kumar

Baba Hari Dass, a Hanuman devotee

Hanuman Quotes from Ramayana

Not getting depressed, frustrated or dejected is the basis for all prosperity and happiness. Giving up one's life produces nothing good, to continue to live is the way to joy and happiness.

A wise man should foresee tragedy or misfortune and take action to prevent or overcome such tragedy or misfortune well before it strikes. Thus only he can enjoy a safe and good life.

One's innermost thoughts and emotions reflect on one's physical appearance which it is difficult to cover up however one may try to do it. Such changes in one's physical appearance forcefully expose such innermost emotions and thoughts.

When Hanuman first met Sri Ram, he says: 'the jeeva is deluded by maya, so I could not recognize my lord in your form'.

On another occasion Hanuman tells Rama: 'when I think of myself as a body, I am your servant; when I think of myself as an individual soul, I am part of you; but when I realize I am atman, you and I become one.'

Hanuman to Tara, wife of Vali: A man reaps the fruits of the actions he has performed: actions whether good or bad, and death grants him these fruits. No man's action depends on those of another. This human body is like a bubble on the surface of water. No one need mourn for another since we are all to be pitied. You are in a pitiable state and you feel sorry for Vali who is dead. There is no cause for grief in this world where everything is transient.

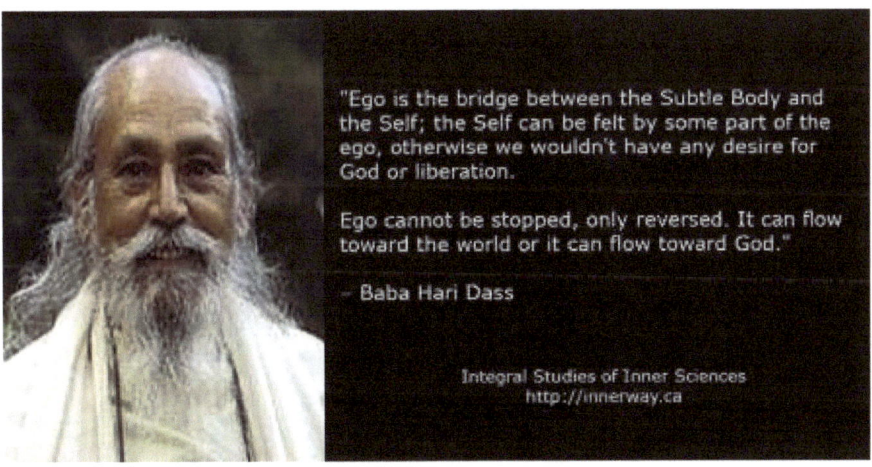

Ego cannot be stopped, only reversed. - Baba Hari Dass

Lord Hanuman Gayatri

We pray to the son of Goddess Anjani and the son of the "Wind".

May Lord Hanuman lead our intellect towards intelligence and "knowing".

Lord Hanuman Gayatri

Hanuman Gayatri is for those who want to develop amazing stamina, the power of selfless love, great physical strength and the power to heal wounds promptly. Hanuman is the embodiment of strength, stamina, wit, loyalty and unwavering devotion. Hanuman is also fearless and never hesitating. Hanuman gayatri is an extraordinary gayatri mantra for those who want to develop qualities like Hanuman. If you are ever in need of strength Hanuman Gayatri is for you. And the strength is both physical as well as inner strength. You can get rid of your fears with Hanuman Gayatri and get rid of doubts too. Your loyalty and devotion will increase manifold and you will also be blessed with clarity of mind to see through things. For where there is clarity of mind, doubts and hesitation will be pushed out of the back door.

ON NAMO HANUMANTE RUDRAVTARAY VISHWARUPAY,

AMIT VIKRAMAY PRAKATPRAKRAMAY,

MAHABALAY SURYA -

KOTISAMPRABHAY RAMDUTAY SWAHA

I pray to Lord Hanuman who is embodiment of Lord Shiva,

covers the whole world, undeletable, courageous, full of

valour, shinning like sun and messenger of Lord Ram.

Lord Hanuman Gayatri

AUM ANJANEYAYE VID-MAHE

VAYU PUTHRAYA DHEEMAHI

TANNO HANUMAT PRACHODAYAT

We pray to the son of Goddess Anjani and the son of the "Wind".

May Lord Hanuman lead our intellect towards intelligence and "knowing".

May Lord Hanuman speak to you in your dreams and bless you!

"One's own thought is one's world. What a person thinks is what he becomes - That is the eternal mystery. If the mind dwells within the supreme Self, One enjoys undying happiness." - Maitri Upanishad

I salute Lord Hanuman, Lord of Breath, Son of the Wind God -

who bears five faces and dwells within us

In the form of five winds or energies

pervading our body, mind and soul,

who reunited Prakrti with Purusa

May He bless the practitioner

by uniting his vital energy – prana –

with the Divine Spirit within.

Hanuman's Birth

Once Shiva and Parvati, ever the adventurous lovers, decided to transform themselves into monkeys and indulge in amorous games in the dense Himalayan forests. During a climactic moment, the seed of Shiva found its mark and impregnated Parvati. Since they were in simian form it was but natural that the offspring born of such a union too would be a monkey. Not desiring to go against the laws of nature, Shiva directed the wind god Vayu to carry his semen from Parvati's womb, and deposit it into that of Anjana - a female monkey, who at that very moment was praying for a male child.

Another slightly variant version of this story in the Shiva Purana states that when Vishnu once disguised himself as the heavenly beauty Mohini, her charms so impressed Shiva that he could not restrain his seed. Vayu then carried the seed and deposited it into Anjana's womb. There was no question of Shiva's potent discharge resulting in an offspring less than extraordinary and the child conceived under such exceptional circumstances was bound to be special, and so it was. The resulting bundle of joy was none other than Hanuman, one of the most celebrated and worshipped figures in Indian thought. Two exceptional traits further marked his birth. The first was that unlike ordinary children, Hanuman was born wearing a loincloth. This was an early pointer to his life-long pursuit of a celibate, almost ascetic lifestyle. The other significant occurrence was the presence of elaborate earrings adorning his ears.

Hanuman's Education

As he grew up, Hanuman sought to educate himself and for this purpose he chose Surya the sun god as his guru saying: "You see everything there is to see in the universe and you know everything there is to know. Please accept me as your pupil." Surya hesitated. "I don't have the time," he said. "During the day I ride across the sky, and at night I am too tired to do anything."

"Then teach me as you ride across the sky during the day. I will fly in front of your chariot, facing you from dawn to dusk." Impressed by Hanuman's zeal and determination, Surya accepted him as his pupil. Thus Hanuman flew before the chariot of the sun god, withstanding the awesome glare, until he became well versed in the four books of knowledge (the Vedas), the six systems of philosophies (darshanas), the sixty-four arts or kalas and the one hundred and eight occult mysteries of the Tantras.

Having become a master of all that he set out to learn, it was now time for Hanuman to pay for his education (guru-dakshina). Surya asserted that watching the devoted pupil study was payment enough for him but when Hanuman insisted on giving something to express his gratitude, the sun god asked him to look after the welfare of his son Sugriva, who was the stepbrother of Vali, the king of monkeys.

Before Vali became the lord of apes, a simian named Riksha ruled over them. Once it so transpired that Riksha fell in an enchanted pool and turned into a woman. Both the sky-god Indra and the sun-god Surya fell in love with her and she bore each of them a son. Indra's son was her first born Vali while Sugriva her second offspring was the son of Surya. After bearing the sons, Riksha regained his male form.

When Riksha died, in accordance with the law of the jungle, the monkeys fought each other for becoming the leader. Vali successfully killed or maimed every other contender to the throne and became the undisputed ruler of the monkey world. As one who had successfully earned his dominant place among the apes, Vali was not obliged to share the spoils of power with anyone, but being of a magnanimous nature he shared everything with his younger brother Sugriva. It was in these circumstances that Hanuman entered the companionship of Sugriva who later became the king of monkeys himself. It was under Sugriva that the massive army of monkeys helped Lord Rama reclaim his wife who had been abducted by the demon Ravana.

Hanuman as Yogachara

If yoga is the ability to control one's mind then Hanuman is the quintessential yogi having a perfect mastery over his senses, achieved through a disciplined lifestyle tempered by the twin streams of celibacy and selfless devotion (bhakti). In fact, Hanuman is the ideal Brahmachari (one who follows the path of Brahma), if ever there was one.

He is also a perfect karma yogi since he performs his actions with detachment, acting as an instrument of destiny rather than being impelled by any selfish motive.

Hanuman - The First to Teach Pranayama and the Inventor of the Surya Namaskar

Pranayama is the ability to control one's breath so that the inhalation and exhalation of air is rhythmic. Vayu, the god of air and wind, first taught pranayama to his son Hanuman, who in turn taught it to mankind.

The Surya Namaskar (salutation to the sun) too, was devised by Hanuman as a greeting for his teacher Surya.

Source: The Mystery of Hanuman - Inspiring Tales from Art and Mythology by Nitin Kumar

Sun salutation (surya namaskar) is a complete physical and spiritual practice in itself. It includes asanas, pranayama, mantra and meditation. All the 12 postures involved in a round of Surya Namaskar are performed in a steady, rhythmic sequence, synchronizing with the breath and mental awareness. This is an effective way of loosening, stretching, massaging and toning up all the body joints, muscles and internal organs.

Surya Namaskar fortifies the whole body, stimulating circulation and giving strength and flexibility to the spine; energizes the nerve channels, heart, lungs, and digestive organs. **See Surya Namaskar with Mantras below; What is Raja Yoga?, page 47; 8 Limbs of Ashtanga Yoga, page 104; Ashtanga Yoga Hand Mudras, pages 138-139; Healing and Returning to Oneness, page 157; Techniques of a Master, page 159**

NOTE: A number of prophets have claimed to have seen Hanuman over the course of the centuries, notably Madhvacharya (13 Century A.D.), Tulsidas (16th century), Sri Ramdas Swami (17th century) and Raghavendra Swami (17th century), Swami Ramdas (20th century), and Shirdi Sai Baba (20th century).

Benefits of Monkey Mind Meditation

Meditation has been around in recorded history for thousands of years. Historically it was used by the sages or spiritual practitioners and new research shows it's good for everyone.

- Improved brain function. Meditation has been found to increase cortical thickness in the hippocampus, which governs learning and memory, and in certain areas of the brain that play roles in emotion regulation and self-referential processing.
- Reduced stress/cortisol levels. Meditation has been found to consistently reduce cortisol levels in the blood. Deep relaxation produced by meditation triggers the brain to release beneficial neurotransmitters, including oxytocin and dopamine.
- Decreased psychological disorders. Studies show that meditation is associated with improvement in a variety of psychological areas, including stress, anxiety, addiction, depression and eating disorders.
- Lowers blood pressure/protects heart. Meditation decreases heart rate, blood pressure, rate of breathing, and muscle tension. Some studies shows it also reduces fatty plaques.

Shri Hanuman Chalisa

Son of the Wind, destroyer of sorrow, embodiment of blessing,

Live in my heart, King of Gods, together with Ram, Lakshman and Sita.

Tulsidas' most famous and wisely read poem of 40 verses (chalisa) was written in praise of Lord Hanuman. Many recite it as a prayer on a regular basis (daily or weekly on Tuesdays and Saturdays). It is said to provide inner-strength and deliverance from ones troubles.

Maharaj-ji said, "Hanuman is the breath of Ram," the breath of God. God is not far away from us but as close as our breath. Symbolically Hanuman represents the breath, our constant companion and aid along the spiritual path. He is the son of the wind, (Vayu) the very essence of prana (vital energy) itself. Whenever we need increased power and vitality Hanuman is there for us, we need only remember him. Our breath is interrelated with prana for it is breath that serves the divine within us all.

Therefore, Hanuman is also called Pranadeva, or the God of Breath or Life.

Shri Hanuman Chalisa

(Invocation)

Shree Guru charana saroja raja nija manu mukuru sudhari

Baranaun Raghubara bimala jasu jo daayaku phala chaari

Having polished the mirror of my heart with the dust of my Guru's lotus feet

I sing the pure fame of the best of Raghus, which bestows the four fruits of life.

Budhi heena tanu jaanike sumiraun pawana kumaara

Bala budhi vidyaa dehu mohin harahu kalesa bikaara

I know that this body of mine has no intelligence, so I recall you, Son of the Wind

Grant me strength, wit and wisdom and remove my sorrows and shortcomings.

Bhajelo Ji Hanuman! Bhajelo Ji Hanuman!

Oh Friend! Remember Hanuman!

(Verses)

1. Jaya Hanumaan gyaana guna saagara

Jaya Kapeesha tihun loka ujaagara

Hail to Hanuman, the ocean of wisdom and virtue,

Hail Monkey Lord, illuminater of the three worlds.

2. Raama doota atulita bala dhaamaa

Anjani putra Pawanasuta naamaa

You are Ram's emissary, and the abode of matchless power

Anjani's son, named the "Son of the Wind."

3. Mahaabeera bikrama bajarangee

Kumati niwaara sumati ke sangee

Great hero, you are as mighty as a thunderbolt,

You remove evil thoughts and are the companion of the good.

4. Kanchana barana biraaja subesaa

Kaanana kundala kunchita kesaa

Golden hued and splendidly adorned

With heavy ear rings and curly locks.

5. Haata bajra aura dwajaa biraajai

Kaandhe moonja janeu saajai

In your hands shine mace and a banner

And a sacred thread adorns your shoulder.

6. Shankara suwana Kesaree nandana

Teja prataapa mahaa jaga bandana

You are Shiva's son and Kesari's joy

And your glory is revered throughout the world.

7. Bidyaawaana gunee ati chaatura

Raama kaaja karibe ko aatura

You are the wisest of the wise, virtuous and clever

And ever intent on doing Ram's work.

8. Prabhu charitra sunibe ko rasiyaa

Raama Lakhana Seetaa mana basiyaa

You delight in hearing of the Lord's deeds,

Ram, Sita and Lakshman dwell in your heart.

9. Sookshma roopa dhari Siyahin dikhaawaa

Bikata roopa dhari Lankaa jaraawaa

Assuming a tiny form you appeared to Sita

And in an awesome form you burned Lanka.

10. Bheema roopa dhari asura sanghaare

Raamachandra ke kaaja sanvaare

Taking a dreadful form you slaughtered the demons

And completed Lord Ram's mission.

11. Laaya sajeevana Lakhana jiyaaye

Shree Raghubeera harashi ura laaye

Bringing the magic herb you revived Lakshman

And Ram embraced you with delight.

12. Raghupati keenhee bahuta baraaee

Tuma mama priya Bharatahi sama bhaaee

The Lord of the Raghus praised you greatly:

"Brother, you are dear to me as Bharat!"

13. Sahasa badana tumharo jasa gaawai

Asa kahi Shreepati kanta lagaawai

"May the thousand-mouthed serpent sing your fame!"

So saying, Lakshmi's Lord drew you to Himself.

14. Sanakaadika Brahmaadi muneesaa

Naarada Saarada sahita Aheesaa

Sanak and the sages, Brahma, gods and the great saints,

Narada, Saraswati and the King of serpents,

15. Yama Kubera digapaala jahaante

Kabi kobida kahi sake kahaante

Yama, Kubera and the guardians of the four quarters,

poets and scholars - none can express your glory.

16. Tuma upakaara Sugreevahin keenhaa

Raama milaaya raaja pada deenhaa

You did great service for Sugriva,

Presenting him to Ram, you gave him the kingship.

17. Tumharo mantra Bibheeshana maanaa

Lankeshwara bhaye saba jaga jaanaa

Vibhishana heeded your counsel

And became the Lord of Lanka, as the whole world knows.

18. Yuga sahasra yojana para bhaanu

Leelyo taahi madhura phala jaanu

Though the sun is thousands of miles away,

You swallowed it, thinking it to be a sweet fruit.

19. Prabhu mudrikaa meli mukha maaheen

Jaladhi laanghi gaye acharaja naaheen

Holding the Lord's ring in your mouth

It's no surprise that you leapt over the ocean.

20. Durgama kaaja jagata ke jete

Sugama anugraha tumhare tete

Every difficult task in this world

Becomes easy by your grace.

21. Raama duaare tuma rakhawaare

Hota na aagyaa binu paisaare

You are the guardian at Ram's door,

No one enters without your leave.

22. Saba sukha lahai tumhaaree sharanaa

Tuma rakshaka kaahu ko daranaa

Those who take refuge in you find all happiness

and those who you protect know no fear.

23. Aapana teja samhaaro aapai

Teenon loka haanka ten kaanpai

You alone can withstand your own splendor,

The three worlds tremble at your roar.

24. Bhoota pisaacha nikata nahin aawai

Mahaabeera jaba naama sunaawai

Ghosts and goblins cannot come near,

Great Hero, when your name is uttered.

25. Naasai roga hare saba peeraa

Japata nirantara Hanumata beeraa

All disease and pain is eradicated,

Brave Hanuman, by constant repetition of your name.

26. Sankata ten Hanumaana churaawai

Mana krama bachana dhyaana jo laawai

Hanuman releases from affliction

those who remember him in thought word and deed.

27. Saba para Raama tapaswee raajaa

Tina ke kaaja sakala tuma saajaa

Ram, the ascetic, reigns over all,

but you carry out all his work.

28. Aura manorata jo koee laawai

Soee amita jeewana phala paawai

One who comes to you with any yearning

obtains the abundance of the Four Fruits of Life.

29. Chaaron juga parataapa tumhaaraa

Hai parasidha jagata ujiyaaraa

Your splendor fills the four ages

your glory is renowned throughout the world.

30. Saadhu santa ke tuma rakhawaare

Asura nikandana Raama dulaare

You are the guardian of saints and sages,

the destroyer of demons and the darling of Ram.

31. Ashta siddhi nau nidhi ke daataa

Asa bara deena Jaanakee Maataa

You grant the eight powers and the nine treasures

by the boon you received from Mother Janaki.

32. Raama rasaayana toomhare paasaa

Sadaa raho Raghupati ke daasaa

You hold the elixir of Ram's name

and remain eternally his servant.

33. Tumhare bhajana Raama ko paawai

Janama janama ke dukha bisaraawai

Singing your praise, one finds Ram

and escapes the sorrows of countless lives.

34. Anta kaala Raghubara pura jaaee

Jahaan janama Hari bhakta kahaaee

At death one goes to Ram's own city

or is born on the earth as God's devotee.

35. Aura devataa chitta na dharaaee

Hanumata se-ee sarva sukha karaee

Give no thought to any other deity,

worshipping Hanuman, one gains all delight.

36. Sankata katai mite saba peeraa

Jo sumire Hanumata bala beeraa

All affliction ceases and all pain is removed

by remembering the mighty hero, Hanuman.

37. Jai jai jai Hanumaana Gosaaee

Kripaa karahu gurudeva kee naaee

Victory, Victory, Victory to Lord Hanuman!

Bestow your grace on me, as my Guru!

38. Jo sata baara paata kara koee

Chootahi bandi mahaa sukha hoee

Whoever recites this a hundred times

is released from bondage and gains bliss.

39. Jo yaha parai Hanumaana chaleesaa

Hoya siddhi saakhee Gaureesaa

One who reads this Hanuman Chaleesa

gains success, as Gauri's Lord (Shiva) is witness.

40. Tulasee Daasa sadaa Hari cheraa

Keejai naata hridaya mahan deraa

Says Tulsi Das, who always remains Hari's servant:

"Lord, make your home in my heart."

Pawanatanaya sankata harana mangala moorati roopa

Raama Lakhana Seetaa sahita hridaya basahu sura bhoopa

Son of the Wind, destroyer of sorrow, embodiment of blessing,

Live in my heart, King of Gods, together with Ram, Lakshman and Sita.

Source: Khrisna Das Translations

How I quiet my mind

We all experience the monkey mind, where our heads are preoccupied with constant chattering of thoughts. The following true stories are my experiences when the monkey mind quiets down via meditation and Qigong.

Four years ago, I had an unforgettable experience that showed the chatter of the monkey mind and the effect of meditation:

I just left my condo to take the sky train to the Vancouver airport for my vacation in the Philippines.

While I was in the sky train, my monkey mind asked, "Are you sure you locked the door key?"

After the question from my monkey mind, out of fear I guess, I noticed myself sweating and my heart beat pacing.

I started to become aware of my breath and started chanting my favorite Hanuman Gayatri mantra to quiet the mind and stop the emotional effect of fear and anxiety brought on by my monkey mind.

After a few minutes of meditation, I started to feel calmer and noticed that my physical and emotional symptoms disappeared.

My higher mind also said, "there is nothing to worry because as a habit you always make sure that you lock the door before leaving a thousand times before."

Two years ago in early spring morning, I was practicing Primordial Wuji Qigong (with Qigong breathing) infront of a giant maple tree in the Victoria park, in North Vancouver, for about ten minutes.

After the practice session, I felt calm, peaceful and blissful. The blissful feeling lasted for three days. That was another unforgettable Qigong energy flow experience.

Every time I do sauna bathing near the swimming pool, I always practice the full three sets of sitting Sheng Zhen Healing Qigong with Qigong breathing. Most of the time I always noticed that my body felt so relaxed and light after the Qigong session followed with blissful joyful feeling.

Baba Hanuman

You are the destroyer of Suffering, the abode of Grace.

According to popular tradition, Hanuman is not only the greatest devotee in terms of loving Rama, but also the greatest in worshipping him, particularly in the devotional chanting known as kirtan that calls upon sacred pranic energies which serve to quiet the mind, remove obstacles, open and heal the heart, and bring us back to the center of our being. According to popular belief, Hanuman is present wherever Rama's name is sung, since taking part in this is his highest bliss.

Baba Hanuman

Namo... Namo...Anjaninandanaaya

I bow, I bow again and again to Anjani's son, Hanuman

Jaya Seeyaa Raama, Jai Jai Hanumaan

Victory to Sita and Ram, Victory to Hanuman

Victory over the darkness of suffering...

Jaya Bajrangbalee, Baba Hanuman

Victory to the one with the body of a thunderbolt

My Baba, Hanuman.

Sankata Mochan kripaa nidhaan

You are home of all Grace.

Destroy all my problems, calamities and sufferings.

Jai Jai Jai Hanuman Gosaaee

Hail My Lord Hanuman

Kripaa karahu Gurudeva kee naaee

You are my Guru, bestow your Grace on me.

Sankata Mochan kripaa nidhaan,

You are the destroyer of Suffering, the abode of Grace

Laala Langotta, Laala Nishaan

You wear a red langotta and carry a red flag

Hare Raama Raama Raama, Seetaa Raama Raama Raama

Source: Krishna Das Baba Hanuman Lyrics

Hanuman leading Kirtan. This image also shows Hanuman as a devotee, holding the hand cymbals that are used during kirtan as rhythm instruments; Rama and Sita are seen outlined on his chest, indicating his total devotion. This peaceful, devotional image stands in marked contrast other martial images, and Hanuman's personality has this complex mix of power and devotion. "Rama" in ancient Sanskrit literally means "Ra" - radiance, and "Ma" - within, or the radiance within an individual.

This is another extremely common contemporary image, and one that also reflects popular piety as epitome of selflessness, humility and devotion for Sri Rama.

Who you meditate on, you become. "Who realizes what? That is realization." - Baba Hari Dass

Epilogue: I believe that the other important reason why I meditate on Hanuman ji is that, as a Shaivite yogi from Sadguru Bhagawan Nityananda lineage, he personifies the grace of Lord Shiva and Lord Rama, and he also has the distinctive power of Rudra (Shiva).

I therefore recommend that the practitioner practice Maitreya (Shiva) Shen Gong and Omkabah Lightbody Activation to imbibe Hanuman ji's blessings and spiritual empowerment for abundance, healing and enlightenment. I also recommend the five niyamas (*disciplines*) and five yamas (*moral prescriptions*) and the *meditation on the gap* taught by Swami Lakshmanjoo, and the Five Agreements by don Miguel Ruiz / don Jose Ruiz to quiet the *mitote* or *maya* – illusion of the mind.

How people tame their monkey mind

I find that most millennials (those born in the year 2000 and earlier) tame their monkey mind by using their cellphones a lot. However, I don't believe that connecting with other people's monkey mind via cell phones will tame their monkey mind but instead increase the chattering of thoughts and emotions rather than taming it.

As a form of walking meditation to quiet their monkey mind, most people can be seen holding and texting on their cell phone while walking in the sidewalk.

Using cellphone a lot not only expose you to harmful wi-fi electromagnetic frequencies but also exposes you to other people's voices of fear, anxiety, worry and other negative emotions which are all detrimental to your health and well-being.

"Every time you feel yourself being pulled over other people's nonsense, repeat these words: not my circus, not my monkeys." - Anonymous

"The soul always knows what to do to heal itself. The challenge is to silence the mind." - Buddha

What is the monkey mind? According to Buddha, 2500 years ago, the human mind is described as being filled with drunken monkeys, jumping around, screeching, chattering on endlessly. Buddha said, we all have monkey minds with dozens of monkeys all clamoring for attention. Fear is an especially loud monkey, sounding the alarm incessantly, pointing out all the things we should be wary of and everything that could go wrong.

What is the best way to quiet or tame the monkey mind? Buddha, a true psychologist, taught his students how to meditate to tame the drunken monkeys in their minds. It's useless to fight with the monkeys or to try to banish them from your mind by talking or use alcohol and drugs because, as we all know, that which you resist persists. Instead, Buddha said, if you will spend some time each day in quiet meditation — simply calm your mind by focusing on your breathing or a simple mantra — you can, over time, tame the monkeys. They will grow more peaceful if you lovingly bring them into submission with a consistent practice of meditation.

Buddha was right. Meditation is a powerful way to quiet the voices of fear, anxiety, worry and other negative emotions brought on by the drunken monkey minds.

"Rest the mind by directing one-pointed attention on a specific object." - The Ninth Gyalwang Karmapa, Mahamudra: The Ocean of Definitive Meaning

"The aim of life is to attain peace. No one can give us peace. We can't buy or borrow it. We have to cultivate it by practicing yama and niyama [yoga restraints and observances]." - Baba Hari Dass

Quotations from the Yoga Scriptures of the Ancient Siddha Lineage Tradition

"One's own thoughts is one's world. What a person thinks is what he becomes - that is the eternal mystery. If the mind dwells within the supreme Self, One enjoys undying happiness." - Maitri Upanishad

May the following quotations from the ancient Shaivite and Vedic scriptures lead you to further additional Kundalini Shakti (Qi) exploration, study, chanting, mantra-repetition, selfless service, satsang, spending time in the company of saints and practice of the Guru principle and their basic centering meditation techniques to purify the mind and break the chain of inner words that will eventually assist you in your spiritual journey and liberation, as the practices have assisted me greatly as a long-time Yoga and Qigong practitioner, toward love, transformation, spontaneous healing and personal freedom through Self-realization or Realization of Buddha nature. Siddha Guru Baba Muktananda writes, "The universe is a garden for us to roam with love. It is not intended as a source of attachment, jealousy, hatred, or anxiety. These only destroy our equanimity. Give up all desires. If something comes, let it come; if something goes, let it go. It is all Shiva's play. This is not a mere universe; it is the image of Him. Knowing it as Shiva, love it. Meditate on the awareness that all conscious beings as well as inert matter are Shiva. Having the knowledge of Shiva, understand that the world is the embodiment of Him."

"It is to attain the bliss of samadhi that we should meditate, that we should have our Kundalini awakened by the grace of a master. We do not meditate to attain God, because we have already attained Him. We meditate so that we can become aware of God manifest within us."

And this is why he always tells everyone, "Meditate on your Self, honor your Self, understand your Self, worship your Self, for God dwells within you as you."

"Ignorance is the root cause of all suffering. It is also the forgetfulness of one's own Self." - Shankaracharya, Aparokshanubhuti, 17

Lokananda samadhi sukham - "The bliss of the world is the ecstasy of samadhi." - Shiva Sutras, I, 18

"Moksa or liberation is nothing else but the awareness of one's true nature." - Abhinavagupta, Tantra I, p. 192

"Neither reject anything, nor accept, abide in your essential Self which is an Eternal presence." Abhinavagupta, Anuttarastika, 2

"Why do you look for Him only in churches or mosques? Do you not see His creation? Where does He not abide? The whole universe made by Him recites His tale." – Sarmad

"He is the real Guru Who can reveal the form of the formless before your eyes; who teaches the simple path, without rites or ceremonies; Who does not make you close your doors, and hold your breath, and renounce the world; Who makes you perceive the Supreme Spirit whenever the mind attaches itself; Who teaches you to be still in the midst of all your activities. Fearless, always immersed in bliss, he keeps the spirit of yoga in the midst of enjoyments." – Kabir

"No religion can grant enlightenment or salvation. Your own faith, devotion, and Love for God can bring about enlightenment. Your spiritual practices and your desire to attain God are the main thing." - Baba Hari Dass

"Life is not a burden, but we make it one when we refuse to accept things as they are." - Baba Hari Dass

"Work honestly, meditate every day, meet people without fear, and play." - Baba Hari Dass

"Like oil in sesame seeds, butter in cream, water in the river bed, fire in tinder, the Self dwells within. Realize that Self through meditation." - Shvetashvatara Upanishad

"Just by repeating the Name, that which cannot be understood will be understood. Just by repeating the Name, that which cannot be seen will be seen." - Jnaneshwar Maharaj

"Contemplate Kundalini, Who is supreme Consciousness, who plays from the base of the spine to the crown of the head, Who shines like a flash of lightning, Who is fine as the fiber of the lotus stalk, Who has the brilliant radiance of countless suns, Who is a shaft of light as cool as hundreds of nectarian moonbeams." - Shri Vidya Antar Yaga

"One's own thoughts is one's world. What a person thinks is what he becomes - that is the eternal mystery. If the mind dwells within the supreme Self, One enjoys undying happiness." - Maitri Upanishad

"Yoga is the stilling of the vrittis [modifications] of the mind." - Patanjali Yoga Sutras, I, 2

"Smaller than the smallest, greater than the greatest. This Self forever dwells in the hearts of all. A person freed from desire, with mind and senses purified, Beholds the glory of the Self and is without sorrows." - Katha Upanishad

"He who continually perceives this entire universe as a sport of the universal Consciousness is truly Self-realized beyond any doubt; he is liberated in this body." - Vasuguptacharya, Spanda Shastra

"There is neither bondage nor liberation for me. Bondage and liberation frighten only those who are ignorant of their essential nature. The universe appears as a reflection in the intellect like the image of the sun in water." - Vijnana Bhairava, 135

"O my blessed beloved, awake! Why do you sleep in ignorance." – Kabir

Baba Muktananda says, "Chanting the divine name is the most sublime way to develop inner love. The divine lover pursues God through his divine name."

"Chant the mantra with great feeling. Chant with all your heart and the bliss will come. No negativities can withstand the bliss of the Lord's name." *OM NAMAH SHIVAYA*

Sadguru Bhagawan Nityananda

Baba Muktananda says: It is the mind with its ceaseless thoughts and fancies that takes the body all over the place. The body runs after thoughts and thoughts run after the mind. The mind gives orders to the body and senses. Why do you punish the body in order to please the mind? Why do you punish *Krishna* when you are angry with *Ram*? What purpose does it serve? I agree that the mind is fickle and unsteady and causes us trouble. It is only to control the mind that so many techniques have been devised. Yogis learn these techniques to bring their minds under control, but they still become votaries of pride and ego, devotees of easy living. They don't find love through these practices, nor do they find inner contentment or joy in their hearts. Everybody says that the mind never stays in one place, and I entirely agree. But at the same time, have you ever shown it a good place to rest? Take the mind to a worthy place and it will stay there. It won't wander here and there.

Dear students, the mind wants real love, complete equanimity, and union with God. The mind wants something captivating; that is why it is restless. It leaves one place of restlessness and goes on to the next. Just as a bee flies from one flower to another collecting honey, the mind, for one reason or another, wanders on and on. But remember that there is a significant quest behind this restlessness of the mind: the mind is looking for perfect repose. The mind will always fluctuate and will never be steady until it is completely dissolved in meditation on the Self. Only when it has become lost in meditation as a gift of *Kundalini* and become one with the inner light will it abandon its unsteadiness and become still. Remember that only when the mind becomes completely still in the Self in meditation, and absorbed in love, will you become the incarnation of supreme bliss. Your direction will change; you will be transformed. A fountain of pure peace will flow inside you.

The mind cannot find perfect repose anywhere except in God. When you meet God, you find everything, and the mind becomes steady. Then, even if you try, it doesn't move. From this point of view, it is the restlessness of your mind, that has never been satisfied by temporary stillness, which has set you on the search for truth and peace. The mind does not become still anywhere except in God. It is this tendency of the mind which has led it to find peace. You should consider this a great service on the part of the mind. The restlessness of your mind is a great asset to you, for it has fostered your interest in meditation and has made you worthy of the grace of the Siddhas. So you should welcome heartily the beneficent grace of the Siddhas.

Instead of trying to control and force your mind, you should lead it lovingly to the river of the ecstasy of the Self. Take it on that pilgrimage to the divine shade of love of the Self, where the luster of true love shines. If you turn the mind to the supremely blissful Self, it will want you to run there as fast as it can, but if you stubbornly try to make it peaceful by force or by austerities, it will become more and more agitated and turn against you. Love the mind, but even before you love it, stop thinking of it as the mind. Regard it as the *Goddess Chiti* who is pulsating as the mind. Give up your antagonism to it and, establishing a true friendship with it, say, "Go to the inner Self." To think like this is actually meditation. If you are going to conquer the mind you must love it, considering that it is filled with *Chiti*. When you think of the mind as ordinary, when you are hostile to it, then the mind conquers you. Therefore, to conquer the mind completely, you must love it. Love is a mantra of victory. It is the magnet that draws God to you. It is the great *jnana* that makes the mind intoxicated and joyful. Love has great power. It makes the impossible possible; it has the power to make the broken whole. Cease to think of yourselves as small and petty. Fill yourselves with love, and you will see your own greatness.

Dear yogis of meditation! Through meditation you can discover what is inside you and what is not inside you. Without meditation you are poor; with it you are rich. So first love yourself and meditate with love.

There was once a Siddha who lived in the forest. One day he was visited by a seeker who said to him, "Maharaj! I want to see God. What *sadhana* should I do?

After studying him carefully the Siddha asked, "Who do you love?"

"Love is an obstacle on the path to God," the seeker replied.

"It is not love that is an obstacle," said the Siddha. "Desire in love is an obstacle, infatuation is an obstacle. Love is the body of God. The love that you have for yourself and your friends and relations should spread out everywhere. That is the true love that takes you to *Ram*. Therefore, love everybody."

Don't waste your life getting trapped in arguments about renunciation and acceptance, since they don't have much value. Only knowledge of the Self has value. Yoga, learning, and knowledge, when they are full of egotism, are the enemies of love. You should totally renounce egotism, and this can be done only through love. When selfless love arises in the heart, one experiences deep peace in one's life. Instead of suppressing the mind, fill it with love, then see what marvelous ecstasy there is within yourself.

Instead of torturing your mind through force or breath controls, simply lead it to the Self, pacifying it with love. Let God be the object of all your senses. *Tukaram* says that the man whose one enjoyment is *Narayana* sees the world filled with love.

Love is your very nature. It is your *sadhana* and your highest attainment. Love is God; love is the universe. God has appeared as the universe – the universe is no different; it is a manifestation of the divine Shakti. Love is a complete *sadhana* for the realization of God. Without love He cannot be attained.

Love is a great inner experience. Seek it within. You will see the divine Shakti darting with speed of electricity through your whole body, through all its fluids, blood, prana. As you experience this Shakti, you will know what love is.

Man should love his Self, which is all-embracing. He should have complete faith in it. Love turns man into an ocean of happiness, an image of peace, a temple of wisdom. Love is man's very Self, his true beauty, and the glory of his human existence. *Muktananda* says, "First love yourself, then your neighbors, and then the whole world." This is *bhakti*; this is the way to the joy of *jnana*; this is the fulfillment of the joy of yoga. All other *sadhanas* are contained in the *sadhana* of love. Bhagawan

Nityananda is that love. He is the supreme bliss that is the reward of all *sadhanas*. He is adored through the grace of the Guru. *May you abide in my heart. May our lives be the play of universal consciousness!*

Source: *The Path of Love* from *Play of Consciousness* by *Baba Muktananda*

Awakening your Kundalini by Raja Choudhury

Do you have a yoga, spiritual, or meditation practice, but are unable to sustain the bliss of inner awakening?

Would you like to discover how you can use your spiritual body to heal yourself and others — and find wellness, balance, and inner peace in your life?

Spiritual seekers have long heard the lore about the rapid spiritual growth that can be sparked when you awaken the Kundalini energy that typically lies dormant at the base of your spine.

This energy is said to enter us at birth and remain latent until ignited, which can occur spontaneously, accidentally, or as a byproduct of intense spiritual practices. Once awakened, Kundalini can lead to higher visions, blissful feelings, and spontaneous movements of the body called kriyas.

The awakening of Kundalini is a subject surrounded by hype, myth, and tales of caution; however, it is possible to connect with this primal force in a way that is grounded, gentle, and powerfully liberating — opening you to mystical awareness and a vast field of blissful energy.

When activated in the right way, there are few things that can accelerate your spiritual awakening faster than tapping into this divine force within you, which is why Tantric teachers have worshipped Kundalini as the Goddess incarnate within us.

As you awaken your Kundalini, you begin to liberate more energy not only for your spiritual life but for your career, your creativity, and your service in the world.

As Raja Choudhury explains, Kundalini can open your body, emotions, mind, and soul to divine energy pouring through your very cells. You can access a more boundless field of love, since accessing Kundalini connects us more deeply with the love-energy of the universe.

Because the awakened kundalini opens the third eye and the heart, you may even develop new capacities of intuition, clairvoyance, clairsentience, or healing capacities — and awaken to a more reverential relationship with the world around you.

* **Kundalini** is a reservoir of energy (prana) stored at the base of the spine. Because it is a spiraling power, kundalini is described as a serpent, coiled three and one-half times around svayambhu lingam. By doing sadhana (spiritual practices) this kundalini energy is activated; it then moves up the subtle spinal channel (sushumna nadi), piercing the energy centers (chakras). So long as the illusion of "I am this body" persists, kundalini power remains inherent but inactive. It awakens only when attachment to the body begins to dissipate, and then it becomes the energy by which Yoga (union) is achieved. – Baba Hari Dass

The seven chakras including their Bija mantras are activated along the Microcosmic Orbit from the root up to the crown chakra.

Read Pancha Kosha, p. 43; Sri Vidya Mantras, p. 76; Becoming a Beacon of Love, p. 92; Shiva and Shakti Meditation, p. 106; Excerpts on Kundalini, p. 121; Sri Yantra Mantras, p. 130; Three Dantiens, p. 133; Microcosmic Orbit, p. 153; Bija Mantras of Seven Chakras, p. 154

Why A Guru is Necessary

Bhagawan Nityananda says, "The heart is the hub of all sacred places, go there and roam." In order to accomplish this, your heart needs to be purified of all the false impressions and dirt deposited there by the impure ego. For this you need a Guru.

According to *Acharya Kedar*, "I am often asked why a Guru is necessary. Some people who come to our programs have expressed concerns about the fact that there are pictures of my Gurudev and the other Siddhas of my lineage hanging on the walls of our Meditation Hall. People want to know why I worship *Gurudev* and why we encourage worship of the Siddhas. There are those who believe that one should only worship the formless God. So, we have this question. "Why?" And it is a very good question which the Disciple must ask.

To be clear, the limitation of your ego is the only thing standing between you and God, the only thing that prevents you from attaining liberation or God-realization.

The only reason to take a Guru is to destroy the limitation of the ego. This ego cannot be destroyed by attempting to worship that which you cannot see or experience through your senses since, in order for the ego to be purified, the senses must also be purified.

Since the function of your senses is to attach themselves to objects of form (people, places, and things) the senses and the ego can only be purified by becoming attached to that which will destroy their limitation in the fire of Yoga. This must be an object with agency, an object with the power to bestow God's Grace. That object is the Guru who is a Siddha.

If you constantly remember that the Guru is not the physical body, but the Grace-bestowing power of God that is being transmitted through the Acharya; and if you worship the Master, remembering this, taking the form of the Guru inside your being in meditation, or meditating on the Acharya's Guru or any of the saints of the Guru's lineage, you will begin to experience a wonderful and powerful purification and opening of the heart.

This leads to a burning devotion to and love for the Guru, which leads to surrender of the impure ego. Once this surrender is complete, you still have an ego, but it is purified ego which proclaims, "I am Shiva, I am Shakti, I am the Absolute, I am Pure, I am Worthy, I am Perfect." You begin to bask in your own natural, free state of divine unconditional love.

That Love has the power to perform miracles and it will transform your entire being and also, over time, heal all your latent illnesses. This Love comes from the Grace-bestowing power of the Guru and your own Self-effort at daily spiritual practice. It is your own Grace, known as Disciple's Grace, that is the foundation for this relationship between Acharya and Disciple. Your Grace is the most important element. Without it, the Master cannot do his work."

"Ego is the bridge between the Subtle Body and the Self; the Self can be felt by some part of the ego, otherwise we wouldn't have any desire for God or liberation. Ego cannot be stopped, only reversed. It can flow toward the world or it can flow toward God."– Baba Hari Dass

Ego, Desire and Attachment

Understanding the ego nature with its desires and attachments within everyone is only half the battle in quieting the monkey mind. I hope that the information by Baba Hari Dass about the psychology of ego and how to quiet it down through meditation, selfless service and living a virtuous life assists you towards the peace and love of your true inner Self.

Quiet and peace is the real nature of a being. It is disturbed by our desires, attachment, and ego. As long as the desires, attachment and ego remain strong, the mind will remain disturbed. So one should practice meditation, or any other spiritual practice, to purify the mind.*

There are three great demons in life called evils: 1) ego, 2) attachment, 3) desire. Without ego, attachment and desire, we can't exist. Ego is the main energy. 'I am, I want, it's mine.' 'I am' is ego. 'I want' is desire. 'It's mine' is attachment.

Desire, attachment and ego is our life. We can't function in the world without these energies.

Desire and attachment are the field of expression of the ego. Ego alone is only the sense of 'I am,' and nothing more. Ego is no different from atman (the Self), except ego is individualized atman, and works through the mind and intellect. If it separates from the mind and intellect, then it discovers its real nature, the Self.

Ego is the most mysterious thing in a human incarnation. It is small in one situation and in the next moment it will be big as a mountain. So one should always keep an eye on the activities of the ego.

The mind's nature is ego, attachment and desire. The ego expresses itself by creating attachment and desires. When attachment and desires are removed, then there will be no selfish identification. Ego expresses its existence by desire and attachment and the ego always seeks for its self-interest.

Ego is strengthened only by negative thinking and actions. By positive thinking and actions, the ego is weakened.

The ego sounds like a bad word in English. Yet it is all we have. When the ego sits in the mind, it becomes the owner of the world. When this ego separates from the mind, it identifies itself with its true nature, the atman.

A watched thief cannot steal. There is always ego. Without the ego, we can't live. The ego that traps us in worldliness, that ego should be watched. Self interest in every action and thought is watched.

Without desires, we can't function. But the question is desires that are obstructing our path and desires that are supporting us on our path. We can't become desireless all at once. First weaken the desires by removing the objects. If there is candy in the refrigerator, the mind will go toward it. If there is no candy, the mind will accept that and the desire will get weaker.

Then the next step is to face it. Facing is only in the mind; it's a test. In life, you always go through tests. If you are trying to remove some habit or desire, you have to test it.

Desire makes the object, all of the objects that are in your life. The only escape from the trap is to realize that the objects and conditions of your life come out of you, that they are illusions projected by you. So why identify with them?

Limit desires. You have a desire to eat sweets. You don't watch it and you don't have a limit. When your mind wants to stop it, then at first you must reduce the quantity of sweets. You put one limit. Then you say, 'I will eat only certain sweets.' And then you say, 'I will eat at certain times.' All these self-imposed limits will remove that habit. This is called austerity or tapas.

Attachment is a feeling in the heart generated by the ego of ownership. It has nothing to do with your outer activities. You still love your partner, children, friends, but you never forget their mortality. You are not attached ignorantly.

We create our own realties. That reality is 'I may live forever and all those who are dear to me will be with me all the time.' It appears very real, and we cover the truth, which is 'neither will I live forever nor will those dear to me remain with me forever.' When this truth is understood, the person still functions as before but doesn't feel the same feelings of attachment as before.

A child is attached to the toy. The toy for an adult has not the same meaning, but the parent still keeps the toy for the child. When we understand the truth, we don't stop our duties in the world.

You are attached to your family and feel a sense of duty. If you deeply reflect on attachment, you will understand the attachment and desires in the world are separate. We express our attachment in a state of ignorance. We think "the family cannot exist without me." This selfish tie doesn't exist if attachment is understood. But the actions and duties will remain the same.

The first step is to develop nonattachment to objects. It will weaken the desires. When attachment and desires are weakened, the ego will lose its control over the mind. Ego is the root cause. But we need steps to lead up to the ego.

The ego appears in millions of faces. All those different faces are based on one ego. Actually, all identifications are the faces of the ego. You don't need to paint all the faces black. Only remove the ego that is reflecting in so many different faces. In a room of mirrors, one candle light is seen as so many. By removing the real candle, all others will be removed. But how? By surrender to God, by selfless service and by living a virtuous life.

*Words in italics are from the unpublished writings of Baba Hari Dass. All of the writings of Baba Hari Dass are copyrighted by Sri Ram Publishing.

Hanuman, Shri Rama, Sita and Lakshmana

Lord Shiva and Parvati

Ganesha

Shiva Lingam

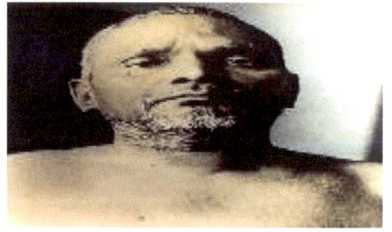

Sadguru Bhagawan Nityananda

Baba Muktananda

Nataraja or Nataraj, the dancing form of Lord Shiva, is a symbolic synthesis of the most important aspects of Hinduism, and the summary of the central tenets of this Vedic religion. The term 'Nataraj' means 'King of Dancers' (Sanskrit nata = dance; raja = king). In the words of Ananda K. Coomaraswamy, Nataraj is the "clearest image of the activity of God which any art or religion can boast of... A more fluid and energetic representation of a moving figure than the dancing figure of Shiva can scarcely be found anywhere," the Dance of Shiva.

The Significance of Shiva's Dance:

This cosmic dance of Shiva is called 'Anandatandava,' meaning the Dance of Bliss, and symbolizes the cosmic cycles of creation and destruction, as well as the daily rhythm of birth and death. The dance is a pictorial allegory of the five principle manifestations of eternal energy – creation, destruction, preservation, salvation, and illusion. According to Coomerswamy, the dance of Shiva also represents his five activities: 'Shrishti' (creation, evolution); 'Sthiti' (preservation, support); 'Samhara' (destruction, evolution); 'Tirobhava' (illusion); and 'Anugraha' (release, emancipation, grace).

The overall temper of the image is paradoxical, uniting the inner tranquility, and outside activity of Shiva.

The Vital Form & Symbolism:

In a marvelously unified and dynamic composition expressing the rhythm and harmony of life, Nataraj is shown with four hands represent the cardinal directions. He is dancing, with his left foot elegantly raised and the right foot on a prostrate figure – 'Apasmara Purusha', the personification of illusion and ignorance over whom Shiva triumphs. The upper left hand holds a flame, the lower left hand points down to the dwarf, who is shown holding a cobra. The upper right hand holds an hourglass drum or 'dumroo' that stands for the male-female vital principle, the lower shows the gesture of assertion: "Be without fear."

Snakes that stand for egotism, are seen uncoiling from his arms, legs, and hair, which is braided and bejeweled. His matted locks are whirling as he dances within an arch of flames representing the endless cycle of birth and death. On his head is a skull, which symbolizes his conquest over death. Goddess Ganga, the epitome of the holy river Ganges, also sits on his hairdo. His third eye is symbolic of his omniscience, insight, and enlightenment. The whole idol rests on a lotus pedestal, the symbol of the creative forces of the universe.

To sum up, here's an excerpt from a beautiful poem by Ruth Peel:

"The source of all movement,

Shiva's dance,

Gives rhythm to the universe.

He dances in evil places,

In sacred,

He creates and preserves,

Destroys and releases.

We are part of this dance

This eternal rhythm,

And woe to us if, blinded By illusions,

We detach ourselves From the dancing cosmos, This universal harmony..."

Source: About.com, Hinduism

Hanuman Qigong, a movement meditation form, is included by Ricardo B Serrano to balance and enhance the flow of energy (Shakti) derived from the non-movement (still) Siddha tantric yoga practices symbolized by Sri Yantra, and the Dancing Shiva Nataraja, a symbolic dance of bliss representation of universal harmony arising from the unity between Shiva and Shakti, yin and yang, non-movement (still) and movement (dynamic), and the individual soul with the universal soul, through Guru devotion with meditation and Qigong. **See Pancha Kosha Meditation below; Hanuman Qigong, page 9**

Pancha Kosha is the concept in yogic philosophy that there are five layers, or sheaths, around the human soul. **See Pancha Kosha, page 43**

Pancha Kosha Meditation by Linda Johnsen

1. Sit comfortably with your head, neck, and trunk in a straight line. Sit upright without straining. You'll feel both alert and relaxed.
2. Close your eyes, withdrawing your awareness from the sights and sounds around you. Bring your full attention to your physical body. Be aware of your head and shoulders, chest and waist, back and abdomen, arms and legs. This is your annamaya kosha.
3. Bring your full attention to the point between your nostrils and feel yourself breathe. Gradually your breath will flow more slowly, smoothly, and quietly. Be aware of the energy pulsing through your body. It's making your heart beat, your lungs expand and contract, the blood course through your veins, your stomach gurgle. The force orchestrating this movement—not your physical body itself—is your prana-maya kosha.
4. Shift your awareness into your brain. Pay attention to the part of your awareness that's regulating your sensory input and motor output. This is the part of you that notices your nose is itching and orders your hand to scratch it. It notes that you're uncomfortable sitting in one position for so long and wants you to move your legs. It generates the reflexive mental chatter that continually fires through your mind. This is your manomaya kosha.
5. Lift your awareness higher inside your skull. Sense the part of your awareness that consciously made the decision to participate in this exercise and right now is commanding you to sit still and complete it. It recognizes the value of expanding your self-awareness and compels you to get up early in the morning to do your hatha postures and meditation, even though lazing in bed might be more pleasant. This is your vijnanamaya kosha.
6. Center your awareness in your heart. Relax deeply; keep breathing smoothly and evenly. Now, taking as much time as you need, allow yourself to settle into a state of complete tranquility. Buried deep in that inner peace is a sense of purest happiness. This is not an emotional euphoria, though as you leave this state it may pour out of you as a sense of great joy and gratitude. It is a space of perfect contentment, perfect attunement, and abiding stillness. There is no sense of lack, or fear, or desire. This is your anandamaya kosha.
7. Now simply be aware of your own awareness. The pure consciousness that is having this experience lies beyond this experience. It is your true inner Self, your immortal being. Rest in your own being for as long as you can hold your attention there.
8. Return your attention to your breath. Breathe slowly, smoothly, and evenly. Open your eyes. Take a moment to relax and absorb this experience before you get up.

A complementary and additional practice to the Pancha Kosha Meditation and Atma (Soul) Yoga Meditation and Qigong Forms is the Lightbody meditation. **Read the Invocation to the Unified Chakra, page 69 and Merkaba Meditation, page 92**

"The dancer in this field of universal dance is his Self of universal consciousness." - Shiva Sutra 3.9

What is this universal dance? It is everything that you experience in your life. It may be coming. It may be going. It may be birth, death, joy, sadness, depression, happiness, enjoyment. All of this forms part of the universal dance, and this dance is a drama. In this field of drama, the actor is your own nature, your own Self of universal consciousness. This Self of universal consciousness is the one who is aware, he is the actor in this universal drama. Those who are not aware are not actors, they are played in this drama. They experience sadness, they experience enjoyment, they become joyful, they become depressed. But those who are aware, they are always elevated; they are the real players in this drama.

So it is your own Self of universal consciousness which is, in fact, the actor. Why? Because he acts. The actor is he who conceals his real nature. When you conceal the real nature of your being and, to the public, reveal another form of your being, that is the behavior of acting. Because when any person, say, a person named Denise, is the real actor and, as an actor, she appears as Lord Krisna, as Lord Siva, as a woman, as a child, as a silly fellow, then the real and actual state of her being is concealed. So for others, the actual state of her being is concealed and a superficial formation is revealed. But for her, the actual state of her being is not concealed. She knows she is Denise. At the time of becoming Lord Krisna or Siva or Jesus Christ, she is aware of her being Denise. In herself, she knows she is really Denise.

"The independent state of supreme consciousness is the reality of everything." - Shiva Sutra 1.1

This first sutra, *caitanyamatma*, states that individual being is one with universal being. The reality of this whole universe is God consciousness. It is filled with God consciousness.

In this sutra, the state of complete independence is indicated and accomplished through the use of the word *caitanya* ... It is only this one aspect, *svatantrya*, that is revealed by the word *caitanya*. This indicates that the word *caitanya* means "the independent state of consciousness."

The independent state of consciousness is the self. It is the self of everything, because whatever exists in the world is the state of Lord Shiva. So Lord Shiva is found everywhere.

"Let Shiva, who is my Self, let Shiva do pranam (bow down) to his real nature – to Universal Shiva, by his own Shakti, for removing the bondage and limitation, which is Shiva." - 1st verse, Shiva Dhristi

Here, Shiva bows to himself, for the removal of obstacles, which are also Shiva, through his own energy (*shakti*) which is one with Shiva, and in the end He resides in the state of universal Shiva. That is the state of Para (Supreme) Bhairava!

TALKS ON DISCIPLINE

The divine discipline is comprised of the five niyamas and the five yamas. You can only gain the protection of the Lord by strictly following the code of conduct set forth in these niyamas and yamas. This is not something I made up but a statement of fact. I will now explain the five niyamas. These are *sauca, santosa, tapasya, svadhyaya,* and *isvara-pranidhana*.

> *The fruit that accrues from maintaining cleanliness (sauca) of body, mind, and action is that you will begin to hate your body and shun contact with other bodies.* – Yoga Sutra 2:40

> *The fruit that accrues from maintaining complete contentment (santosa) is that you attain complete peace in this lifetime.* – Yoga Sutra 2:42

> *The fruit acquired through practicing self-control and tolerance (tapas) is that all impurity in your body and organs will vanish and you will become filled with power.* – Yoga Sutra 2:43

> *The fruit that accrues from continuously striving for self-knowledge by constant study of the scriptures is that the Lord whom you seek (istadeva) will shine before you.* – Yoga Sutra 2:44

Whether your Lord is Siva, Rama, or Krishna, He will reveal Himself to you, either in the dreaming state or in wakefulness.

> *I bow to those devotees who in their dreams experience Lord Siva, the bestower of all bliss and peace, with the crescent moon shining on His forehead.* – Stavacintamani 13

Isvara-pranidhana is the final phase and supreme *niyama* (discipline). It means love and devotion to God. The love of Lord Siva creates devotion. If you love Lord Siva and devoted to Him, it is not possible for Him to neglect you. He will reveal Himself to you and purify you with his glorious eighteen arms. He will help you enter into the realm of God consciousness.

> *Through devotion to Lord Siva, mystical rapture (samadhi) is effortlessly attained.* – Yoga Sutra 2:45

To enable yourself to be protected by the eighteen arms of Lord Siva, you must endeavor to protect yourself through the above niyamas. Do not worry about material things or about your family or relatives. You must concentrate one-pointedly on God. When you do so, God will most certainly reveal himself to you.

The five yamas, the five moral prescriptions:

Ahimsa (non-violence), *satya* (truth, both objective and internal), *asteya* (not being dishonest), *brahmacarya* (maintenance of mental and physical character), and *aparigraha* (absence of the habit and disease of hoarding).

Source: *Self-Realization in Kashmir Shaivism* by Swami Lakshmanjoo

Golden Rule: Do not do unto others what you do not want others to do unto you. Do unto others what you want others to do unto you. **Law of Karma**: What you sow is what you reap.

The master (guru) is the means. – Shiva Sutra 2.6

The two powers, the power of creative energy (*mantra virya*) and the power of establishment in that creative energy (*mudra virya*) can be attained only through the master (*guru*), no one else. But who is the master?

The one who demands his disciples donate money to him or who requires his disciples to provide service to him, all in the guise of attaining enlightenment, is not the *guru*. Then who is the *guru*? The *guru* is that person who puts before you the reality of God consciousness. It is said that the *guru* is the means here because only he can make you realize the fullness of these two awarenesses, mudra and mantra.

Lord Siva tells Parvati, "That master who is the cause of your attaining the creative energy of Lord Siva and who then establishes you in that state is as good as me." – Malinivijaya Tantra 2.10

In other words, that master is one with Lord Siva

I bow to that supreme and wonderful world of the master that gives rise to manifold ways of supreme thought that carry the disciple across the ocean of all doubts. – Spanda Karika 4.1

Some other masters think, because of the teachings of the Malinivijaya Tantra, that the master is not a worldly being. For them, the master is, in the real sense, the supreme energy of Lord Siva. In this regard, it is said in Malinivijaya Tantra:

That is the wheel of all energies and that is the mouth of the master where everything is obtained.

In the Trisirobhairava Tantra, it is said:

The great energy of that great Lord is said to be the mouth of the master; hence, that energy, being the cause of understanding, is the means (*upaya*).

Source: *Shiva Sutras Supreme Awakening* by Swami Lakshmanjoo

TALKS ON PRACTICE

On the pathway of your breath, maintain continuously refreshed and full awareness on, and in the center of, the breathing in and breathing out. This is force and this is internal asana. – Netra Tantra 8:11

Your concentration has to be on the center. You must practice on the junction (*sandhi*). You must concentrate on the word of the master (*guru-sabda*) with full devotion and be aware of the center of the inhaling and exhaling of the breath. You should not only concentrate on the center when the center is reached at the end point of exhaling; but from the beginning of the breath until the end point of exhaling. The effort is to be one-pointed in the center. You must meditate in this way for your efforts not to be wasted.

Exhaling and inhaling also refer to day and night. That is, the best time to practice meditation is not during the day or during the night, but in the center between the two, in the morning when the goddess of the dawn meets the day, and in the evening, when the dusk meets the night, when the sun seems to sink into the horizon. I swear by Absolute Reality that if you practice meditation in this way you will never fail.

There can be no one-pointedness of continuously fresh awareness in absolute day or absolute night. Even if you remain conscious while exhaling and inhaling you will achieve nothing.

Do not worship the Lord during the day. Do not worship the Lord during the night. The Lord must be worshipped at the point of the meeting of day and night. – Quoted in Tantraloka 6

Do not worship God during the day or the night; do not meditate during the day or the night; do not maintain awareness upon exhaling (day) or inhaling (night). Concentrate on the center. The Lord of gods must be worshipped where day and night meet. This is meditating on the junction (*sandhi*).

If you meditate upon your Self ceaselessly, remaining always attached to Me, thinking of Me alone, you will gain that peace which is residing in My own nature and which will effortlessly carry you to liberation. – Bhagavad Gita 6:16

You must have full faith and complete attachment to meditation. It must not become a routine or a chore. When you are about to meditate you must feel excitement and be thankful to God that you have received this opportunity of beginning meditation. Unless you fall in love with meditation and approach it with total enthusiasm, attachment, and longing, you cannot enter the realm of Awareness. All your efforts to achieve Awareness are likely to fail. They will be useless and futile.

The aspirant who is dedicated to this glorified state of Awareness, and maintains peace and harmony, will attain that *nirvana* which abides in the Kingdom of the Lord.

You must unravel all the various kinds that exist in your mind. For example, if you are feeling jealousy, thinking that the *guru* is concerned with another disciple more than you, then you have are not thinking properly. You should not think this way. You must concentrate on your *guru* and not on your *guru*-brother. Thoughts of this kind are full of avarice and jealousy. Through these thoughts you deviate and wander adrift in the desert. You should not look to see whom your *guru* is looking at. Keeping your mind absolutely pure you should concentrate on your *guru* alone.

Breath is extremely important in meditation, particularly the central breath (*madhyamam pranam*). This central breath is neither the exhaling breath nor the inhaling breath. It is the center of these two, the point existing between the inhalation and exhalation. This central point cannot be held by any physical means like a material object can be held by the hand. The center between the two breaths can be held only by knowledge, *jnana*. This knowledge is not discursive knowledge, it is that knowledge which is pure awareness. When this central point is held with continuously refreshed awareness – which is knowledge, and which is achieved through devotion (*bhakti*) to the Lord – this is, in the true sense, settling into your *asana*. *Asana*, therefore, is the gradual dawning of the Awareness which shines in the central point between inhalation and exhalation.

This Awareness is not gained by a person who is full of prejudice, avarice, or envy. Such a person, being filled with negative qualities, cannot concentrate. The prerequisite of this glorious achievement is, therefore, the purification of your internal sense of self. It must become pure, clean, and crystal clear. After you have purged your mind of all prejudice and have started settling with full awareness into that point between the two breaths, then you are settling into your *asana*.

If when breathing in and breathing out you maintain a continual awareness on the center of between the incoming and outgoing breath, then your breath will spontaneously and progressively become more refined. At that point you are elevated to another world. That is pranayama. – Netra Tantra 8:12-13

After assuming the *asana* of meditation, the refined practice of *pranayama* arises. *Pranayama* is not vigorously inhaling and exhaling like a bellows. Like *asana*, *pranayama* is internal and very subtle. There is an uninterrupted continuity in moving your awareness from the point of *asana* into the practice of *pranayama*. When, through your awareness, you have settled in your *asana*, then you automatically enter into the practice of *pranayama*.

The second form of the practice of *asana-pranayama* is *cakrodaya*.

This cakrodaya, *which I have described according to my own experience, the teachings of my master, and the explanation of the scriptures, must be undertaken with the most refined awareness.* – Tantraloka 7:71

You must maintain the awareness which is the most subtle awareness. This is neither external awareness nor internal awareness, but the awareness that is in the center of the depths of these two. This is the meaning of the words "the most refined awareness."

In *cakrodaya* there exists the gross movement of breath. It is breath with sound. Through practice, this gross movement of breath is refined and, with the passage of time, becomes more and more subtle. This can only be accomplished through one's own will and concentration. Even the *guru*'s grace (*guru-kripa*) will not help a seeker unless he is determined and fully devoted to maintaining awareness and concentration. This grace of the *guru* helps those who are simple, and simple are those who have awareness and consciousness. The spiritual aspirant who waivers and becomes disturbed gains nothing.

If you undergo these practices for one thousand centuries without full awareness and concentration you will have wasted all one thousand of those centuries. The movement of breath has to be filled with full awareness and concentration.

God consciousness is not achieved by means of the scriptures nor is it achieved by the grace of your master, God consciousness is only achieved by your own subtle awareness. – Yogavasistha

The scriptures will not lift a seeker nor can his master elevate him, but when his consciousness is fixed in his own awareness then his soul becomes visible.

By maintaining the constantly refreshed continuity of your awareness in the center of the two breaths through the practice of either *ajapa-gayatri* or *cakrodaya*, you settle in your *asana* and *pranayama* commences. The movement of your breath becomes very subtle, very refined, as if thin. At this stage you feel like going to sleep, but it is not really sleep. You are proceeding towards the subtle state of awareness (*suksma-gati*). Your awareness will not allow you to fall asleep. At this point you enter the fourth state (*turya*) which is neither the waking state (*jagrat*), the dreaming state (*svapna*), nor the deep sleep state (*susupti*). This is the beginning of *paramaspanda-tattva*. About this *Sankaracarya* has said,

If you maintain your awareness at that point which is found between waking and sleeping, you will be focused on that supreme felicity which is the supreme bliss of God consciousness. – Slokastaka

This is that point, which is found at the ending of wakefulness and the beginning of sleep, the point between waking and sleeping. This junction is very important, it is the entrance into the state of *turya*, which has opened as a result of settling into your *asana* and undergoing *pranayama*.

Long ago I composed these lines:

There is a point between sleep and waking

Where you must remain alert without shaking.

Enter into the new world where hideous forms will pass.

They are passing. Endure.

Do not be taken by the dross.

Then the pulls and pushes about the throttle, all those you must tolerate.

Close all ingress and egress.

Yawnings there may be.

Shed tears, crave, implore, and you will not prostrate. A thrill passes and that goes down to the bottom.

It rises – may it bloom forth. That is Bliss. Blessed Being! Blessed Being! O greetings be to Thee!

In these verses, Swami Lakshmanjoo reveals his experience of the dawning and unfolding of that supreme mystical experience known as *kundalini*. Here, Swami tells us that the journey of rising begins when the seeker maintains his awareness in continuity by concentrating on the center and enters the junction, the gap, found between sleep and waking. You must not fall asleep. Then you will begin to experience the death of your limited self (ego) in preparation for the awakening of your universal Self. Here you attain that supreme state of the bliss of Enlightenment and recognize the reality of the Self.

Source: *Self Realization in Kashmir Shaivism* by Swami Lakshmanjoo

Pancha Kosha

Pancha Kosha is the concept in yogic philosophy that there are five layers, or sheaths, around the human soul. The term comes from the Sanskrit pancha, meaning "five," and kosha meaning "sheath."

Pancha Kosha consists of:

1. Annamaya kosha - the body sheath
2. Pranamaya kosha - the prana sheath
3. Manomaya kosha – the emotion sheath
4. Vijnayanamaya kosha - the intellect (wisdom) sheath
5. Anandamaya kosha - the bliss sheath

The path of yoga is said to heighten one's understanding and awareness of these sheaths. Eventually, the aim of yoga is to move inward, taking a journey through these sheaths and uncovering one's true nature, or Atman (the inner Self). Then one finds unity as the relationship of Atman with Brahman (the universal Consciousness) is realized.

The model of Pancha Kosha comes from the Taittiriya Upanishad and is said to be one of the most ancient conceptualizations of the human being. The Pancha Kosha can be thought of as hiding one's true nature. Once they are removed, they leave a void, which also needs to be removed to reveal Atman.

One of the ways of working with Pancha Kosha is to undertake a Pancha Kosha meditation, which takes one's awareness through the five sheaths, on the path to Self-realization. See **Pancha Kosha Meditation, page 37**

Each of the koshas have their own way that they relate to our sense of Self:

1. Annamaya kosha - This is the physical body which needs food and nourishment to thrive. It is said to be the most vulnerable of the koshas and manifests any deficiencies on the other layers. Practicing Hatha yoga asanas works primarily with the annamaya kosha.
2. Pranamaya kosha - This is the sheath that exists within the physical body and is composed of life force energy, or prana. It flows in the circulatory, lymphatic and nervous systems. Pranayama works with this kosha.
3. Manomaya kosha - This is the mind which governs perception of the world and it is where one's sense of Self develops, along with the way it behaves. Mudras such as hand mudras with Gayatri mantra and Surya Namaskar with mantra transcend the two outer koshas to allow the manomaya kosha to be penetrated.
4. **Vijnayanamaya kosha** - This is the conscious body and intellect which governs one's sense of yamas and niyamas or ethics and morals. It is also responsible for inner growth and the acquisition of knowledge, which can occur through studies of sacred texts. **See Ego, Desire and Attachment, page 33; Talks on Discipline, page 39**
5. Anandamaya kosha - This is the most subtle body and is generally only perceived in brief flashes of bliss. It is where we experience unity with the universal Consciousness. This experience can only be realized when consciousness is expanded deeper than the material world. Meditation and Qigong with Hand Mudras and Surya Namaskar every day for at least 20 minutes is said to help experience anandamaya kosha.

To be grounded in the Self, to be at home with the Self, to be established in the Self, then the wisdom of the body awakens and guides you. That is the yogic concept of healing. **See Awakening your Kundalini, page 31; Notable Quotations, page 160**

See Surya Namaskar, page 16; Raja Yoga, page 47; 8 Limbs of Ashtanga Yoga, page 104; Koshas – the Five Sheaths that Wrap Your Soul, page 135; Gayatri Mantra and Hand Mudras, page 138-139; Healing and Returning to Oneness, page 157; Techniques of a Master, page 159

Notable Quotations from Meditation Masters

The following quotations are derived from *Swami Muktananda*'s book *The Perfect Relationship* which on the whole deals with general suffering through meditation principles from great meditation masters such as *Lord Buddha, Khrisna, Narada, Jnaneswar Maharaj, Kabir, Sunderdas, Jesus, Gurumayi*:

Lord Buddha's story will shed light on his reason for following his meditation path to freedom and self-realization which have been giving his devotees their own path to salvation from internal suffering which everyone of us shares no matter what station in life anybody is in.

When *Lord Buddha* saw the suffering of the world, he said, "All that I see in this world is birth and death. Death follows birth, disease follows health, old age follows youth. As one watches this pain and constant suffering, one ultimately sees that there are only faults in the world and becomes afraid of it." The *Bhagavad Gita* describes this understanding as "perception of the evil of birth, death, old age, sickness and pain." To have this perception is the greatest of all worldly attainments. When *Lord Buddha* began to see the world in this way, he decided to relinquish his kingdom; he was convinced that there could not be any more suffering in the forest than on the throne. With this understanding, he left his palace accompanied by *Channa*, the keeper of the royal stables, who was an ordinary man of the world. When they reached the forest, *Lord Buddha* ordered *Channa* to leave. *Channa* pleaded, "O prince, do not do this. You are still a young man. You have had no experience of life. Do not run away out of fear of the world. Do not give up your kingdom. There is so much joy in life! You are the prince – you have elephants, horses, wealth! Where will you go after giving these up? Even a poor, small man like me is not ready to leave this life, and you are a sovereign. Turn around and look at your kingdom! What do you lack?"

Lord Buddha looked back and then said to *Channa*, "I see nothing there except pain and intrigue. I have thoroughly experienced the palace life and the activities of the kingdom which appear to be joyful to you. To you they are a show, but to me they are a source of pain. That which seems pleasurable to you has brought only sorrow to me. Suffering is hidden behind the face of pleasure. *Channa* return!"

There is pain in a poor man's life; his poverty is the means by which he hides the true source of his suffering. Similarly, anguish lies beneath the ostentatious wealth of a rich man, who displays riches in order to disguise his pain. In the course of their lives people often greet pain in silence. One person conceals his torment in a hut and another in a palace (*princess Di*); one hides it in a solitary place and another among people. But suffering is the same everywhere.

What is the source of this pain? We experience it because we beg for happiness where it does not exist; instead of wanting that which is right for us, we seek that which we can never attain. We desire to make the impossible possible. This world is like a boarding house or a Hilton Hotel in which we are temporary guests. Trying to find eternity here is like trying to stop a river whose very nature is to flow. We seek outer love, which is transitory. We want that love to be undying, but how can we attain undying love from something ephemeral? In fact, if we consider this matter with understanding, we will realize that we experience our greatest suffering in the name of love. "God dwells in the heart." But although God, the embodiment of love, resides within us, most people are so unfortunate that they do not see love even in their dreams. Even a person who has labored all his life to attain love is unhappy; in the name of love, he experiences only pain. Without true love, everyone suffers – renunciants, sensualists, those who have great wealth, and those who have nothing. A poor person suffers because he has no wealth. A rich person suffers because he has too much wealth. You may look for a truly happy person, but you will never find one.

You will attain happiness only if you stand firmly in the face of the anguish that you encounter. Do not run from it. Look pain squarely in the face; then you will understand it. Know that without knowledge or meditation, without discovering the inspiration of the Self, you will experience only heartache and the misery of living without love for God. Without meditation, life is filled with sorrow. Without the bliss of the Self, there is unquestionably nothing but suffering.

Lord Buddha said, "A life without knowledge is painful." Old age and death are miserable when one lacks knowledge of the Self. In fact, without this knowledge, all of life – from one corner to the other, from east to west, from north to south, above and below – is filled with anguish.

The following teachings from Kashmir Shaivism also sheds light on the necessity of the practice of meditation to help people find peace, love, happiness from within themselves rather than focus their dependency from outside.

The sages and saints have said that to end suffering and attain happiness, one must have knowledge of the Self, which is the true source of joy. "Knowledge is the supreme state." The bliss of the Self is attained only through knowledge. In the *Bhagavad Gita* the Lord says, "In the world, there is nothing as pure as knowledge."

"God exists in one's feeling." There is great power in a person's feeling. Through it he can make God manifest. Because his feeling is the result of his understanding, right understanding is the source of all attainments, mundane as well as spiritual. "The supreme state comes only from knowledge." Through knowledge a wise person turns poison into nectar: *Mirabai* drank poison, considering it God's nectar, and was unaffected by it. But through his non-awareness, an ignorant person turns nectar into poison. The truth is that there is neither nectar nor poison in poison. Everything depends on one's attitude and understanding. For a person who has the supreme knowledge of God's all-pervasiveness, even a dark forest is a celestial garden and even a prison is a wide-open space. But for one who does not know his own Self, who does not regard others as himself, even a celestial garden is like a prison.

That is why it does not matter where you are or where you live, but rather who you are and what your inner state happens to be. The problem lies in your ignorance of your own essential nature. You will gain nothing by changing your country, town, or home; since you take your own destiny with you, you will only be welcoming pain again. It is very good to want freedom, but instead of looking for it in the wrong place, you must discover where it really dwells. The difference between a spiritual being and a politician is this: The politician says, "Bondage is external – break it and then you will obtain the joy of freedom." But the knower of the Truth says, "O my friend, bondage is not outside, but within you." No matter how much you try to break your outer fetters, your bondage will only increase. Therefore, you must go where there is supreme freedom – to the inner Self in the heart.

You are entirely responsible for your own state of dependency; in fact, you have become addicted to it. Because you think that the elixir of love is found in dependency, you have made it the abode of your love, and if you were ever to tear down the wall of dependency, you would only build another one somewhere else. However, you must free yourself in every way. *Lord Buddha* said again and again, "You can certainly come to me, but do not become bound by me." In the same way, when people ask me, "Is it alright to meditate on you?" I tell them, "Meditate on your own Self." Although it is difficult, you must escape from the prison of the non-Self. Who is a Hindu? Who is a Jain, a Buddhist, a Sufi, or a Christian? If you are imprisoned in one of these false identities, how can you find freedom of the Self? That is why *Lord Khrisna* said, "Give up all religions and take refuge in me (our inner consciousness) alone." Discard all false identification with religion. Go to the inner Self for shelter and revel there.

Our undisciplined mind is where it all starts. All the negative conditioning or programming from childhood and past lives have to be cleansed through the practice of meditation before the full brilliance of the light of consciousness within can shine forth. Pride, arrogance, hate, fear, anger, lust, greed, addictions, compulsions, inhibitions, and other negative thieves of the heart have to be purged out of the energy body through the universal energy (Qi) of love of meditation before self-realization can take place.

Remember that as long as your clogged mind has not been cleaned out, as long as your vessel has not been emptied and washed, you will not be able to fill it with God's nectar, nor will you be able to digest that nectar. It is important that your vessel be empty and completely purified in the fire of meditation and knowledge.

The following benefits of meditation are expounded by the great meditation masters which will give students of meditation a reason, a goal and a vision to strive for.

As the divine sage *Narada* (*Bhakti Yogi*) said: "After attaining love, a person has no desire for anything else." A being who has found the inner love neither suffers nor becomes excited over trivial matters. He neither hates nor becomes attached to anything. Why should he become trapped in delusive dramas when he holds the source of the world, the center of bliss, in his hand? Why should he take interest in the wrong path? Why should he criticize any religion, sect, or person?

Jnaneshwar Maharaj wrote, "One tastes and attains this elixir by stealing it from the senses." When the senses become free from all outer contacts, for the first time in one's life one experiences the inner sensation of joy that lies at the core of one's being. When one sees and hears one's Self, one touches that inner love. When one tastes one's own Self, one experiences *satchidananda* (being, consciousness and bliss). Whoever has tasted this sublime elixir has tasted the mystery of life and the essence of the entire world.

The divine sage *Narada*, author of *Bhakti sutras* (*Yoga of Love*), said, "Knowing this, the devotee becomes intoxicated and still, reveling in the Self." By attaining and experiencing the nectar of the Self, which is supreme love, one becomes ecstatic. One who is completely established in the Self becomes utterly quiet and serene; he becomes the Self. When the love of God, the ambrosia of the Self, is revealed, one finally attains the Truth and begins to dance like a madman. The intoxication that arises from the love of the divine Self is overwhelming. I often say, "Why do you use marijuana, opium, and cocaine? If you want real intoxication, drink the elixir of the Self. That will take you higher and higher; you will never come down from it."

When a flowing river merges into the ocean, it becomes the ocean and so takes on the ocean's delight. The ocean of the Self is complete in itself. Intoxicated with love, it billows ceaselessly with its own joy. A person who is immersed in the Self becomes drunk with love. Sometimes he is lost in a state of overwhelming bliss. At other times, he is engrossed in discussing the Self. *Narada* said, "The love of the inner Self is nectarian by nature." That inner love is not far from us; since its source lies within us it is not, and cannot be concealed. We ourselves have obscured it. Our blindness makes us think that it is hidden, but it is manifest within us.

Ultimately, a true living spiritual teacher is very much a must to seek and have because without one meditation would be unfruitful, unsafe, unprogressive, and a waste of time. The following statements will help you realize the importance of having a true Siddha or Arhat Guru [whose teachings are energy (Qi, prana, shakti) based with a true lineage of Siddha (enlightened) masters] in your path to freedom.

Therefore, before you set out on a pilgrimage to the infinite, reflect upon your undertaking with great care. If you go alone, your journey will be confined to the realm of the mind. If you want to go beyond the mind, you will need a companion who has himself transcended the mind and can therefore take you by the hand and lead you on a journey. A small child needs a wise person to give him self-confidence and a helping hand, someone to kindle faith in his heart so that he can eventually stand up and walk straight on the path. Similarly, a seeker of Truth needs a strong hand and a firm support. *Kabir* wrote: Think this over and understand it. The path is very narrow and precarious; it is so subtle that you need the Guru's help to discern it. Jesus also said, "Straight is the way and narrow is the path." Its subtlety is such that it is beyond your experience and understanding. When this is the case, how can you walk on it? You cannot find the path by clever thinking; thoughts are not sufficiently subtle. As long as you do not give up your mental cleverness, as long as your thought-waves do not subside, you will neither experience nor recognize the bliss of *That*. This is why *Kabir* said that one needs the *Guru*'s help in order to find the way.

> When the kingdom of fantasies collapses, only the *Guru* remains as the support of all. In one of his poems, *Sunderdas* wrote, "the *Guru* has revealed the perfect *Brahman*, who alone is all-pervasive. To whom can you be attached? Whatever exists is *That*. The root of everything pervades everything. All the thoughts and doubts of the mind have been obliterated. Through the contemplation of *That*, the *Guru* has firmly established me in the Truth. He has washed away all my filth and made me pure. When I meditate on my *Guru*, my heart is filled with ecstasy."

Let me quote from *Gurumayi Chidvilasananda*'s book *Kindle My Heart*, "Once a commuter who wanted to catch the ferry arrived too late at the dock. Dashing to the end of the pier and leaping across the water, he just made it onto the boat.

"Why didn't you wait?" asked the deckhand. "We were just pulling into the ship!"

This is a good metaphor for our human life. We work so hard: we always want to feel we have done something. Particularly if you live in Manhattan – although the red lights always turn green, and the green lights always turn red – somehow, just before the lights turn, we always make a mad dash. "Ah! I just made it!"

We try to use the same strategy, to take the same shortcuts, on the spiritual path. And through the merits of many, many lifetimes, we might succeed, but this happens very rarely. There is no reason for all that urgency. The scriptures say there must be longing for the experience, then you need a *Master*, or a *guide* to show you the path."

"A *Guru* is like a cable car that will speed us to our destination," said my teacher *Master Choa Kok Sui*.

What is Raja Yoga?

The word Yoga is synonymous with Truth, One-ness, Samadhi, Nirvana, or Moksha. Oftentimes today the term Yoga is used to describe what is in fact Hatha Yoga or Yoga Asana and Pranayama etc. That is, a series of physical postures (asanas) and other techniques that are part of a Hatha/Raja Yoga practice.

The word Yoga is derived from the Sanskrit word yuj which means 'to join'. Yoga is a means to bring unity and harmony to the body, mind and emotions; and in spiritual terms a means to bring about the union of the individual consciousness with the universal consciousness. For the Wave to realise it is and was always the Ocean.

Different Yogic philosophies discuss many paths to achieve Yoga (or Self Realisation) and it is understood that all paths lead to the same endless Ocean. Understanding this we are free of judgment of ourselves and others. We all have our own path.

All systems of Yoga are based on developing our awareness and learning to respect and accept who we are. This Body and Mind of ours is an instrument to marvel, to understand, and to care for. It may not be perfect but it is what is required for us. The more we understand it and care for it the better we can manage our life and realise our purpose. When we do not accept ourselves and others we suffer. The cause of all suffering is ignorance. Knowledge is that which can remove suffering. This same Body and Mind that experiences this suffering is the very same instrument that will allow us to experience the Self that is Truth. So the call comes to "Wake Up" and not to waste the opportunity this life has given you. The four divisions of Yoga: Jnana Yoga, Karma Yoga, Raja Yoga and Bhakti Yoga

Raja Yoga (Ashtanga Yoga)

Raja yoga is the eightfold path (Ashtanga Yoga) or the royal path is usually related to Patanjali's Yoga System, the way he described it in his Yoga Sutras (2nd century BCE).

Raja Yoga is the path of meditation providing the scientific and practical methodology to acquire the subtle perceptions required to reach Truth. It does not deny the existence of facts that may be difficult to explain, and it warns us that attributing such facts to supernatural beings will bring dependence and spiritual decay, fear and superstition. It teaches that all knowledge is based upon experience and Yoga is the science that teaches us about religion, that allows us to experience Truth for ourselves, to realise and know truth, not simply follow that which our forefathers tell us is so. Raja Yoga teaches the method to this understanding, this experience. It shows us how to observe the internal states, how to direct the power of attention, how to analyse the mind, how to concentrate to obtain knowledge. This knowledge is that which takes away misery. No faith or belief is necessary to study Raja Yoga, it never asks what our religion is. We are human beings and have the right to seek religion and have our questions answered by ourselves. Raja Yoga teaches us to believe nothing until we have found it out for ourself. Anything that is presented as secret or mysterious in these systems of Yoga should be rejected. Discard all things that weaken you, strength is vital. It takes much effort to concentrate and to move inwards and study the mind, it takes time and constant practice – some of this practice is physical but most is mental.

Raja Yoga is divided into eight steps as follows: Yama: such behaviour as non-violence, truthfulness; Niyama: such behaviours as cleanliness, contentment, self-study, surrender to Truth, and sustained practice; Asana: postures ("any posture that is easy and steady is an Asana") *; Pranayama: management and control of Prana (breathing exercises may be involved here but Prana is not breath, Prana is the vital life force); Pratyahara: withdrawal of the senses within; Dharana: concentration and fixing the focus on a single spot without distraction; Dhyana: Meditation that is all encompassing; Samadhi: Bliss, Truth, One-ness. Once we reach Dhyana and prepare the foundations we continue to practise and the experience of Samadhi will come when the time is right.

*It may be seen that Asana is that which is similar to Hatha Yoga but it should be realised that Hatha Yoga is a very physical practice to make the body strong and healthy and to live long, it takes a long time to achieve much spiritual growth and practices can be difficult. In Raja Yoga asana is mainly to achieve a firm seat or foundation, to purify the nerves, and keep the spine column free and straight and the chest open.

Yoga and the Ocean

As an analogy, we can compare Yoga to that of the Ocean; as a vast body of water; endless and eternal. In the Ocean all is one and never separate though there are often Waves. We can compare these Waves to the human birth and the ego that makes us feel we are separate to others. As soon as we feel this separation we suffer all the limitations and fear of associating ourselves with the individualised Body and Mind, of being the Wave and not the Ocean. We become stuck there, and we forget that we have always been the Ocean. There are many Waves but they are never separate from the Ocean, and it is only due to Karma/Maya we (the Body and the Mind) assume the form of Waves.

Identifying and practising seriously an appropriate technique to attain Yoga will help us re-connect and re-unite to the Ocean that we are and have always been. The practice will help us develop discipline and equanimity, allowing us to realise our potential and our true Self beyond the Body and the Mind. Nevertheless we must understand, control, and manage the Body and the Mind as instruments to experience the Self that is Truth. These are the only tools we are given to allow us to experience that which we are here to experience in this life span. **See 8 Limbs of Ashtanga Yoga, page 104; Universal Prayer, page 105; Epilogue, page 113; Ashtanga Yoga Hand Mudras, page 139**

Pancha Kosha (Five Sheaths that wrap your Soul) See p. 43

INVOCATIONS for Divine Blessing and Healing

Invoking Divine Blessings

To the universal supreme God, To my respected spiritual teacher, To all the spiritual teachers, To all the holy masters, To all the holy angels, To all the saints, spiritual helpers, all the great ones, To my higher soul, my divine Self, Thank you for the divine blessings, Thank you.

Affirmation on I AM

I AM not the body. I AM not the emotion. I AM not the thought. I AM not the mind. The mind is only a subtle instrument of the soul.

I AM the soul. I AM a spiritual being of divine intelligence, divine love, divine power.

I AM one with my higher soul. I AM that I AM. I AM one with the divine spark within me.

I AM a child of God. I AM connected with God. I AM one with God. I AM one with All.

Affirmation for Receptivity

"Lord, Thou art the source and fountain of life. I humbly invoke your divine blessing and healing. I fully accept your divine healing energy. With thanks and full faith." Repeat three times.

The *Invoking Divine Blessings* is the first affirmation invoked to ask for divine blessings, followed by the *Affirmation on I AM* to connect with you higher soul and God, followed finally by *Affirmation for Receptivity* to be receptive to God's divine blessing and healing. Repeat these invocations as many times when needed. *Always connect your tongue to your upper palate before meditation and invocation*.

For those who practice meditation, the following will have to be avoided to prevent *kundalini* syndrome:

1. Eating pork, eel and catfish
2. Smoking
3. Excessive consumption of alcoholic drinks
4. Addictive and hallucinogenic drugs

Kundalini syndrome may manifest as:

1. Chronic fatigue
2. Overheating of the body
3. Chronic insomnia
4. Depression
5. Skin rashes
6. Hypertension

Source: Pranic Psychotherapy by Master Choa Kok Sui, 2000.

THE FIVE AGREEMENTS

NOTE by Ricardo B Serrano, R.Ac.: With thanks and acknowledgement to don Miguel Ruiz and don Jose Ruiz, my Nagual teachers of Toltec wisdom from the Eagle Knight lineage, as expressed by the Five Agreements below:

BE IMPECCABLE WITH YOUR WORD

Speak with integrity. Say only what you mean. Avoid using the word to speak against yourself or to gossip about others. Use the power of your word in the direction of truth and love.

DON'T TAKE ANYTHING PERSONALLY

Nothing others do is because of you. What others say and do is a projection of their own reality, their own dream. When you are immune to the opinions and actions of others, you won't be the victim of needless suffering.

DON'T MAKE ASSUMPTIONS

Find the courage to ask questions and to express what you really want. Communicate with others as clearly as you can to avoid misunderstandings, sadness, and drama. With just this one agreement, you can completely transform your life.

ALWAYS DO YOUR BEST

Your best is going to change from moment to moment; it will be different when you are healthy as opposed to sick. Under any circumstances, simply do your best, and you will avoid self-judgement, self-abuse, and regret.

BE SKEPTICAL, BUT LEARN TO LISTEN

Don't believe yourself or anybody else. Use the power of doubt to question everything you hear: Is it really the truth? Listen to the intent behind words, and you will understand the real message.

Source: The Fifth Agreement by Don Miguel Ruiz and Don Jose Ruiz, 2010.

"We can never be someone else, we can only ever be ourselves. When we master what we are not, we are far from truth. We must all follow our own individual path, another person's way won't lead us to enlightenment. Enlightenment comes from within us, by accepting and loving ourselves and the expression of our art wherever we go." – don Jose Ruiz

"The Toltec wisdom of don Miguel Ruiz is included with Meditation and Qigong to help us purify and quiet the *mitote* – *maya* or illusion – of the mind, break the self-limiting agreements that create needless suffering and replace them with agreements that bring us personal freedom, happiness, and love." - Ricardo B Serrano

REFERENCES:

The Mystery of Hanuman - Inspiring Tales from Art and Mythology by Nitin Kumar

Hanuman Gayatri mantras by Anamika S (http://anamika.hubpages.com)

Valmiki Ramayana by Sundara Kanda (http://valmikiramayan.net)

Hanuman Chalisa and *Baba Hanuman* mantras by Krishna Das Translations (http://krishnadas.com)

Hanuman Qigong by Master Li Jun Feng, 2012.

Why a Guru is necessary by Acharya Kedar (http://bhagawannityananda.org)

Nataraj, Dancing Shiva by Subhamoy Das (http://hinduism.about.com)

Self Realization in Kashmir Shaivism of Swami Lakshmanjoo by John Hughes, 1994.

Shiva Sutras by Swami Lakshmanjoo, 2007.

Kashmir Shaivism by Swami Lakshmanjoo, 2007.

Five Agreements by don Miguel Ruiz and don Jose Ruiz, 2010.

Where are you going? by Swami Muktananda, 1989.

Play of Consciousness by Swami Muktananda, 1978.

The Perfect Relationship by Swami Muktananda, 1979.

Concise Yoga Vasistha by Swami Venkatesananda, 1984.

Kindle my Heart by Swami Chidvilasananda, 1996.

Inner Teachings of Hinduism Revealed by Master Choa Kok Sui, 2004.

Pranic Psychotherapy by Master Choa Kok Sui, 2000.

Raja Choudhury, Ricardo's Kundalini teacher

Acknowledgements and Parting Thought: With thanks and acknowledgements to Raja Choudhury and the authors of the above books for their assistance and contributions to my enlightenment as a Siddha yogi and especially to the completion of this book. Please view the Hanuman mantras and Qigong via the Youtube videos at my blog keystohealing.ca

May this book help you to some degree realize the importance and relevance of Sri Vidya meditation practices to our health, happiness and well-being as conveyed by the saints and meditation masters like Guruji Amritananda. Traditionally, the great Masters imparted their teachings in secret to only a few, hand-picked disciples, however, because of their great love and empathy for humanity's disposition, they are now starting a new meditation revolution for students who are ready, therefore, let us be grateful for their teachings and contributions to alleviate humanity's suffering. My contribution is integrating Qigong with Sri Vidya meditation for rooting or grounding the Kundalini Shakti to Mother Earth – to avoid kundalini syndromes and for healing Mother Earth. Ricardo B Serrano, R.Ac., North Vancouver, B.C., Canada, April 30, 2018

Buddha's Four Noble Truths:

1. Life is suffering - everything that changes brings suffering
2. Cause of suffering - selfish desire
3. End of suffering - free of selfish desire
4. Eight-fold Path that frees us from suffering:

1. Right understanding - seeing life as it is
2. Right purpose - learning to live that is in line with life as it is
3. Right speech - speaking kindly
4. Right conduct - acting kindly
5. Right occupation - living for the welfare of all
6. Right effort - constant endeavor to train our mind; we become what we think
7. Right attention to *here* and *now*
8. Right meditation to train your mind

Lord Buddha said, "This, brothers, is the path that I myself have followed. No other path so purifies the mind. Follow this path and conquer Mara (*tempter*); its end is the end of sorrow. But all effort must be made by you. *Buddhas* only show the way."

"By this path of the *Guru*, knowledge of one's *Self* rises." – *Guru Gita*, v.110

I truly believe that the original root and beginning of my spiritual journey toward liberation started since attending the *Siddha Shaktipat* intensive with *Gurumayi Chidvilasananda* in Vancouver, B.C. in *June 15, 1989*. My spiritual search and journey within a span of 20 years also finally culminated after including *Siddha* meditation (*Gurukripa Yoga*) with my Enlightenment Qigong Forms – for rooting or grounding the *Kundalini Shakti to Mother Earth* – to avoid *kundalini* syndromes and for healing Mother Earth – as my form of *seva* (*selfless service*) to my beloved *Sadguru Bhagawan Nityananda*, the *Guru* of our *Siddha* lineage.

From my spiritual oneness experience as a *Siddha* yogi for over twenty years, I believe that without the *grace* of a *Siddha*, a *Sadguru*, like *Bhagawan Nityananda* you cannot realize God. A *Siddha Master* said, "You may be successful at reducing stress or even attaining states of relative happiness. But without the *Guru*, these will be fleeting at best. By reading scriptures and attending lectures you may be able to understand and express philosophy like so many preachers that we encounter day-in and day-out. But you won't have a lasting experience of the philosophy that you are preaching. To become completely absorbed in God, to liberate yourself from *ego* bondage in order to bask in the rays of total freedom from this ignorance of pain and pleasure, you must be guided by a *Siddha* (perfected being) until you are set on your own path. It is only by the g*race* of such a *Sadguru* that you can undergo permanent spiritual transformation."

Return to Oneness with Shiva

You Hold the Healing Codes

Invocation to Unity

I am a Christed Being; I am in unity with Spirit

I am a Christed Being; I am in unity with All That Is

The Light of my own Being shines upon my path

I am a Christed Being; I am in unity with All That Will Be

I hold the shining Light of the Source within my heart

I walk in unity with Spirit

I laugh in unity with the Source

I love in unity with my fellow beings

I am a Christed Spirit; I am a bridge between heaven and earth

By Ricardo B Serrano, R.Ac.
8/27/2012

Dedication and Disclaimer:

Ricardo B. Serrano has dedicated this work to the present and future generations of eclectic Wu Ji Qigong practitioners and bodhisattvas who want to experience spiritual enlightenment, ascension, healing and heaven on earth.

You Hold the Healing Codes

© Ricardo B Serrano, R.Ac.

Published by Holisticwebs.com

August 27, 2012

ISBN 978-0-9880502-1-1

Disclaimer: The healing conscious mind encodements are not intended to replace expert medical care. Consult with your physician or licensed health care practitioner regarding the treatment of any medical condition. The author is not held responsible for any negative effects of the meditation practices.

INTRODUCTION

The main emphasis of the second part of the book – You Hold the Healing Codes – is the use of the two step process – Hologram of Love Merkaba energy ball of light for your lightbody activation, and for encoding the abundance code or healing codes inside the hologram of love energy ball of light you're holding with your hands which is then moved to the diseased part of the body.

Once the Hologram of Love is activated through the Omkabah Heart Lightbody Activation and Maitreya (Shiva) Shen Gong followed by one of the Enlightenment Qigong forms, the merkaba assists us in accessing our natural Qigong state of ascended consciousness. The heart awakens and opens more to unconditional love during healing sessions and this opening continues during your normal life.

The Hologram of Love Merkaba energy ball of light is the divine dimensional medium that allows us to connect to the higher levels of consciousness. It has the ability to heal and rejuvenate any form of creation as it is the living conscious holographic pattern of God Source vibration.

The abundance and healing codes are commands to program or direct God's universal energy which comes from the unconditional love within the heart when it is opened through the practice of Merkaba meditation, Qi-healing and Enlightenment Qigong forms.

For your abundance meditation, write down three things that you would like to manifest in your life at this present time.

The abundance code is: *I now encode this Hologram of Love I'm holding to retrieve my original request which was "_____" and replace it with my new request which is "_____." Please let this manifest if it is for my divine higher good. I accept that these requests are now given to me and I give thanks to God. So be it.*

Each of the healing code is used for a particular specific disease(s) you wish to heal for yourself and others. See Healing Conscious Mind Encodements

You can add this command to each healing code: *I command this hologram of love healing process to permanently cleanse and heal my multidimensional bodies from my past, present and parents, now.*

SPECIAL CALL

I, as son or daughter of the new age awakening now upon the earth command forth in the name of my mighty 'I AM' presence that my holy Christ Self flow forth into my human mind and perform the work of reuniting me to its God receiver.

Oh come into me now, oh Christed one, and raise me back up to my source. Bring forth God energies necessary for me to know, only the perfection of God's love, life, and light this day, in all I see, speak, and do. So be it done, in the name of my mighty 'I AM' presence. KODOISH KODOISH KODOISH ADONAI TSEBAYOTH 3x. The Mantra of Salutation from the Brotherhoods of Light. This mantra has been given to man as both a greeting and a protection from the influences of negative consciousness.

The Theory behind the Abundance and Healing Codes Using the *Hologram of Love Merkaba* Energy Ball of Light

"Where awareness (or attention) goes, energy flows. Where energy flows, awareness follows." – Qigong expression

All we need to do to receive direct help is to ask. Didn't Christ also say: "*Ask, and it shall be given you: seek and ye shall find; knock and it shall be opened unto you. Everyone that asketh receiveth; and he that seeketh findeth*?"

The creative process involves four steps to attracting all your desires:

1. Ask – You must know what you want. The universe can't deliver without first knowing what it is that you want to have manifested into your life.
2. Believe – You need to truly believe that what you are asking for will become yours. Doubts need to be pushed away. The idea that failure is a possibility will mess up the delivery.
3. Receive – It is important that you become an active player in reaching your goals. When opportunity comes your way you must not hesitate.
4. Energize – Energizing your heart's desire (thought forms) through the *merkaba* energy ball of light for abundance and healing is the critical energetic part in manifesting the desire.

As Bodhisattva Padmasambhava says: "*Complete devotion brings complete blessing; absence of doubts brings complete success.*"

The use of the merkaba energy ball of light you're holding after *Hologram of Love Merkaba* activation in manifesting your heart's desire for abundance and healing works for the following reasons:

"*A man is but the product of his thoughts what he thinks, he becomes.*" – Mahatma Gandhi

"The Heart is the Supreme Master of the organs and is the home of *shen*, the Spirit. If the Master is brilliant, his subjects are peaceful. If the Master is disturbed, his twelve officials [the body's organ systems] are endangered."

"Our true Spirit, which the Chinese call *shen*, is the spark of divinity that resides within the heart of every human being and manifests as love, kindness, compassion, generosity, giving, tolerance, forgiveness, mercy, tenderness and the appreciation of beauty.

It is the Spirit of a human being as the divine messenger, the channel of God's will and love. *Shen* is the purpose of all spiritual paths. It is the Buddha's desire to end suffering and it is Christ's love and compassion... *Shen* manifests only when the heart is open. Once the heart is open, *shen* manifests as light that illuminates the path of a man or woman in life's journey toward the spiritual goal and along the spiritual path." – quotes from Ron Teeguarden's book *Radiant Health*

"All diseases belong to the heart." – ancient Chinese sage

"The basis of the techniques is the activation of the Hologram of Love Merkaba, a rotating lightfield awakening your spherical consciousness. This will actually raise one's quotient of light vibration within the human atomic cell structure. Once activated, the merkaba assists us in accessing our natural Qigong state of ascended consciousness. The heart awakens and opens more to unconditional love during healing sessions and this opening continues during your normal life. The tool of the Hologram of Love is a high dimensional Divine manifestation of living that allows one to access all levels of consciousness. It has the ability to heal and rejuvenate any form of creation as it is the living conscious holographic pattern of God Source vibration." - Master Thoth

Hologram is an energy interference pattern. Within this pattern, every piece contains the whole. - Dr. Richard Gerber

Quotes from Vibrational Medicine book on Holograms, Vibrational Medicine, Spiritual Healing, Personal & Planetary Evolution by Dr. Richard Gerber, MD

The holographic model sets a precedent for new ways of understanding Einsteinian medicine and provides a totally new way of looking at the universe. Utilizing the holographic model, it is possible to arrive at conclusions one might not come upon by utilizing simple deductive reasoning and logic.

Etheric matter is referred to in the Eastern esoteric literature as "subtle matter," or matter which is less dense than physical, i.e., of a higher frequency nature. The etheric body appears to be a subtle counterpart of the physical body, possibly somewhat like the phantom leaf. Our etheric body is an energy interference pattern with the characteristics of a hologram. It is likely that there are subtle counterparts to the physical universe made up of matter of higher frequencies. If the energy interference pattern of a single etheric body acts as a hologram, might not the entire universal energy interference pattern represent a vast cosmic hologram? If this is true, then by virtue of the holographic principle whereby every piece contains the whole, there are profound implications for information being stored within the seemingly empty space around us! The fact that limitless amounts of information might be enfolded into the structure of the universe is an idea gaining more and more attention from theorists such as Nobel prize-winning physicist David Bohm. Bohm has presented convincing scientific arguments for what he calls the "implicate order" of the holographic universe. In such a universe, higher levels of order and information may be holographically enfolded in the fabric of space and matter/energy.

If indeed there exists a cosmic hologram, then every piece of the universe contains information concerning the makeup of the entire cosmos. Unlike a static hologram, the cosmic hologram is a dynamically moving system that changes from microsecond to microsecond. *Because what happens in just a small fragment of the holographic energy interference pattern affects the entire structure simultaneously, there is a tremendous connectivity relationship between all parts of the holographic universe.* If one were to view God as "all there is," then, through the holographic interconnectivity of space, God could simultaneously be in contact with all creations. The ultimate question, of course, is how does one tap into this information about the cosmos which is enfolded into the structure of space within and around us? How do we decode the cosmic hologram?

By decoding a small piece of the universal hologram, one may unfold information about the whole universe stored within the matrix.

The selective focusing of consciousness via psychic attunement (Merkabah) may hold the potential for such decoding of the universal hologram.

The Einsteinian viewpoint of vibrational medicine sees the human being as a multidimensional organism made up of physical/cellular systems in dynamic interplay with complex regulatory energetic fields. Vibrational medicine attempts to heal illness by manipulating these subtle-energy fields via directing energy into the body instead of manipulating the cells and organs through drugs or surgery.

The recognition that all matter is energy forms the foundation for understanding how human beings can be considered dynamic energetic systems. Through his famous equation, $E = mc^2$, Albert Einstein proved to scientists that energy and matter are dual expressions of the same universal substance. That universal substance is a primal energy or vibration of which we are all composed. Therefore, attempting to heal the body through the manipulation of this basic vibrational or energetic level of substance can be thought of as vibrational medicine.

Although the Einsteinian viewpoint has slowly found acceptance and application in the minds of physicists, Einstein's profound insights have yet to be incorporated into the way doctors look at human beings and illness.

Vibrational medicine seeks to reunite the personality with the Higher Self in a more meaningful, connected way. Vibrational modalities help to strengthen the energetic connections between the personality and the soul itself, by rebalancing the body / mind / spirit complex as a whole. Not all vibrational healing tools work at the higher energetic levels, but it is the intent and goal of the vibrational healer / physician to seek and assist this alignment within his or her patients.

Spiritual healing (holographic healing) *attempts to work at the level of the higher subtle bodies and chakras* to affect a healing from the most primary level of disease origins. *The spiritual healer (holographic healer) works as a power source of multiple-frequency outputs to allow energy shifts at several levels simultaneously.* It is theorized that there may be a transient energy link between the chakras of the healer and the patient. This chakra-to-chakra link may allow for a direct resonant transfer of multiple subtle frequencies, which can shift the multidimensional energy structure of the patient back toward a perfect balance of mind, body, and spirit. *While most magnetic healers work strictly at the level of the body, spiritual healers (holographic healers) usually work with the many levels of mind and spirit as well.* The nature of this higher dimensional energy is that it transcends all limitations of space and time by virtue of the fact that levels from the etheric and higher energies are in the domain of negative space / time. As such, the energies working at these levels move in a dimension which is outside of the usual references of ordinary (or positive) space / time to which the conscious mind is limited in its perception. However, the frequencies at which spiritual healing takes place often extend to the same levels at which the Higher Self exists and operates.

"Spiritual healing" (holographic healing) works not only at the physical and etheric levels, but also helps to rebalance the astral, mental, and higher energetic levels of dysfunction as well. In addition, spiritual healing (distance healing) may be performed either in the presence of the patient or at great distances which may separate the patient and healer.

If we are beings of energy, then it follows that we can be affected by energy.

Vibrational healing modalities are effective because of their ability to impact upon the subtle unseen hierarchical levels of human physiology, which include the physical and etheric bodies, the acupuncture meridians, the chakras and nadis, and the astral, mental, causal, and higher spiritual bodies. Having described the function and integration of these many levels of energetic and spiritual physiology, *we must now ask how all of this information fits in with our divine purpose upon the planet Earth.* An understanding of the higher levels of subtle anatomy and their influence upon our daily lives and health will help us to comprehend how we are all intimately linked with the continually evolving divine energies of the soul.

Our physical and higher bodies are specialized vehicles which allow the expression of the soul's consciousness upon the dense Earth plane. The consciousness of each soul is actually a particularization of that greater spiritual consciousness which we refer to as God. Various spiritual philosophies look to the time of our universe's creation as the period when God created all souls simultaneously. Mixing cosmic evolution with theology, one might view the Big Bang as more than just the creation of primordial interstellar hydrogen and light. It was also the time at which the Creator gave birth to the billions of human souls that would inhabit the new universe through an explosive particularization of the divine conscious energies. It is said that God created human beings in the divine image. As each soul was created in that first moment, God separated into smaller beings of light which were energetic representations of the original vast beingness. *Through the conscious evolution of these lesser gods and the holographic connectivity of the universe, God could enrich and develop the tremendous potential for diversity and self-knowledge inherent in supreme consciousness*. These primal beings of light, or souls, developed ways of manifesting the ethereal energies of their consciousness through denser forms of expression. The denser forms, called the physical bodies, would allow them to experience through their senses the wonders and beauties of the evolving planets. Also, it would allow them to experiment with the expression of their emotional nature through interactions and relationships between themselves, their environment, and the other sentient life forms manifesting upon the planets on which they chose to incarnate.

Because no entity could develop itself in all possible ways through the course of a single life span of these dense vehicles of expression, a continuous cycle of regeneration and rebirth, known as reincarnation, was created. During each lifetime, the incarnating soul is able to partake of many diverse experiences which allow it to explore the wonders, joys, and sorrows of human existence. Through hit or miss, and reward or punishment, the consciousness of the soul, projected through earthly bodies, can learn and experience planetary life through every conceivable variation of the human form. Via the reincarnation cycle, each soul comes to know the splendor and achievements, as well as the difficulties and sadnesses, of each of the existing races and colors of peoples. All souls come to experience life as the pinnacle of high society as well as the simplicity and daily toil of the farms and fields. All conscious entities find out how life differs between being male and female in the different societies. Through each of these varied experiences, the soul comes to know itself and to better understand its own emotional, physical, and spiritual nature, as well as the many different expressions that physical human life allows. *Perhaps most importantly in its earthly sojourns, the soul comes to appreciate and experience the nature of love in its many different forms, and develops a greater compassion and caring for all of God's creations*.

Personal and spiritual transformation are dependent upon the opening of the heart chakra. As our heart centers open wider and we begin to feel greater compassion and empathy for all living things, we move closer to expressing the divine unconditional love of the Christ Consciousness, which is the supreme facet of spiritual awakening towards which we are all gradually evolving.

Of the chakra blockages that are known to occur, dysfunction in the heart chakra can be the most devastating. *The heart chakra is the central energy center in the chakra / nadi system*. It is an integral link between the three higher and the three lower chakras. In another sense, it is also the center of human existence, because it is the major chakra from which we are able to express love. *The expression of love is perhaps one of the most important lessons that humans have incarnated upon the physical plane to learn. Without love, existence can be dry and meaningless. It is necessary that we learn to love not only those around us but also ourselves.*

All souls are spiritual beings of light which remain energetically connected to the Creator and the Creator's universe through a holographic connectivity relationship. All souls have evolved as unique but diverse manifestations of the single divine principle (also known as the Law of One). As the souls become enriched through their experiences, so too does the Creator come to grow and evolve in a greater knowing of self in infinite expression. In spite of this unity with God and the universe, the souls temporary lose the memory of their spiritual origins after incarnating into dense physical bodies. *In reality, the higher spiritual bodies of the souls maintain a cosmic awareness and connection to the God-force. Only the projected fragment of the soul's total consciousness which inhabits the dense physical form loses the memory of its origins.*

The earthly personalities forget that they are manifestations of the one supreme intelligence, as the perceptual mechanisms of their brains and bodies create a physical sense of separation from each other as well as from their Creator. Partly because of this sense of separation from God, human beings have created religion and its rituals in an attempt to reunite themselves with the creative forces of nature and the physical universe which seemed outside of themselves. Human beings forget that the kingdom of God is already within each of us. Jesus (Lord Sananda) incarnated to teach and remind us of this simple forgotten truth.

The reincarnational cycle has built-in safeguards that prevent the perpetuation of wrong thinking and negative actions toward fellow journeyers upon the soul quest of self-discovery and enlightenment. This system of energy credits and debits, based on positive and negative deeds and actions, has been referred to as the Law of Karma. The subtle nature of higher dimensional anatomy and its controlling influence upon the creation and physiological maintenance of the physical body, allows the negative energies of past-life misdeeds to be carried over to future lifetimes by causing subtle abnormalities in the human physical and emotional structure.

By working through physical handicaps and illnesses, individuals are able to "burn away the karma" of their negative deeds and redeem their souls for the evils, torments, and suffering that they may have caused others in previous lives.

Karmic illness is worth mentioning because it is an area of disease upon which vibrational medicine is able to have certain impacts, at least in creating an awareness of the reasons behind some diseases and handicaps. Again, this returns us to the concept of self-responsibility in accepting the consequences of our actions, whether they originate from this life or a past one. Few would dream that the negative emotions and malicious deeds of their previous lives would come back to haunt them in their present lives as some form of illness. But it is possible, nonetheless.

The most important things that Jesus (Lord Sananda) taught - learning to love ourselves and others, to forgive, and to pray and give thanks to the Creator - are just as important today as they were 2000 years ago. We have seen how distortions of our emotional nature, and blockage of our ability to love and forgive, can cause disturbance and imbalance of our chakras and subtle-energy anatomy. When one combines weakness of the body's energetic physiology from emotional, mental, and subtle imbalances, with infectious or toxic environmental factors, illness is often the result. Through the sophisticated New Age technologies which spiritual scientists are using to document the existence of our subtle anatomic framework, we are finally beginning to understand the true spiritual significance of what Jesus (Lord Sananda) and many others have taught throughout the centuries since the time of Lemuria and Atlantis. *The discoveries that we are making today are, in fact, reincarnational expressions of older spiritual knowledge which originated in these ancient yet advanced civilizations.*

The basic principles of holistic and natural healing, as well as vibrational medicine, are actually thousands of centuries old, dating back to the times of Atlantis and Lemuria. Through the continuous cycle of regeneration and rebirth, these ideas have surfaced *once again to produce methods of spiritual healing (such as holographic healing) that may help to alleviate much of the disease that humanity seems to have inflicted upon itself*. It is only because of a gradual shift in consciousness within the new guard of the medical and scientific community that the intellectual and spiritual environment has ripened to the point that these powerful healing modalities may again surface to see the light of day.

The expression of love is perhaps one of the most important lessons that humans have incarnated upon the physical plane to learn. Without love, existence can be dry and meaningless. It is necessary that we learn to love not only those around us but also ourselves."

Dr. Richard Gerber, MD, **Vibrational Medicine: New Choices for Healing Ourselves**, 1988

Activating the Hologram of LOVE - A New Spiritual Science?

An Interview with Alton Kamadon of the Alpha, Omega Order of Melchizedek by Olga Sheean of Shared Vision (Feb/98)

OS: What exactly is the hologram of love - the basis of your teachings?

Alton: The hologram of love (or Merkaba) is the sacred geometric pattern which gave birth to the whole universe. It is based on unconditional love, so it must be the pattern of unconditional love, because everything in the universe resonates to it, no matter what it is or what dimension it's in. That means that you and I, as human beings, also have that pattern within us, so we are actually walking, talking unconditional love. We always have been, we've just never recognized it.

However, you can't really measure this in third dimensional terms. This is a high concept of divine creation that you intuitively resonate to. It's not something to be analyzed by the left brain. Those who are drawn to this intuitively find that, as soon as they apply it, they have the most extraordinary experiences and their whole body changes. They meditate in a way that activates the Holographic Merkaba with light, invoking a special frequency of 13:20:33 into that field of continuous time.

OS: What is this 13:20:33 frequency?

Alton: Part of what we came to learn as human beings was how to live with limitation, and the 12:60 timing that we have allowed ourselves to be encompassed within is a timing of limitation. It was brought in through the Gregorian calendar, and represents the 12 months of the year, the 60 minutes in the hour, etc. I work with a different frequency - 13:20:33 - a frequency of no limitation. If you study the human body, you will find that this frequency is harmonized through it. We have 13 major articulations in the body - ankles, knees, hips, wrists, elbows, shoulders and the neck - and 20 fingers and toes. When you add 20 and 13, you arrive at the master number of 33, which is also the number of vertebrae in the spine - the center of the body. The ancient Mayans used the frequency of 13 and 20 for their calendar of time, awakened God Consciousness within themselves, and enabled them to access the center of the universe and merge with it. The process provides a spherical perspective called omni perspective which, in turn, helps individuals live in non-judgement and to be the witness in our illusionary physical world. They thus become galactically aligned and empowered.

OS: How is this frequency applied?

Alton: If our ultimate goal is to merge back with God, then God our Creator made our bodies to transcend this physical world by providing keys and formulas within us to achieve this. When you relate this key to the hologram of love, you'll see that those two concepts together make up the ultimate key to ascension. The frequency of 13:20:33 is the frequency of no time. The hologram of love is symbolic of the time continuum because it's all made up of curves. When you try to measure linear time, or anything in this world, it has straight edges or angles. But when we work with the hologram of love, we are working with the curves of continuous time. You look at that design and see that it goes into itself continuously, circle after circle. When you put it into a hologram, you end up with sphere after sphere, and there is no beginning or end. That is the pattern of our human body. If you put those two things together - 13:20:33 and the Hologram of Love (utilizing the curves of time) - you can create a whole new body form and consciousness.

OS: What exactly is the time/space continuum?

Alton: As we make our transition into our light body or form of creation, we withdraw from linear time (measured in a straight line, with a beginning and an end), and we move into the time continuum, which is time-less spiritual existence, with no beginning or end. According to the Egyptian spirit guide Thoth, the time/space continuum is attached to the spine. This makes it very easy to withdraw yourself from your physical body within a meditation through your own time/space continuum. Thoth teaches us that we are already in unity consciousness - and always have been - and it's a complete illusion that we are not, because we are always attached to God through the time/space continuum and always have been. We have just not allowed ourselves the expansion of consciousness to accept there is something else (the time continuum) that is part of our body.

OS: In practical terms, what can the hologram of love do for people?

Alton: First of all, it will open up their psychic abilities through their pineal gland. It will activate a rotational field of life that encompasses this dimension and all the others beyond us. It also provides a completely different perception of creation, expanding consciousness, and exerting an amazing effect on your heart. As soon as you use the hologram of love, it activates the love center, and opens up your heart spontaneously, so that you can express and receive much more love. You can also use this technique to heal yourself permanently.

OS: What about a degenerative condition caused by poor diet, for example?

Alton: You are working with holograms which are thought-induced. If you work with the time/space continuum of the hologram of love, you immediately change the timing around the physical body. In other words, your physical self resonates to a 12:60 illusionary memory. Now if you use this other concept, you change the memory of the cell and you bring it into the time/space continuum where everything is perfect. It is only down at this third-dimensional level that we have imperfection.

What's marvelous about this is that if a person has created an illness through incorrect eating, and the illness is healed with this particular technique, this changes the thought pattern in the person so that they then begin to change their diet. It happens automatically, changing the memory cell. This is what makes this process so extraordinary. We're talking about permanent changes in people - not something that will re-manifest.

OS: Can you give some example of that?

Alton: Yes, I have worked with two cancer cases recently, both of which were totally healed in a relatively short period of time. They were treated with 30-minute sessions for five days, until the cancer was completely gone. One individual, with cervical cancer, felt as if her insides were being sucked out of her. This was all done with the hologram and thought, with no other modalities used. There are many different hologram modalities out there, but none of them use this particular pattern and frequency which are the key to the permanent and total healing achieved with this approach. Anyone can do this. It's a three-breath activation, very quick and extremely effective. The energy in this hologram of love is much more refined - as it should be, as a higher vibration beyond the third dimension. The simplest form can be learnt by anyone within an hour or less. Once the hologram is activated and locked into your heart, it becomes part of you, breathing with you, and is very soft and malleable, like an outer skin. Once it's there, we simply take one focused breath and it is immediately re-activated. You just have to think about it, and you see and feel it.

According to Thoth, unconditional love is a powerful magnetic force which, once activated through the hologram of love, makes you truly magnetic within every cell of your body. As a result, you begin to attract all you need to become a cosmic vibration of higher wisdom. If we could understand time and love together, Thoth said, we would have the answer.

Healing Conscious Mind Encodements

"The energy ball is your magical ally for power and guidance."

The Healing Conscious Mind Encodements are healing codes that are used every time the Merkaba field is activated through the use of Qi-healing, Enlightenment Qigong forms, Maitreya (Shiva) Shen Gong and Omkabah Heart Lightbody Activation. Each of the following healing code is used for a particular specific disease(s) you wish to heal for yourself and others.

The Healing Conscious Mind Encodements are the healing commands that program or direct the universal Qi healing energy which comes from the unconditional love within the heart when it is opened through the practice of the Enlightenment Qigong forms and Qi-healing discussed in the two DVDs: Maitreya (Shiva) Shen Gong and Omkabah Heart Lightbody Activation; and in the four books: Meditation and Qigong Mastery, Return to Oneness with the Tao, Return to Oneness with Spirit, and Keys to Healing and Self-Mastery according to the Hathors.

INFECTIOUS AND PARASITIC DISEASES
- I now command freedom from any and all infections or infestations.
- I command full immune competence and full function of all white cells, T-cells and lymphocytes, which are present in normal numbers.

IMMUNOLOGIC AND ALLERGIC DISORDERS
- I command harmonious relationships of all parts of my body to each other and to all substances that I ingest.

CARDIOVASCULAR DISORDERS
- I command my heart and circulatory system are strong, balanced and clear.
- I command my blood to flow freely, bringing vitality to all parts of my body; to every cell, molecule, and atom of this body.

PULMONARY DISORDERS
- I command that I breathe deeply, freely and effectively, bringing oxygen to every tissue, organ and cell in my body.
- I command my chest, lungs and circulation to be effective, balanced and strong.

GASTROINTESTINAL (GI) DISORDERS
- I command my intestinal tract, from entrance to exit, to be in harmonious balance in all of its movements and in its absorption of nutrients.
- I command my intestinal tract to absorb fully all nutrients, and eliminate fully all substances that this body no longer needs.

LIVER AND BILE DISORDERS
- I command my liver to metabolize and detoxify fully all substances presented to it.
- I command my bile to flow freely and without obstruction into the gastrointestinal tract, leaving no sediment behind.

ENDOCRINE DISORDERS
- I command my endocrine glands work in perfect balance to produce the hormones that heal and stabilize this body and keep this body in perfect health.

HEMATOLOGIC (BLOOD) DISORDERS
- I command perfection in the fluids, proteins and cells within the blood at all times, in perfect balance.

URINARY SYSTEM
- I command my kidneys function freely and fully to filter and purify the blood.
- I command that I eliminate all wastes fully, freely and fluidly.

MUSCULOSKELETAL AND CONNECTIVE TISSUE DISORDERS

- I command my muscles and joints to be strong, flexible and in beautifully balanced alignment, free of any pain or inflammation.
- I command my connective tissue, tendons and ligaments to be strong, flexible, and of perfect chemical composition, free of any pain or inflammation.

NEUROLOGIC DISORDERS
- I command perfect function of my mind, brain, spinal cord and muscles, accomplishing any and all actions and functions that I decree.

PSYCHIATRIC DISORDERS (upper, middle and lower dantians)
- I command perfectly balanced integration of body, mind and spirit, to be joyous and enthusiastic about life, and I command that I open to allow this joy throughout the day.

EAR, NOSE AND THROAT
- I command perfect hearing and clear breathing.
- I command that I speak my truth freely, clearly and beautifully.

OPTHALMOLOGY (EYE) DISORDERS
- I command that I receive fully all vision and perception. I see clearly with no judgement or limitation. I welcome the beauty that the world offers.

DERMATOLOGIC (SKIN) DISORDERS
- I command my skin to be clear, smooth, and beautiful and place no barriers between me and the outside world.
- I command that I love and accept myself as a divine child of God created in perfection and beauty.

DENTAL DISORDERS
- I command my jaw to be fully relaxed and functional; the joints work freely and fluidly.
- I command my teeth and gums to be clear, strong and functional.
- I command that I love and care for them daily, blessing them and accepting their perfection.

REPRODUCTIVE SYSTEM
- I command that I accept myself as a Divine child of God endowed with the beauty of reproduction.
- I command the balanced function of all my reproductive organs operating in harmony with God's Divine Plan.

ADDICTION and CODEPENDENCY (upper, middle and lower dantians)
- I command that I accept, forgive, and love myself as a divine child of God in harmony with All That Is.
- I command that I accept, forgive, and love others who have done wrong to me in the past.
- I command that I live in the present awareness most of the time, do the best I can, be impeccable with my word, not make assumptions, not take anything personally, and be skeptical but learn to listen.

INSTRUCTIONS: Daily do the Maitreya (Shiva) Shen Gong and Merkaba meditation followed by one of the Enlightenment Qigong forms, and then:

1. Visualize holding a Merkaba Energy Power Ball of Light
2. The specific healing code(s) is encoded inside the Merkaba Energy Ball of Light you are holding with your hands
3. Touching the tip of your tongue to your upper palate, move the energy ball from the top of your head down to a specific chakra, dantian or part of the body in need of healing
4. End the session with grounding the energy ball to your lower dantian (tanden) connecting to the heart center of Mother Earth

By Ricardo B. Serrano, R.Ac. You Hold the Keys to Healing
http://qigongmastery.ca http://keystohealing.ca

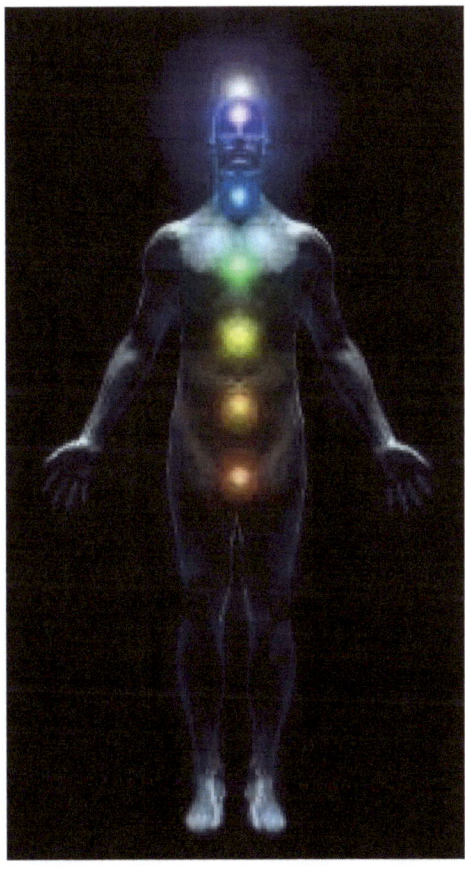

With thanks and acknowledgement to Chakras photo, Alton Kamadon for his Merkaba teachings, my meditation and Qigong teachers and to Dr. Richard Gerber for the quotations from his book "Vibrational Medicine." With thanks and acknowledgement also to *Lucis Trust* for the use of the Triangles Work and the Great Invocation, to Tony Stubbs for quotes from his book *An Ascension Handbook, and* other owners of the photos used in the book.

YOU HOLD THE KEYS TO HEALING

"Awareness and intention are powerful factors for personal transformation and healing."

Now that the five books by Ricardo B Serrano have been published, *Meditation and Qigong Mastery, Return to Oneness with the Tao, Return to Oneness with Spirit through Pan Gu Shen Gong, Keys to Healing and Self-Mastery according to the Hathors* and *Return to Oneness with Shiva,* the important questions are, what makes these books different from other related meditation and Qigong books? What will you learn from reading these books?

These five books have the same goal: to offer readers how-to-techniques to manage stress in their daily lives and spiritually awaken when stress is cleared and released. These keys to your healing - are the *non-sectarian* how-to-techniques that have been personally practiced and developed for 30 years by the author, Ricardo B Serrano, and have been tested in clinical setting by him, his clients, and other Taoist, Buddhist and Yoga meditation and Qigong practitioners of every *pantheistic* - All is God - tradition for centuries for healing and personal transformation.

The first book *Meditation and Qigong Mastery* elaborates on the meditation and Qigong principles that masters use to activate and develop their lightbodies, also called EMF (electromagnetic fields), Wei Qi or merkaba, which is the missing mastery principle not discussed by eastern authors in their meditation and Qigong books. Omkabah heart lightbody activation and Maitreya (Shiva) Shen Gong are introduced. Quotations on inner mastery by meditation masters are included to guide the readers toward the path of inner mastery. Powerful mantras are also included to unite the meditation practitioners to the spiritual divine energy of the ancient lineage of the Siddha and Buddhist Masters. Lastly, the merkaba energy ball of light with holographic sound healing is taught for healing and spiritual awakening.

The second book *Return to Oneness with the Tao* elaborates on the Taoist meditation and Qigong inner alchemy techniques such as lower dantien breathing, Microcosmic Orbit Qigong, primordial wuji Qigong, meditation on twin hearts, and Tibetan Shamanic Qigong to cultivate the Three Treasures Jing, Qi and Shen. An important addition to this book is the understanding of a most important principle - awareness and intention are powerful factors for personal transformation and healing. When we are aware of what is - the emotional root cause of disease that is blocking the flow of Qi - we can intentionally release it through meditation and Qigong to effect a process of change for personal transformation and healing.

"*God Consciousness is the reality of everything.*" - Shiva Sutra 1.1

The third book *Return to Oneness with Spirit through Pan Gu Shen Gong* elaborates on the use of Pan Gu Shen Gong together with the EFT Qi-healer's Method to effectively clear and release the emotional debris held in the body, cultivate the Three Treasures Jing, Qi and Shen, and strengthen one's self-awareness through an integrated combination of Toltec wisdom, Qigong, Qi-healing, emotional freedom technique therapy, ear acupuncture, and Chinese tonic herbs. We are sick because we are not aware. Awareness is the key to healing.

The goal of the fourth book *Keys to Healing and Self-Mastery according to the Hathors*, a supplementary book to Holographic Sound Healing taught at the *Meditation and Qigong Mastery* book, and the *Omkabah Heart Lightbody Activation* video, is to build the Ka and offer readers an effective Hathor's emotional mastery technique to manage emotional stress, the main cause of disease, in their daily lives and spiritually awaken when emotional stress is cleared, released and stabilized. Doing this practice will provide a fast, safe way to stabilize your chaotic emotions such anger or fear. Holographic Sound Healing with the Four Sacred Elements is integrated with Ka(Merkaba) Meditation to complement Holographic Lightbody activation, and build the Sahhu or immortal golden lightbody. Dr. Johanna Budwig's *Diet for Cancer and Chronic Diseases* and *Sun gazing* are included as adjunct keys to healing.

The goal of the fifth book *Return to Oneness with Shiva* is to offer a solution to most people whose life challenge is battling their monkey-mind (ego) which I believe is the cause of suffering and can be conquered by becoming like Hanuman whose love and devotion to his Sadguru is shown by the application of Hanuman Qigong and Hunaman ji's mantras and self-realization teachings of Kashmir Shaivism. Healing with the hologram of love merkaba energy ball of light encoded with the healing conscious mind encodements is also included. Who and what you meditate on, you become.

In summary, the five books *Meditation and Qigong Mastery, Return to Oneness with the Tao, Return to Oneness with Spirit*, and *Keys to Healing and Self-Mastery according to the Hathors*, and *Return to Oneness with Shiva* form a strong basic foundation, so to speak, of dietary and energy-based psychoneuroimmunolgy or neuroimmunomodulation strategies to effectively heal substance abuse and chronic diseases mainly caused by emotional stress, diet that is high in trans-fatty acids and low in Essential Fatty Acids, and unhealthy lifestyle. These strategies bring the physical, mental, emotional, and spiritual aspects of a person into homeostasis, and at the same time spiritually awaken a person in the process of being in the flow because the individual being is one with universal being.

The reality of this whole universe is God consciousness. It is filled with God consciousness. This world is nothing but the blissful energy of the all-pervading consciousness of God. God and the individual are one, to realize this is the essence and goal of meditation and Qigong.

Whatever the diagnosis of your disease, you do not have to expect the worst. For every problem, there are solutions. You hold the keys to healing.

ENLIGHTENMENT QIGONG FORMS for Returning to Oneness

Ricardo welcomes you to this non-denominational page that is dedicated to the spread of non-denominational integrative Enlightenment Qigong forms throughout the world for awakening our true inner selves to return to oneness by opening the heart to unconditional love.

The Enlightenment Qigong (Wuji Qigong) forms synthesized and taught by Master Ricardo B. Serrano, R.Ac., a Qi-healer and certified Qigong instructor, are Pan Gu Shengong, Primordial Wuji Qigong, Sheng Zhen Wuji Yuan Gong, and Maitreya (Shiva) Shen Gong supplemented with spontaneous Tibetan Shamanic Qigong, a formless Qigong, together with Merkaba meditation and Shaktipat meditation to further develop the lightbody (energy bubble).

Through their ancient lineages, these four Enlightenment Qigong forms, applied individually or in combination, have been clinically tested and proven together with the formless spontaneous Tibetan Shamanic Qigong and Merkaba / Shaktipat meditation by myself and their practitioners to provide a strong basic foundation for understanding and experiencing spiritual enlightenment and healing self and others through contemplations with movements, and non-moving meditation to return to oneness by connecting oneself with heaven, earth and humanity.

May the regular practice of these four complementary Enlightenment Qigong forms together with the formless spontaneous Tibetan Shamanic Qigong and Merkaba / Shaktipat meditation provide spiritual healing and enlightenment to yourself as they have provided to myself and fellow practitioners spiritual enlightenment and healing by purifying the physical body, calming the emotions, and opening the heart/ elevating the spirit, together with building the Three Treasures - Jing, Qi and Shen.

"Pan Gu Shengong, also known as the Heaven, Earth, Sun and Moon Qigong, has its fundamental philosophy and practice rooted in kindness and charity. It is designed to absorb the essence of Qi (energy) from the universe. It regulates and intensifies life force and the human immune system.

PGSG, which is a complete set of Qigong exercises, consists of a Moving Form, a Non-moving Form (meditation) and an Advanced condensed Form. The Moving Form is the basis, which only takes you 20 minutes to finish. The Non-moving Form is a meditation, focusing on the regulation of the nervous system and the spirit. The Advanced condensed Form is a condensed form which takes less time but produces more powerful effect.

Qi-healing is an energy treatment offered by a Qigong Master. The energy emitted by the Master works on the patients' body, fighting the disease and improving the immune system." - Pan Gu Shengong Master Ou Wen Wei

Primordial Qi Gong opens the heart to the true force of unconditional love emanating from Wuji, the Supreme Unknown." - Wuji Qigong Master Michael Winn

"In the Sheng Zhen forms of qigong, opening one's heart is the primary purpose. The qi is the vehicle of unconditional love, of Sheng Zhen.

"Love can transform people's hearts. Love can dissolve hate. Love can affect the environment. Unconditional love is the best medicine and the highest power." - Sheng Zhen Qigong Master Li Jun Feng

"*Historically, all styles originated at one time or another from a primordial foundation of Qigong that was deeply rooted in Shamanic Medicine Dances*." - Qi Dao Master Lama Tantrapa

"... tantra is the right practice for Westerners and of the utmost need in this twentieth century. After all, the Buddhas wanted us to have as much perfect pleasure as possible; he certainly didn't want us to be miserable, confused or dissatisfied. Therefore we should understand that we meditate in order to gain profound pleasure, not to beat ourselves up or to experience pain. If entering the Buddhist path brings you nothing but fear and guilt then it's certainly not worth the effort."

"Maitreya is the manifestation of the love of all the buddhas - the supreme beings who have achieved limitless, universal love. When we practice the yoga method of Buddha Maitreya we unify with the universal love energy that is Maitreya by developing to their ultimate extent the limited qualities of love, compassion and purity that presently lie within us." - Lama Yeshe

"The hologram of love (or *Merkaba*) is the sacred geometric pattern which gave birth to the whole universe. It is based on unconditional love, so it must be the pattern of unconditional love, because everything in the universe resonates to it, no matter what it is or what dimension it's in. That means that you and I, as human beings, also have that pattern within us, so we are actually walking, talking unconditional love. We always have been, we've just never recognized it.

With the breath and thought intention, the hologram of love will obey your every command and you will transverse the angles of linear time and into the higher dimensions of no time and endless love." - Merkaba Master Alton Kamadon

"Spiritual energy is needed for expansion of consciousness and traveling in the inner worlds. Stillness and awareness are not enough. No spiritual energy, no expansion of consciousness. Spiritual empowerment or

Shaktipat is the transference of tremendous spiritual energy to enable the consciousness of the disciple to be able to travel to the different levels of the inner world. This transference of tremendous spiritual energy is called spiritual initiation in modern esoteric books. Shaktipat is an Indian term for spiritual empowerment." - Master Choa Kok Sui

"One must seek the shortest way and the fastest means to get back home - to turn the spark within into a blaze, to be merged in and to identify with that greater fire which ignited the spark." - Bhagawan Nityananda

"*Qi-healing and Enlightenment Qigong forms are both meditation in motion practices to achieve spiritual oneness*." - Master Ricardo B. Serrano, R.Ac.

"*Let Love Light Your Path, Truth Guide Your Way and Joy Sing From Your Soul.*" – Sananda

* Enlightenment is another term for Qigong state, ascension, illumination or spiritual oneness, wherein the incarnated soul is achieving a higher degree of oneness with the higher soul, and a certain degree of oneness with God and oneness with all, experienced as expansion of consciousness accompanied with blissful joy, inner peace and quiet mind.

* The Supreme Being is known by many names God, Origin, Primal Mother, Tao, Shiva, Pan Gu, Dream Being, Source at the center of all sacred space called Wu Ji, Void, Nothingness, supreme unknown, the primordial space.

* Qigong is an interexchange of Qi (universal life force) between men and the universe. As an integral system of Oriental medicine, Qigong is based on the coherence of human energy fields within the universal flow of Qi, or life force. Qi comes from the power of love, Qi and love are never separate, and Love is the Source of All. Enlightenment Qigong is also called Wuji Qigong, meaning "skill at entering the Supreme Unknown."

The complete integrative Enlightenment Qigong Forms taught by Ricardo B. Serrano in his Qigong workshops:

1. Pan Gu Shengong with foundation Yuan Qi

2. Primordial Wuji Qigong with Tao immortals

3. Sheng Zhen Wuji Yuan Gong

* Awakening the Soul Qigong

* Zhongtian Yiqi Gong and Nine Turns Qigong

* Kuan Yin and Jesus standing Qigong

* Jesus, Kuan Yin and Mohammed sitting Qigong

* Mohammed and Lao Tzu's Return to Spring standing Qigong

* Sheng Zhen Healing Qigong 1, 2 and 3, and Hanuman Qigong

4. Maitreya (Shiva) sitting Qigong with Shaktipat Meditation on Twin Hearts

* The above four Enlightenment Qigong forms are supplemented with Merkaba meditation, Toltec wisdom and spontaneous Tibetan Shamanic Qigong, a formless Qigong, to spontaneously go with flow of Qi thereby master being in the flow and experience personal freedom. Qigong and *Six Wing Chun Forms* (Siu Lim Tao, Chum Kiu, Biu Gee, Dummy, Butterfly Knives, and Six & 1/2 pole) both have health and life-saving self-defense. benefits.

To have a greater sense of well-being and spiritual awakening, it is necessary to include and practice Merkaba meditation with spontaneous formless Tibetan Shamanic Qigong, the root of the entire Qigong tree, with the six branches of the Qigong tree and the most proven enlightenment Qigong forms - Taoist, Buddhist, Medical, Martial Arts, Confucianist and Tantric Qigong - shown from the Pan Gu Shengong, Primordial Wuji Qigong, Sheng Zhen Wuji Yuan Gong, Maitreya (Shiva) Shen Gong, and Qi Dao martial arts forms practiced since time immemorial.

Dedication and Acknowledgement: Ricardo B. Serrano has dedicated this work to the present and future generations of eclectic Wu Ji Qigong practitioners and bodhisattvas who want to experience spiritual enlightenment, healing and heaven on earth. It is in blessing that you are blessed. It is in giving that you receive. It is in going with the flow of Qi and surrendering to it that you master being in the flow. This is the law or principle - "*Where energy flows, awareness follows*" - followed by Qigong masters to become enlightened! WARNING: The Meditation and Qigong practices may lead to overwhelming love, joy and happiness. Namaste!

Invocation to the Unified Chakra

"Use this invocation to get centered, before using any of the other tools, and before performing any activity involving Spirit. Unifying to the eleventh chakra is often sufficient, but on occasion, you may want to unify to the twenty-first and invite the Christ Oversoul into your fields. Pay particular attention to opening your Alpha and Omega chakras." - Archangel Ariel

Use this invocation to get centered, before using any of the other tools, and before performing any activity involving Spirit. Unifying to the eleventh chakra is often sufficient, but on occasion, you may want to unify to the twenty-first and invite the Christ Oversoul into your fields. Pay particular attention to opening your Alpha (eight inches above your head) and Omega chakras (eight inches below your spine).

I breathe in Light through the center of my heart, Opening my heart into a beautiful ball of Light,

Allowing myself to expand.

I breathe in Light through the center of my heart, Allowing the Light to expand,

Encompassing my throat chakra

And my solar plexus chakra

In one unified field of Light

Within, through, and around my body.

I breathe in Light through the center of my heart,

Allowing the Light to expand,

Encompassing my brow chakra

And my navel chakra

In one unified field of Light

Within, through, and around my body.

I breathe in Light through the center of my heart,

Allowing the Light to expand,

Encompassing my crown chakra

And my base chakra

In one unified field of Light

Within, through, and around my body.

I breathe in Light through the center of my heart,

Allowing the Light to expand,

Encompassing my Alpha chakra above my head

And my Omega chakra below my spine

In one unified field of Light

Within, through, and around my body.

I allow the Wave of Metatron to resonate between them,

I AM a unity of Light.

I breathe in Light through the center of my heart,

Allowing the Light to expand,

Encompassing my ninth chakra above my head

And my thighs

In one unified field of Light

Within, through, and around my body.

I allow my emotional body to merge with my physical,

I AM a unity of Light.

I breathe in Light through the center of my heart,

Allowing the Light to expand,

Encompassing my tenth chakra above my head

And my calves

In one unified field of Light

Within, through, and around my body.

I allow my mental body to merge with my physical,

I AM a unity of Light.

I breathe in Light through the center of my heart,

Allowing the Light to expand,

Encompassing my eleventh chakra above my head

And to below my feet

In one unified field of Light

Within, through, and around my body.

I allow my spiritual body to merge with my physical,

I AM a unity of Light.

I breathe in Light through the center of my heart,

Allowing the Light to expand,

Encompassing my thirteenth chakra above my head

And to below my feet

In one unified field of Light

Within, through, and around my body.

I allow my Oversoul to merge with my unified field,

I AM a unity of Light.

I breathe in Light through the center of my heart,

Allowing the Light to expand,

Encompassing my twenty-first chakra above my head

And to below my feet

In one unified field of Light

Within, through, and around my body.

I allow the Christ Oversoul to merge with my unified field,

I AM a unity of Light.

I breathe in Light through the center of my heart,

Allowing the Light to expand,

Encompassing my twenty-sixth chakra above my head

And to below my feet

In one unified field of Light

Within, through, and around my body.

I allow the I AM Oversoul to merge with my unified field,

I AM a unity of Light.

I breathe in Light through the center of my heart,

Allowing the Light to expand,

Encompassing my thirty-third chakra above my head

And to below my feet

In one unified field of Light

Within, through, and around my body.

I allow the Source Presence to move throughout my unified field,

I AM a unity of Light.

I breathe in Light through the center of my heart, I ask that the highest level of my Spirit radiate forth

From the center of my heart,

Filling this unified field completely.

I radiate forth throughout this day.

I AM unity of Spirit.

The *Invocation to Light* assists you to 'lock' the Unified Field into position and increases Light absorption. It is a powerful statement of intent.

Invocation to Light

I live within the Light.

I love within the Light.

I laugh within the Light.

I AM sustained and nourished

By the Light.

I joyously serve the Light.

For I AM the Light.

I AM the Light.

I AM the Light.

I AM. I AM. I AM.

As far as the physical food that you eat, it is helpful to add Light to it as well. We do this by reciting the *Invocation to Water* over our food. Like our bodies, our food is about 75% water, so the Invocation will allow us to absorb more pure Light frequency into our body with everything we eat or drink.

Invocation to Water

I take this, the Water of Life,

I declare it the Water of Light.

As I bring it within my body,

It allows my body to grow.

I take this, the Water of Light,

I declare it the Water of God. I

AM a Master in all that I AM.

(above information courtesy of Tashira Tachi-ren)

NOTE: The unified chakra and aligned energy fields are very important, not just for survival, but – more importantly – as vital tools for ascension, healing and channeling. Working with the unified chakra, you unify the higher and the seven lower chakras into one so that they all function in accordance with the *frequency of love-based energy flowing through the heart center*. One of the benefit is that the unified chakra allows fast and easy alignment and unification of your energy bodies. Another benefit is that you can now bring much more energy through the unified chakra into your unified field. And most importantly, the unified chakra allows you to embody even more of your *Spirit-self*. According to Master Tehuti (Thoth), *Your conscious role is to clean out your lower fields, get them aligned, and prepare them to handle the massive influx of high-frequency Light energy. Spirit's role is to flood these fields with your own energy and complete their alignment. Everything is Spirit, of course. It's just a matter of how much distortion your ego-self imposes when it expresses Spirit.*

Basically, the process involves breathing Light into the heart chakra. On each outbreath (using SOHAM mantra), you visualize your heart chakra becoming larger, opening in all directions like a sphere. You expand it to include each succeeding pair of chakras as you breathe in and out: third and fifth, second and sixth, first and seventh, omega and alpha, ninth and your knees, tenth and your ankles, and the eleventh and your feet. Your unified chakra is now a sphere of golden light, about 20 to 50 feet in diameter, and forms the center of your unified field, which could be several miles in diameter. Read the *Hologram of Love Merkaba Meditation* on page 92

You can experience yourself as a truly multi-dimensional being by expanding your unified chakra to include the thirteenth chakra (your Oversoul, Higher Self), the twenty-first chakra (the Christ oversoul), the twenty-sixth chakra (the I AM Presence), and the thirty-third chakra (God Source).

It is recommended that you unify your chakras several times a day. With a little practice, you'll be able to say, "Unify" to yourself, and instantly snap your chakras to one unified chakra.

The ultimate goal is to be anchored and balanced in *Love* and synchronized with the *Here* and *Now*.

Source: What is Lightbody? Archangel Ariel, channeled by Tashira Tachi-ren, New Leaf, 1999. Please note that the chakras are not the same as the book due to the usage of the 33 chakra system model and the use of the SOHAM mantra for the Integral Studies of Inner Sciences Workshop. *With thanks and acknowledgement to Tachi-ren.*

Divine Light Invocation for Healing and Ascension

NOTE: I would like to acknowledge and thank Swami Sivananda Radha for the Divine Light Invocation taken from her book "Kundalini Yoga for the West." Do the *Invocation to the Unified Chakra* first before doing the *Divine Light Invocation*.

I AM CREATED BY DIVINE LIGHT

I AM SUSTAINED BY DIVINE LIGHT

I AM PROTECTED BY DIVINE LIGHT

I AM SURROUNDED BY DIVINE LIGHT

I AM EVER GROWING INTO DIVINE LIGHT

Use the imagination to *see* yourself standing in a shower of brilliant white Light. See the Light pouring upon you, into the body through the top of the head, filling your entire being. Mentally repeat the Invocation.

During the second repetition, with the arms beside the body, concentrate on *feeling* a warm glow of Light suffuse your entire body, outside as well as inside. Acknowledge silently to yourself:

"*Every cell of this, my physical body, is filled with Divine Light; every level of consciousness is illumined with Divine Light. The Divine Light penetrates every single cell of my being, every level of consciousness. I have become a channel of pure Light. I am One with the Light.*"

The Divine Light invocation is an exercise of will, as well as an act of surrender. Be receptive to the Light and accept that you are now a channel of Divine Light. Express your gratitude with deep feeling. Have the desire to share this gift with someone whom you wish to help. Turn your palms forward. See **Sri Vidya Mantras, page 76**

You can now share the Divine Light with any friend or relative. See him or her standing before you. Mentally open the doors of your heart and let the Light stream forth towards the feet of this person. The Light encircles the body, spiralling upwards in a clockwise direction, enveloping the body completely. See the spiral moving high up into the sky, taking his or image along with it. Finally the person merges into the source of the Light and becomes one with Light. You may even lift your head to follow the spiral of Light, keeping the eyes closed. When the person has passed from your view, relax and silently give thanks for having the opportunity to help someone in need. Remember, in helping others we are helping ourselves. You can do the *Divine Light Invocation* followed with Triangles Work (see page 108) with the Great Invocation (see page 125).

CONCLUSION

I hope that you keep building your Ka (pranic body, lightbody or energy bubble) through the Merkaba meditation, Invocation to the unified chakra, and Enlightenment Qigong practices recommended in this book not only to have a healthy and strong body, mind spirit but also manifest your dreams of abundance and healing through the abundance and healing codes taught. May the following research findings of mine, and quotations from the Hathors, Masters of Sound and Love, and sound healer Renee Brodie hopefully enlighten you.

Merkaba activation is best integrated with Maitreya (Shiva) Shen Gong to build the Ka, pranic or energy body, and life-force (Qi), to open one's heart to the divine energy of unconditional love, to rewire and gradually develop the capacity of the body's Qi circuitry (meridians and 8 extraordinary meridians) and higher subtle bodies to absorb minute dosages of intense divine energy, and gradually strengthen the Qi connection and oneness with one's Higher Soul, the **spiritual teachers**, humanity, the universe (earth, sun, moon, planets and stars), and God Source.

Merkaba activation is also best integrated with the Enlightenment Qigong forms taught at the Qigong workshops to build the Ka, pranic or energy body, and life-force (Qi), to open one's heart to the divine energy of unconditional love, to rewire and gradually develop the capacity of the body's Qi circuitry (meridians and 8 extraordinary meridians) and higher subtle bodies to absorb minute dosages of intense divine energy, and gradually strengthen the Qi connection and oneness with one's Higher Soul, the spiritual teachers, humanity, the universe (earth, sun, moon, planets and stars), and God.

According to the Hathors, "You must build the Ka, you must build the life-force.

In building the Ka, you want to raise that energy by methods that will allow you to experience sexual bliss and ecstasy without depleting the life-force.

The ancient techniques for raising this energy can be found in books on Taoist yoga, tantric yoga, and kundalini yoga. We would say that in using our methods, which became the underpinnings of Egyptian alchemy, you literally raise the life-force into your higher centers by bringing that life-force into all of your body. If you allow the pranic life-force to express itself as a release of sexual fluids and energy only, then the prana is released through those lower centers, is not elevated, and will not have a long term positive upon the Ka.

If you express your sexuality too often through the sexual act without retaining the sexual energy so it can circulate upward, you actually deplete the Ka. This will, in turn, deplete the organs of your physical body, deplete the immune system, and create other various decreases of energy within yourself as an energy system. Let us be very clear, however, that we are not saying to deny yourself sexual pleasures. There are methods that have been developed by Taoist sages and tantric yogis which allow you to experience profound states of sexual bliss and ecstasy without depleting the Ka. In fact, these practices strengthen your life-force and elevate consciousness. We suggest you explore these methods."

According to Renee Brodie, "We need to work on the idea of marrying *sound and colour and movement*. In truth, the three are not really separate, but work together, complementing each other to make us whole. This means that the colour (of a high vibration) is connected with Light and affects the higher subtle bodies. It touches the soul, body and higher mental bodies (*merkaba*). Add to these two the movement (of Chi through the practice of Tai Chi or Qi Gong), and this then touches the physical and etheric bodies. Why chi? Because it reaches into all the meridians (as opposed to dance, which touches vibrations, but not as deeply as chi energy – essential energy of living organisms and the Universe)."

Thank you for reading and using the abundance and healing codes recommended. As I said, "The energy ball is your magical ally for power and guidance," and "The **GURU** is the grace bestowing power of God."

SUPPLEMENTARY MATERIAL ON GURU YOGA

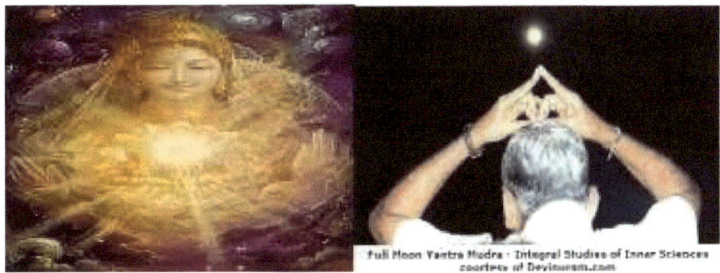

Sri Vidya Mantras by Sri Amritananda

1. Guru: Imagine Guru's feet on top of your head, washing them and bathing in the waters. That purifies you and invokes grace. Best done as soon as you get up before getting up from bed.

Aeem Hreem Shreem – Aeem Kleem Souh – Hamsah Sivah Soham- Hasakhaphrem- Hasakshamalavarayum Hasoum – Sahakshamalavarayim Sahouh – Svaroopa Niroopana Hetave Sva Gurave – Sri Anna Poornamba Sahita Sri Amritananda Natha Sri Guru Sri Padukam Poojayami Tarpayami Namah

2. Ganapati. There are eight bijas separated by hyphens. With each bija imagine a ball of light going down the spine to hit and penetrate the earth. This unlocks the Sushumna channel, grounds you and removes obstacles. If you recite the bijas slowly and aloud, it becomes pranayama of short breathing in and long exhaling. You will feel heat in the base chakra.

Om – Shreem – Hreem – Kleem – Gloum – Gam – Ganapataye Vara Varada – Sarva Janam Me Vasham Aanaya Svaha

3. Subrahmanya: For best results, press on genital area exerting a light comfortable pressure.

Om – Shreem – Hreem – Kleem – Aeem – Soum – Saravana Bhavaaya Namah

4. Chandi: This circulates energy to heart centre. "Aeem" is at the cervix, "Hreem" is at left nipple, Kleem is at right nipple, Chaamundayai is at navel, and Vichche is at clitoris. Keep circulating awareness in these centers to a slow chant of beejas. It is natural to feel sexual arousal and or a release. Offer the pleasure to Goddess in you.

Aeem - Hreem - Kleem Chamundayai – Vichche

5. Krishna: Alternate between the two nipples as you utter the beejas. The attitude is of surrender of ego to Krishna and embracing life. Alternate mantra is **Maha Lakshmi mantra**, page 130

Kleem Krishnaaya Govindaaya Gopijana Vallabhaaya Svaaha

6. Datta: Communications center is the neck where entire attention should be placed. Imagine waves after waves of sounds of beejas going out to infinite distances, to the very edge of cosmos and returning as echoes.

Om Hreem Dram Dattatreya Hare Krishna Unmattaananda Dayaka - Digambara Mune Baala Pisacha Jnaana Saagara – Dram Hreem Om

Combined with Maha Kali Mantra: **OM HREEM STREEM HUM PHAT 3x**

Om Hreem Dram Dram Hreem Om

7. Siva: Imagine a laser beam shooting out of your third eye giving life by emitting nectar OR setting fire to any evil you see with your third eye open. Alternate Mantra: **OM Na Ma Shi Va Ya**

Om Hreem Houm Namah Shivaaya

8. Panchadasi: Srishti-entry, Sthiti-being, Laya-withdrawal. It is the mantra of union between Siva- universal Male and Shakti- universal female archetypes. To create a pillar of light, chant the **Panchadasi mantra with Full Moon Yantra Mudra resting on the crown of the head.**

Ka e I la Hreem – Ha sa ka ha la Hreem – Sa ka la Hreem - Shreem

9. Baala: It is the strength of the Goddess. "Aeem" is on tip of the tongue, "Kleem" is placed on the nipples, and "Souh" is placed on the clit. The energy moves up and down among these spots, making clear the divine plan for you, nurturing it and manifesting it through you.

Aeem Kleem Souh Souh Kleem Aeem

General tips: Goddess and Guru are in and with you. Have no fear. Do what you like. Don't have more than three ideas to execute at a time. Prioritize them. See them through to the end.

See Awakening your Kundalini, p. 31; Becoming a Beacon of Love, p. 92; Sri Vidya Mantras, p. 126; Lakshmi Mantra, p. 130

SUPPLEMENTARY MATERIAL ON GURU YOGA (Part 2)

If you want to know your past life, look into your present condition; if you want to know your future life, look at your present actions.

I am present in front of anyone who has faith in me, just as the moon casts its reflection, effortlessly, in any vessel filled with water.

The eagle that is flying high in the sky should not forget that it should come down one day to see its shadow. [Essence of Karmic causes and effects]

Empty cognizance of one taste, suffused with knowing, is your unmistaken nature, the uncontrived original state. When not altering what is, allow it to be as it is, and the awakened state is right now spontaneously present.

On the northwest border of the land of Orgyen,

Arisen in a lotus flower's heart,

With wondrous siddhi perfectly endowed,

And celebrated as the Lotus Born,

You are encircled by a throng of dakinis (yoginis).

We follow in your footsteps practicing.

Come, we pray, and grant your blessings.

As soon as one's mind is known to be of the Wisdom of the Voidness, concepts like good and evil karma cease to exist. Seek, therefore, thine own Wisdom within thee. It is the Vast Deep.

When the degenerate age of this aeon arrives,

people are their own deceivers, their own bad counsel,

the makers of their own stupidity, lying to and fooling themselves.

How sad that these people have human forms but possess no more sense than an ox!

Now when the bardo of dying dawns upon me,

I will abandon all grasping, yearning, and attachment,

Enter undistracted into clear awareness of the teaching,

And eject my consciousness into the space of unborn Rigpa (primordial non-dual awareness);

As I leave this compound body of flesh and blood

I will know it to be a transitory illusion.

Although my view is higher than the sky, My respect for the cause and effect of actions is as fine as grains of flour.

For anyone, man or woman, who has faith in me, I, the Lotus Born, have never departed — I sleep on their threshold.

Seeing me, all the buddhas are seen,

Accomplishing my practice, the practice of all the buddhas is accomplished,

For I am the embodiment of all the sugatas (fully enlightened beings).

[The Secret Guide to Accomplishing the Guru]

Unstained by objective clinging,

Unspoilt by the grasping mind,

Sustaining the naked and empty awareness

Is the wisdom mind of all the buddhas!

Do not investigate phenomena: investigate the mind.

If you investigate the mind, you'll know the one thing which resolves all.

If you don't investigate the mind, you can know everything but be forever stuck on one.

May I recognize all the manifestations

that appear to me in the bardo (intermediate state)

as being my own projections;

emanations of my own mind.

When the bardo of the moment of death appears

may I abandon attachments and mental fixations,

and engage without distraction in the

path which the instructions make clear.

Mind projected into the sphere of uncreated space,

separated from body, from flesh and blood,

I will know that which is impermanence and illusion.

When the moment is upon me

May I not be frightened

By the collection of peaceful and wrathful aspects:

Emanations of my own mind.

When I am in the bardo of birth till death,

May I waste no time;

Abandoning laziness, may I engage without distraction

In the study, assimilation of,

And meditation on the teachings,

May I practice, integrating on the path

Appearance and mind.

Without thinking that death will come,

I am absorbed in plans for the future.

After having done the many and futile activities of this life

I will leave utterly empty-handed

What a blunder;

as I will certainly need an understanding of the excellent Dharma (proper conduct).

So why not practice now?

Guru Rinpoche, Buddha of the three times, Lord of all siddhis who is the one of great bliss,

Dispeller of all obstacles, wrathful tamer of Mara (demon),

We supplicate you; please grant your blessings.

Grant your blessings that outer, inner and secret obstacles be pacified And that our intentions be spontaneously accomplished.

Bodhisattva Padmasambhava: Guru Rinpoche

Bodhisattva Padmasambhava came from Kashmir, on the side of what is known as Pakistan, "close to the border with Afghanistan and Tajikistan. More precisely, his homeland is often cited as Swat Valley, an area called Udyan." In 747 A.D., he went to Tibet upon the invitation of King This-srong-detsan and started teaching Tantric Buddhism. According to the accounts of Christopher Beckwith, a western historian:

One may also conclude that a major reason for so many Indian Buddhist sages coming to Central Tibet from Kashmir, and notably, the famous Padmasambhava from Udyana, was the simple fact that Tibet then ruled much of this region.

The name of Padmasambhava, literally means "*born of the lotus flower*." This means to be born fully illuminated.

Bodhisattva Padmasambhava has been a Great Teacher for aeons and aeons of time. Under his direct and indirect tutelage are also Taoist immortals and yogis, the siddhas and mahasiddhas in India, and other great spiritual teachers from other traditions.

Invocation of Guru Rinpoche

HUM! In the northwest of Uddiyana,

On the centre of a lotus

Was found supreme, wondrous attainment.

One Renowned as "Lotus-born"

Encircled by vast retinues of dakinis·

Be with us in blessing and inspiration so that

following you, we may achieve [awakening.]

GURU PADMA SIDDHI HUM!

Ricardo's NOTE: Tibetan Tantric Buddhist Master Mahaguruji Bodhisattva Padmasambhava (also known as *Lotus-Born*) with his priceless quotations and invocations with short autobiography above are generously shared to the readers for their contemplation and spiritual benefit.

The above quotations and invocations of Bodhisattva Padmasambhava were collected selectively from Lord Padmasambhava's *Tibetan Book of the Dead* and different Tibetan Buddhist related websites in the internet. With great heartfelt thanks!

With acknowledgements and thanks to Master Mike Nator, Master Choa Kok Sui, Master Djwhal Khul and to Lord Padmasambhava (*Master Mei Ling*), Ricardo B. Serrano's beloved ascended immortal Tibetan Master spiritual guides, for their divine blessings, guidance, help and protection.

Guru Rinpoche

"Spiritual oneness means the incarnated soul is achieving a higher degree of oneness with the higher soul, and a certain degree of oneness with God and oneness with all. Through the regular practice of Meditation on Twin Hearts, your degree of connectedness and oneness with your higher soul is increased. The size of your spiritual cord becomes bigger. You're able to tap your higher soul for inner guidance, inner peace and inner power." – Master Choa Kok Sui

Also known as Chenrezig (Tibetan),

Avalokiteshvara (Sanskrit)

smiling within your inner hearts

The Dharma-body of Kuan Yin is neither male nor female.

Even the body is not the body, what attributes can there be?

Let It be known to all Buddhists:

Do not cling to form.

The bodhisattva is you:

Not the picture or the image.

- *Chinese poem*

OM MANI PADME HUM By His Holiness the Dalai Lama

It is very good to recite the mantra Om Mani Padme Hum, but while you are doing it, you should be thinking on its meaning, for the meaning of the six syllables is great and vast. The first, Om is composed of three letters, A, U, and M. These symbolize the practitioner's impure body, speech, and mind; they also symbolize the pure exalted body, speech, and mind of a Buddha.

Can impure body, speech, and mind be transformed into pure body, speech, and mind, or are they entirely separate?

All Buddhas are cases of beings who were like ourselves and then in dependence on the path became enlightened; Buddhism does not assert that there is anyone who from the beginning is free from faults and possesses all good qualities. The development of pure body, speech, and mind comes from gradually leaving the impure states arid their being transformed into the pure.

How is this done?

The path is indicated by the next four syllables. Mani, meaning jewel, symbolizes the factors of method - the altruistic intention to become enlightened, compassion, and love. Just as a jewel is capable of removing poverty, so the altruistic mind of enlightenment is capable of removing the poverty, or difficulties, of cyclic existence and of solitary peace. Similarly, just as a jewel fulfills the wishes of sentient beings, so the altruistic intention to become enlightened fulfills the wishes of sentient beings.

The two syllables, Padme, meaning lotus, symbolize wisdom. Just as a lotus grows forth from mud but is not sullied by the faults of mud, so wisdom is capable of putting you in a situation of non-contradiction whereas there would be contradiction if you did not have wisdom. There is wisdom realizing impermanence, wisdom realizing that persons are empty, of being self-sufficient or substantially existent, wisdom that realizes the emptiness of duality - that is to say, of difference of entity between subject an object - and wisdom that realizes the emptiness of inherent existence. Though there are many different types of wisdom, the main of all these is the wisdom realizing emptiness.

Purity must be achieved by an indivisible unity of method and wisdom, symbolized by the final syllable hum, which indicates indivisibility. According to the sutra system, this indivisibility of method and wisdom refers to wisdom affected by method and method affected by wisdom. In the mantra, or tantric, vehicle, it refers to one consciousness in which there is the full form of both wisdom and method as one undifferentiable entity. In terms of the seed syllables of the five Conqueror Buddhas, Hum is the seed syllable of Akshobhya – the immovable, the unfluctuating, that which cannot be disturbed by anything.

Thus the six syllables, Om Mani Padme Hum, mean that in dependence on the practice of a path which is an indivisible union of method and wisdom, you can transform your impure body, speech, and mind into the pure exalted body, speech, and mind of a Buddha. It is said that you should not seek for Buddhahood outside of yourself; the substances for the achievement of Buddhahood are within. As Maitreya says in his Sublime Continuum of the Great Vehicle (Uttaratantra), all beings naturally have the Buddha nature in their own continuum. We have within us the seed of purity, the essence of a One Gone Thus (Tathagatagarbha), that is to be transformed and fully developed into Buddhahood.

The Six-Syllable Mantra *'OM MANI PADME HUM'* is the heart mantra of Bodhisattva Avalokiteshvara as well as all the Buddhas. Avalokiteshvara is the compassionate embodiment of all the Buddhas and Bodhisattvas; the mantra is the essence of the 84,000 (literally means uncountable methods) of Buddha's teachings.

Reciting "OM MANI PADME HUM" is all-powerful and brings blessings to all sentient beings in the six realms of existence.

The benefits of reciting the "OM MANI PADME HUM" are:

Purifying our negative karma, removing obstruction, bad habits and ignorance.

Closing the door to the six realm of reincarnation.

Removing physical and mental sickness.

Repelling demonic forces.

Liberating us from samsara and thus allowing us to be reborn in Pure Land.

Lady Kuan Yin is the Bodhisattva of Compassion, and she is known as one of the most popular deities in all of Asia. Her name in Chinese roughly translates as "The One who Hears the Cries of the World." Many believe that she is the female representation of Avalokiteswara, the Tibetan and Nepalese Bodhisattva of Compassion.

In Asia, statues of Lady Kuan Yin can be found in front of, or on the grounds of, many Taoist and Buddhist temples. She is a Bodhisattva, a person who has earned the right to leave this world of suffering and enter nirvana, but has chosen instead to stay on this earth to help others reach enlightenment first. Because of her willingness to help, Lady Kuan Yin is the patron saint of barren women and protects those whose lives depend on the elements, such as farmers and fishermen. It is not unusual to see Lady Kuan Yin in various forms and poses. She always appears cloaked in white, the color of purity, and her gowns are long and flowing. Often she will be holding a rosary in one hand, a symbol of her devotion to Buddhism and its tenets. She will also have either a book (The Lotus Sutra, which refers back to her origins), or a vase, which symbolizes her pouring compassion on to the world.

With great acknowledgement and thanks to Bodhisattva Avalokiteshvara (*Kuan Yin*), Ricardo B. Serrano's beloved ascended immortal Tibetan Master spiritual guide, for Her divine blessings, guidance, help and protection.

Benefits of Guru Yoga of Tibetan Buddhism with Zhan Zhuang Qigong

1. A miraculous healing that happened when I spiritually healed with pranic healing, through the assistance of Bodhisattva Padmasambhava and my late Pranic Healing teacher Master Choa Kok Sui, my 70 year old sister-in-law Julie Taniega with Guillian Barre Syndrome from New Jersey, USA last June, 2007. This is essentially, I believe, how Lin Kong Jing, the empty force, manifests when called on for healing or self-defense. The "void power" or "empty force" becomes more potent when Zhan Zhuang Qigong is combined with Guru Yoga which develop one's energy bubble (lightbody).

2. Ricardo's dramatic healing experience with his left eye pain.

3. Culminating in a state of Awakening which the Buddhists refer to as the Attainment of Self-Realisation through the cultivation and fusion of the subtle energies between Heaven (tian), Earth (di) & Man (ren).

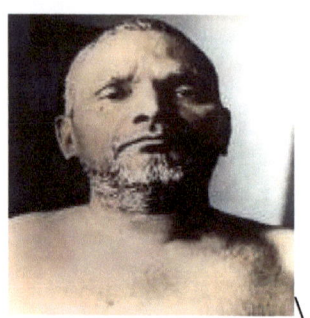

GURUKRIPA YOGA

"The Guru is the Grace-bestowing power of God." - Shiva Sutras

The following quotes were taken from the article on Gurukripa Yoga at BhagawanNityananda.org

"Gurukripa Yoga is the yoga in which the disciple relies in the Grace of the Guru or Acharya (which is God's Grace) to carry him/her to liberation. The Shiva Sutras state "Gururupayah;" the Guru is the means. The Guru who has attained Self-realization is the only one who can help the aspirant acquire it. Gurukripa Yoga and Bhakti Yoga are one and the same because they both emphasize the process of drawing God's Grace to you through Selfless Service and complete Devotion/ Surrender to the Acharya. In this way, over time, you learn to take complete refuge in God...

For this reason, the Saints of the Gurukripa path all state that all the other forms of yoga (Jnana Yoga, Karma Yoga, Bhakti Yoga, and Hatha Yoga) are contained in Gurukripa. Gurukripa Yoga is the Yoga of Bhagawan Nityananda. It is the Yoga of Supreme Love. For this reason, Baba referred to it as Raja Yoga, the yoga in which all the other yogas are contained.

Without the Grace of a Siddha, a Guru, you cannot realize God. You may be successful at reducing stress or even attaining states of relative happiness. But without the Guru, these will be fleeting at best. By reading scriptures and attending lectures you may be able to understand and express philosophy like so many preachers that we encounter day-in and day-out. But you won't have a lasting experience of the philosophy that you are preaching. To become completely absorbed in God, to liberate yourself from bondage in order to bask in the rays of total freedom from this ignorance of pain and pleasure, you must be guided by a Siddha (perfected being) until you are set on your own path. It is only by the Grace of such a Guru that you can undergo permanent spiritual transformation.

Bhagawan Nityananda was a MahaAvatar (a being who is born God-realized) of the 20th century. His disciples believe him to be an incarnation of Lord Shiva and also Lord Vishnu. As lovers and disciples of Bhagawan Nityananda, we want to share our experiences of Gurukripa, His Grace, which had transformed the lives of so many across the globe. We take refuge in His authority, not our own. We do not claim to know everything. However, we do have intimate knowledge and first-hand experience of how Love for Bhagawan Nityananda can transform one's entire being...

We are certain that this journey will lead all those who take it Liberation from the bondage of ignorance that keep one separate from God. Like the ocean, the Grace of the Guru is always available to those who sincerely want to know the Truth. Even if you let go of the Acharya's hands, he will never let go of your hands. The Guru will stand by you, no matter what. That is why we call this Gurukripa. Once you surrender to the Acharya, your Liberation is certain.

What does it take to complete this journey? Prem (unconditional love), Shrada (unshakable Faith), Tyag (sacrifice/ discipline), and Anyanasharanam (total surrender to the God/ Guru). These four cannot be understood intellectually. They have to be experienced through the Grace of your own effort at sadhana (daily spiritual practice) and the Grace of the Guru. Love everyone, have faith in the Self and make your life good. Cultivate discipline in sadhana and the will to excel in wordly affairs, remembering always to give the glory, not to yourself, but to God..."

Shaktipat Meditation

Like oil in sesame seeds,

butter in cream,

water in the river bed,

fire in tinder,

the Self dwells within.

Realize the Self through meditation.

Shvetashvatara Upanishad

People of all religions and all philosophies are not just welcome, but respected. Each of us has a right to believe whatever we want to believe, to follow any religion or philosophy we want to follow. It doesn't matter whether we believe in Christ, Moses, Allah, Brahma, Buddha, or any other being or master; everybody is welcome with love and respect.

"The basic tantric yoga teachings of Shaktipat Meditation in Maitreya (Shiva) Shen Gong are primarily based on the ancient, time-honored principles and practices of Kashmir Shaivism, an established oral tradition having its roots in the relationship between Master and Student." - Siddha yogi Ricardo B Serrano

Shaktipat meditation is the means to realize the Self by spiritual empowerment and stilling the mind.

The real secret of meditation on the Self is Shaktipat or spiritual empowerment. If you want meditation to come easily and naturally, your inner Shakti, the Kundalini, must be awakened through Shaktipat or the grace of a Siddha Guru. Then you will no longer have to struggle for meditation. The Shakti will center your mind and your consciousness will naturally and easily be carried inward, toward the Self.

However, you must meditate regularly and persistently, to strengthen your self-awareness. Along the way, you may have many kinds of experiences, but the ultimate state is beyond all experiences. In the Self-realized state there is only bliss. True meditation is to become immersed there.

Our lives are filled with stress reflected by our mental attitude and emotional experience. Because of our own ignorance, we look for love, happiness, peace, joy and contentment outside where they are not. Shaktipat meditation is a simple and direct means to experience within you an ocean of love, peace, joy, happiness and well-being in a continuous basis.

He is the real Guru

Who can reveal the form of the formless

before your eyes;

Who teaches the simple path,

without rites or ceremonies;

Who does not make you close

your doors, and hold your breath,

and renounce the world;

Who makes you perceive

the Supreme Spirit

wherever the mind attaches itself;

Who teaches you to be still

in the midst of all your activities.

Fearless, always immersed in bliss,

he keeps the spirit of yoga

in the midst of enjoyments.

- KABIR

"The heart is the hub of all sacred places, go there and roam." – Sadguru Bhagawan Nityananda

"God and the individual are one. To realize this is the essence of Kashmir Shaivism." – Swami Lakshmanjoo

"To actually know who you are is a big problem. You have to find out yourself where you are situated. It happens by the grace of Lord Siva, or by the grace of a master, or by the grace of the scriptures (*sastras*)." - Swamiji Lakshmanjoo

"As long as your body is healthy and strong, as long as your senses still function, do something for yourself. Why wait? Contemplate the Self and attain it now. Know that life is very short. You were not born into this world just to eat and drink and die." - Bhartrihari, *Vairagya Shataka*, v.75

Qigong, a movement meditation form, is included by Ricardo B Serrano to balance, ground, root the Shakti to Mother Earth, and center and enhance the healing flow of energy (Shakti) in the body derived from the non-movement (still) Siddha tantric yoga practices such as Shaktipat Meditation, and avoid Kundalini Syndromes.

I truly believe that the original root and beginning of my spiritual journey toward liberation started since attending the Siddha Shaktipat intensive with Gurumayi Chidvilasananda in Vancouver, B.C. in June 15, 1989. My spiritual search and journey within a span of 20 years also finally culminated after including *Shaktipat* meditation or *Gurukripa Yoga* meditation with my Enlightenment Qigong Forms for Returning to Oneness as my form of seva (selfless service) to my beloved Sadguru Bhagawan Nityananda, the Guru of our Siddha lineage.

Acharya Ricardo's powerful inner blissful transformative experiences with Sadguru Nityananda's Grace while performing the tantric and Siddha spiritual practices during his three month's vacation, from November, 2009 till February 2010, in the Philippines, which drove him to write about it, have convinced him that he has become just like a Siddha or an Acharya with the ability to do Shaktipat. These experiences include dreams where he met face to face his late mother and Siddhas in Siddhaloka, and Self-Realization experiences such as overwhelming God's love and universal oneness, inner peace and quiet mind he hasn't felt before. The most powerful and unforgettable experience while practicing Shaktipat was being in the flow of a powerful loving Shakti (Qi) opening his heart greatly to God's (Shiva's) unconditional love and expansion of his consciousness uniting with the universal or Cosmic consciousness. He has to ground himself, connecting with Mother Earth, with Qigong to enable his physical body to handle this powerful expansion of consciousness and overwhelming Qi flow. This liberating and enlightening experience through the Grace of **Bhagawan Nityananda** or **Baba Hari Dass** would be similar to a pond of water (you) reuniting and becoming one with the vastness of the ocean (God) through a river path (Siddha).

Without God's grace through a Siddha, represented by his energy or spirit ("Shakti"), there can be no fulfillment or realization (enlightenment, liberation).

What is Guru?

The Guru is like a boat that takes us across the ocean of worldliness toward oneness with God. Sadgurunath Maharaj Ki Jay (Hail the true Guru).

"A person is in bondage by his own consciousness, so he can be free by his own consciousness. It's only a matter of turning the angle of the mind. If you think you can do it, then you will do it. It takes firm determination. For keeping determination alive, we need regular sadhana, faith, devotion and satsang. Always watch yourself. How desire comes. How a thought builds a long story. How hate, anger and greed come. Watch all these things; this is the real yoga." - Baba Hari Dass

The human mind being purified by service to the Guru and assimilation of the teachings becomes serene and calm and then faithfully reflects the Atman (Pure Consciousness).

Guru is your own Self which is projected onto a person who is more knowledgeable and capable of teaching. In the beginning an aspirant seeks support from outside, which is given by the teacher. But when the aspirant begins meditating honestly, his or her own Self is revealed as the Guru. Then the aspirant starts turning inward and finds the path, which is shown by the voice of the heart.

Nothing is greater than going within [to know the Self]. The real guru is your own Self. If you don't know the Self, then the physical guru is just another object. - Baba Hari Dass

"The world is not a burden; we make it a burden by our desires. When the desires are removed, the world is as light as a feather on an elephant's back." - Baba Hari Dass *See Why a Guru is Necessary, page 32; Ego, Desire and Attachment, page 33*

Baba Hari Dass, a Hanuman devotee

The master (guru) is the means. – Shiva Sutra 2.6

"The independent state of supreme consciousness is the reality of everything." - Shiva Sutra 1.1

This first sutra, *caitanyamatma*, states that individual being is one with universal being. The reality of this whole universe is God consciousness. It is filled with God consciousness.

In this sutra, the state of complete independence is indicated and accomplished through the use of the word *caitanya*... It is only this one aspect, *svatantrya*, that is revealed by the word *caitanya*. This indicates that the word *caitanya* means "the independent state of consciousness."

The independent state of consciousness is the self. It is the self of everything, because whatever exists in the world is the state of Lord Shiva. So Lord Shiva is found everywhere.

"Let Shiva, who is my Self, let Shiva do pranam (bow down) to his real nature – to Universal Shiva, by his own Shakti, for removing the bondage and limitation, which is Shiva." – 1st verse, Shiva Dhristi

Here, Shiva bows to himself, for the removal of obstacles, which are also Shiva, through his own energy (shakti) which is one with Shiva, and in the end He resides in the state of universal Shiva. That is the state of Para (Supreme) Bhairava!

"Focus the mind on a being who has risen above passion and attachment."

"He should be considered as the real Sadguru who makes the disciple experience perfect calmness of mind by making him realize his own Self. For no other reason should one person be considered as the Sadguru of another." – Eknath Maharaj

The predominant sign of such a yogi is joy-filled amazement. – Shiva Sutra 1.12

This yogi is filled with joy and amazement. The Sanskrit word *vismaya* means "amazement completely filled with joy." Just as a person seeing some wonderful object is amazed, in the same way, this yogi is filled with amazement who, in the objective world of senses, experiences entry in his own self filled with consciousness, which is unique, intense, always fresh and uncommonly charming, and by which entry all his varieties of organs are filled with blooming, ever smiling, one-pointed joy.

What kind of amazement is this? This yogi, upon entering into that limitless state of bliss (*ananda*), is never satiated with the experience. On the contrary, he feels bathed with the amazement of joy. This is the predominant state of yoga of a yogi who has become one with the supreme Lord, the supreme *tattva*, Siva *tattva*. And by this, you can surmise that he has ascended to the state of Siva.

May this short essay on my spiritual practices assist those on the path to Self-realization. Thank you for taking the time to read this short essay which is dedicated to my beloved Sadguru Bhagawan Nityananda who through his Gurukripa, his Grace, was instrumental in my enlightenment and liberation or Self-realization. As a final note, I leave you with a quote from my beloved Siddha Guru Baba Muktananda:

"After Shaktipat, when the disciple becomes fully aware of the nature and importance of the Shakti, total devotion to the Guru springs up in his heart naturally. If the disciple were to become aware of the fact that the Kundalini Shakti which pervades the universe, which has limitless power, which creates the universe, is now running through every cell and fiber of his being since the Guru has awakened it in him – in fact, it is the Guru himself who entered him in the form of Shakti – devotion would arise in him spontaneously." – Baba Muktananda

May all who read these words be uplifted and filled with God's Grace and the All-Pervasive Love of the Endless One, Bhagawan Nityananda (everlasting bliss) of Ganeshpuri.

May your heart merge into the heart of the Divine.

The heart is the hub of all sacred places, go there and roam.

Sadgurunath Maharaj Ki Jay! **OM NAMAH SHIVAYA**

Ricardo B Serrano, R.Ac

Melchizedek, Eternal Lord of Light

Sananda, the Christ and Third Eye

I personally have been blessed to experience Ascended Master Sananda's unconditional love during a Merkaba meditation workshop with Alton Kamadon in Vancouver, BC, 2000. When Alton Kamadon was channeling Sananda, everybody in the room was crying when we felt his outpouring love and presence. He said that he can only give us so much love because we wouldn't be able to take more of the love he can give us. I personally saw his radiant golden body behind Alton Kamadon.

As the epiloque to this book, I would like to introduce and share with you information about Sananda, the Cosmic Christ, the Taoist immortals and Cosmic Christ consciousness for experiencing ascension, spiritual healing and whole body enlightenment. I hope that this little introduction assists you as it has greatly assisted me in my search for a solution to my long standing quest on *"how do I attain ascension, spiritual healing and whole body enlightenmen?"*

Sananda, the Cosmic Christ I'm referring to is the historical Jesus most Christians know as the Son of God, the Saviour who died in the cross. I know Sananda, the Sanskrit name for Jesus -- the one with love and bliss,as an ascended master whose teaching "The Kingdom of God is within you" *literally means that ascension, healing and whole body enlightenment can be realized through meditation, Qigong, and energy healing which parallels the ancient Taoist immortals' philosophy. "As above, so below; as without, so within"*. Our multi-dimensional (physical, mental, emotional, spiritual) Qi (Chi) body is the temple of our soul which expands infinitely uniting with the Cosmic Christ consciousness by gathering universal forces inside the space within our Qi or energy body.

The Cosmic Christ consciousness is the infinite primordial space which occupies the outside and inside of our body and beyond, (Void) and is the medium which makes it possible for experiencing unity or expanded consciousness (*ascension*), healing and whole body enlightenment by awakening the third eye through kundalini awakening to access the Cosmic Christ Consciousness. "If thine eye be single, thy whole body shall be full of light." – Christ (Matthew 6:22) See Awakening your Kundalini, page 31

One solution to the problem or process of how to reconnect our energy body for ascension, healing and whole body enlightenment is by communicating or reconnecting the universal forces around us within our body through the *pillar of Light*, core channel or pranic tube, and Cosmic Christ consciousness with the assistance of the centuries known ascended masters such as Sananda, the Cosmic Christ and the Taoist immortals and their inner alchemy techniques.

According to J.J. Hurtak's *The Keys of Enoch*, "Jesus/Joshua 'the Christ' 'Eternal Divine Son of the Father appointed to bring 'Sonship' to the children of God and to activate the work of Je-ho-vah Y-H-W-H Ab-ba, his Father, over creation negated by the **Fall** (Matt. 4:10 John 20:17; John 4:23,24). The Only-Begotten Son of God for this aeon of existence who will offer up the earthly kingdom of God to the Father's Throne. The Head of the Office of the Father's Throne. The Head of the Office of the Christ encompassing the 144,000 Ascended Masters. Divine Love from the Elohistic Garment of Life annointed as the vehicle of Ransom/Redemption (Eph. 1:7; John 3:16; 1 John 4:9,10) so that forgiveness and salvation for eternal life is possible to those 'becoming Christed' through Christ in oneness with the Father and the Son (John 1:29; Acts 10:43; Rev. 7:9,10,14-17). The Sons of Light, as the Order of Melchizedek, will return to Earth to unite the scattered brotherhoods of Melchizedek and establish the Kingdom of God with Jesus who is the eternal Son and High Priest after the 'Order of Melchizedek' (Heb. 6:20)."

For me personally, Sananda, the Cosmic Christ, Lady Kuan Yin and the Taoist immortals are the heart-opening personification of unconditional love, acceptance, compassion, inner smile and expanded consciousness as I have experienced them through the *pillar of Light*, core channel or pranic tube, and Cosmic Christ consciousness during my sitting and moving meditation (*qigong and tai chi*), and energy healing practices.

I believe that Truth can only be known by EXPERIENCE, not by belief or thoughts. Knowing how to experience the flow of Qi energy safely for ascension, healing and whole body enlightenment from a master teacher/guide and not be dependent from drugs, a GURU or anybody is the only empowering way I know to attain mastery simply because the quality of our Qi is the quality of our life, it is the natural way of the Tao, and it is our birthright.

May Sananda, the Cosmic Christ, *Kuan Yin, Lalitha Tripura Sundari* and the Taoist immortals smile within your inner hearts!

By surrounding yourself with the clockwise rotating *Hologram of Love Merkaba*, and linking your heart through the *pranic tube* or *pillar of light* to the source of Father God (Sun) and to the heart center of Mother Earth allows you to draw the spiritual energies of Sun God source and Earth together to manifest a high frequency unconditional love healing energy that uplifts the human body and etheric bodies into a state of receptivity for spiritual ascension, and healing. You also flush-out the noisy and negative thoughts and emotions of your ego-mind within your energy bubble (aura) to experience inner calmness which is a prelude to the practice of inner stillness.

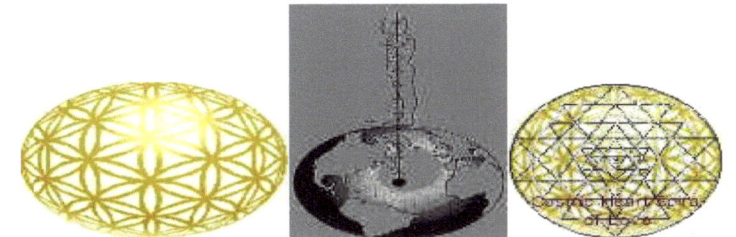

Hologram of Love Merkaba Energy Ball of Light with Unified Chakra *and* Pranic Tube (Pillar of Light)

Becoming a Beacon of Love

Awakening the Kundalini energy requires two things — energy and breath. You need to bring the energy that is all around you into your body in order to wake up the dormant Kundalini energy inside you.

This energy outside and inside your body is called prana — and as you bring it into yourself, a certain vitality comes into your life. You start radiating an energy... your skin begins to glow... you feel less tired, more focused, and less fearful...

You're also better able to control your emotions and your reactions — your sexual desires, your hunger, your food needs... all these kinds of things come under your control.

Through this experiential map of awakening the Kundalini energy and welcoming bliss consciousness, you may be wondering whether you'll be so blissed out that you'll lose the desire to act in the world.

Just the opposite is true. The purpose of awakening the Kundalini energy is not to transcend your day-to-day life, it's to purify and prepare your body, mind, and spirit to welcome the Divine into your life — and then embody and express that divinity in every moment, with every breath.

With your Kundalini energy awakened, you'll become an observer of everything... and when you observe everything, and see through the drama to the role you're playing, you gladly play your part with a deep sense of gratitude while staying continuously aware of your center and your stability.

You don't become useless in the world, you actually become more active and engaged, with a heart full of bliss. When others cross your path, your beacon of love can set their flickering lanterns ablaze.

Kindle the light in others and your own heart glows ever more brightly. The more you give of your love, the more love you have to give. You cannot look anywhere without seeing opportunities to help, comfort, or inspire others. Your mere presence becomes an act of service.

Yet the world needs more from you than service. It needs your creativity, your innovation, and your dreams. Waking up the Kundalini energy within you unleashes these creative latent powers.

Awakening the Kundalini energy frees your spirit to transcend the body-consciousness of the ego and align with Spirit. Pressure, fear, and struggling give way to peace, love, and bliss. You'll feel more joyously and passionately alive than you ever have before, and empowered to go forth and change the world with the gifts that only your awakened self can offer.

Read Awakening your Kundalini, p. 31; Pancha Kosha, p. 43; Shiva and Shakti Meditation, p. 106; Excerpts on Kundalini, p. 121; Sri Yantra Mantras, p. 130; Three Dantiens, p. 133; Microcosmic Orbit, p. 153; Bija Mantras of Seven Chakras, p. 154

Master Djwhal Khul

Channeled Messages from *Master Djwhal Khul*:
Thank you for including me and my works – *Triangles Work* and the *Great Invocation* in your book *Return to Oneness with Shiva*. The spiritual unfoldment of lightworkers world-wide will be greatly hastened with the addition of your Merkaba meditation with the Qigong forms and tantric non-dualistic teachings of *Kashmir Shaivism* elaborated on the pages of your book.

As a student of my late channel Mang Mike Nator, your dedication to his SUFI-ISIS work is noteworthy, indeed.

Your work including the Merkaba meditation and Enlightenment Qigong forms are excellent adjuncts to the work I started with my late channel Alice Bailey who was promulgating the *Triangles Work* and the *Great Invocation* which is best used with the *Meditation on Twin Hearts* promoted by your teachers *Master Choa Kok Sui* and *Mang Mike*.

As a Tibetan spiritual teacher myself, I also salute you in including the works of my co-worker *Guru Padmasambhava* known to your *Arhatic Yoga* and Pranic healing lineage as *Master Mei Ling*. Thank you also for including the work of *Lama Tantrapa* known as *Tibetan Shamanic Qigong* in your Enlightenment Qigong forms.

When lightworkers practice the *Triangles Work* while invoking the *Great Invocation, I and the* spiritual co-workers of what you call the Great White Brotherhood or Divine Hierarchy are ever- present assisting in the spiritual *ascension* of Mankind and Mother Earth.

The words of the *Great Invocation* are similar to light and conscious encodements with messages similar to what you understood in *An Ascension Handbook* channeled by Tony Stubbs, "The *Great Invocation's* three levels operate in the realms of Light, Love, and Will. It is a series of coded invocations. In the first paragraph, The Light of Truth opens the mind to its own God-self. The "descent of light" results in each person's alignment with his or her Higher Self. The second paragraph invokes the opening of the heart for compassion and understanding. The stream of Love into your heart results in alignment with the *Christ Oversoul*. "May Christ return to Earth" invokes the opening of each of us to the *Unity Band*, or *Christ Consciousness*. The third paragraph opens you to being a *Divine Servant*. When your will is aligned with Divine Will, you become a Divine Instrument. Becoming a Divine instrument is the "purpose which the Masters know and serve." Coming into your mastery aligns you with your *I AM Presence*. "The Plan of Love and Light" refers to ascension. "Sealing the door where evil dwells" refers to the dissolution of the veil of separation. When each one of us has dissolved our veil of separation, the illusion will be banished and the Plan will work out. The last statement is a final invocation to Truth, Love, and Power in the *ascension* process." My Blessings to you and the readers of this book! I am your *Shamballa* master servant *Djwhal Khul*. June 2, 2012

Read the *Triangles Work* on page 108 *and* the *Great Invocation* on pages 125 and 141

Swami Lakshmanjoo

Taoist Immortals

Swamiji Lakshmanjoo said, "When, by the grace of Lord Siva or the grace of his master, this limited being comes to the real understanding of his nature, then he knows that he is one with Paramasiva. At that point there is no difference between him and Paramasiva. Your consciousness becomes filled and adjusted with the reality and truth that this whole universe is only God. Nothing is experienced as being outside of God. This is the unification of your individual God Consciousness with Universal God Consciousness."

"He becomes just like Siva." - Shiva Sutra 3.25

According to Swamiji Lakshmanjoo, "He becomes like Lord Siva. Why is it said that he becomes like Lord Siva? Why not say that he becomes one with Siva? It cannot be said he becomes one with Siva because he has a body, a physical frame. As long as his physical frame is existing, he is *just like Siva*, he is not *one with Siva*. His having a physical frame will divert him toward inferior states. For instance, he may cough, have headaches, experience muscle pain, stomach aches, ulcers, or fever. Siva does not have these ailments or suffer these physical discomforts. So, as long as the yogi possesses a body, he can only be like Siva, not one with Siva. When he casts off this physical frame composed of the five elements, then he becomes one with Siva.

Because his physical body is existing, even when he becomes like Siva, that action (karma) that has brought his body into existence is ended by enjoying that action, not by casting it aside. Prarabdha karma cannot be overcome unless it is enjoyed. For an embodied being, prarabdha karma is unavoidable. He may be just like Siva or he may be an ordinary person; prarabdha karma must be overcome by being enjoyed. It cannot be cast aside or abandoned.

So, for the remainder of his life, he must continue to exist with this physical frame. He must welcome whatever comes to him, whether it be good or bad. Whatever he gets to eat, he must eat. It is not worthwhile to cast his body aside. For such a yogi, this body is to be maintained until the time of death."

According to Yoga Vashista, "The self is not revealed either by the scriptures or by the instructions of a preceptor, and the self is not revealed without the instructions of a preceptor and without the help of the scripture. It is revealed only when all these come together. It is only when the scriptural knowledge, instructions of a preceptor and true discipleship come together that self-knowledge is attained."

"Meditate on your Self, honor your Self, understand your Self, worship your Self, for God dwells within you as you." - Baba Muktananda

"By this path of the Guru, knowledge of one's Self rises." - Guru Gita, v.110

However, Ricardo's real Shaktipat initiation (2009) was with Baba Muktananda while he was viewing "Muktananda - The Guru's Touch" video, filmed during Baba Muktananda's 1976 visit in England, when he experienced yoga, reconnecting his soul (inner Self) to his Divine Soul (Higher Self), and awakening his heart to kundalini shakti's love.

After the awakening yoga experience because of Shaktipat initiation that re-created and recognized God within his consciousness, Ricardo has now been made aware that man is a living being, a living material expression, and a living soul (inner Self). And that the material body of man is but a container, a shell for the soul (inner Self) within as explained by the ontological law (Gen.2:7): "God breathed into the nostrils of man the breath of life and man became a living soul."

"Always remember, the Shakti, the energy of our lineage, comes from Bhagawan Nityananda.

A person receives Shaktipat from the Guru according to his attitude." - Baba Muktananda

"Shaktipat is the secret initiation of the greatest sages, and it has been passed on from Guru to disciple since primordial times. It is not the monopoly of the Indian tradition. Great beings of every religious tradition had their own inner energy awakened and could awaken it in others; some spoke of it specifically, while others did not. If Jesus moved his hand over someone, that person would be transformed, and great love and happiness would arise in him. That was nothing else but Shaktipat. *Saint Francis* also had this power. And it was through Shaktipat that *Ramakrishna Paramahamsa* gave his disciple *Swami Vivekananda* an instantaneous experience of the Absolute." - Baba Muktananda

"When the Kundalini is awakened, She unites with the pranas and moves through the body, purifying all the nadis and making our system strong and fit for spiritual sadhana. This process of purification is very important. Physical diseases, as well as such negative qualities as anger, lethargy, envy, and greed, are caused by impurities blocking the flow of prana in the nadis. Once the nadis are purified and the prana can run smoothly through the body, the body is rejuvenated and the mind becomes pure." - Baba Muktananda

"A Guru is one who has saturated himself with the divine power of grace and has become just like the divine. He also has the power of transmitting grace into others, and enables them to become just like himself... A Guru is one who has power of Shaktipat, and who can pierce all the spiritual centers of a seeker, and who can stabilize his mind in his sahasrara. A Guru is videhi, he is above body-consciousness, and he is totally serene. He removes all the blockages, and he transmits knowledge as thoroughly outlined in all the scriptures." - Baba Muktananda

According to Swami Shankarananda in Nityananda: the Living Tradition, "The specialty of Bhagavan's yoga is shaktipat, the awakening of the kundalini energy that lies dormant in every person. The gurus of this lineage awaken the kundalini energy by look, touch, word or thought. Once this energy is awakened by one of the Siddha gurus and the grace of Bhagavan Nityananda, a seeker evolves rapidly, ultimately attaining permanent repose in the Self.

Bhagavan died physically in 1961, but for his devotees and the Ganeshpuri villagers, his spiritual power is completely present and available even now. Indeed, his samadhi shrine, his place of burial, is a perpetual dynamo, a cauldron of Shakti... This lineage produced enlightened beings in earlier generations, and it continues to produce them today. Though each person's realisation is uniquely their own, the realisers of the Nityananda tradition have a quality that is characteristic of the great Shakti-based lineages. Their enlightenment is based on the recognition of the Self within, and on the freedom that arises from being centred beyond the mind. But it is also centred in love, seeing the Divine in others. Its core is the transmission of Shakti, and while it may make a devotional affirmation of the world, it is ultimately non-dual. The realisers of the Nityananda tradition blend love, wisdom and Shakti in a matchless dynamic.

Our lineage makes a great and unique contribution. It brings the Divine within reach of everyone. The gurus of our lineage have awakened the kundalini shakti of thousands of seekers. They have offered us a direct path to God, and also given us the experience of the Self."

Bhagawan Nityananda Samadhi Shrine

The Sri Yantra or Shri Chakra is a yantra formed by nine interlocking triangles that surround and radiate out from the central (*bindu*) point, the junction point between the physical universe and its unmanifest source. It is drawn by the super imposition of five downward pointing triangles, representing **Shakti** ; the female principle and four upright triangles, representing **Shiva** ; the male principle. It is a tantric symbol that is based on the non-dualistic philosophy of *Kashmir Shaivism* which states that the reality of this whole universe is God consciousness. It is filled with God consciousness. This world is nothing but the blissful energy of the all-pervading consciousness of God. God and the individual are one, to realize this is the essence and goal of meditation and Qigong.

Quotes from Kashmir Shaivism

"Kundalini shakti is the concealing and revealing energy of *Lord Shiva*. Para (supreme) kundalini is the heart and existence of *Shiva*, in fact it is the life and glory of *Shiva*, it is *Shiva* himself." - *Kashmir Shaivism, the Secret Supreme*

"*Kashmir Shaivism* proclaims that there are three means (upayas) for entering into the state of Universal God consciousness, i.e. shambhavopaya (supreme), shaktopaya (medium), and anavopaya (inferior). The difference is, in anavopaya you take the support of everything as an aid to strengthening awareness. In shaktopaya you begin in the center and become established there. In shambhavopaya no support is needed, you reside at your own point, the rest is automatic. It is important to realize that although these means are different, they all lead to the state of one transcendental consciousness."

"Creating, protecting, destroying, concealing and revealing are the five great acts of *Lord Shiva*. The individual soul also accomplishes these five acts and feels he is acting according to his own will, but, in reality his actions are dependent to the will of God, *Lord Shiva*. Still, as long as he has ego and feels that he is the actor, the limited individual is responsible for his own actions.

In the kingdom of spirituality *Lord Shiva* creates masters and disciples through his act of revealing, also known as grace or shaktipata. There are three types of grace, intense (tivra-tivra), medium (tivra) and inferior (madhya). Within each of these there are three levels which means *Lord Shiva* bestows grace and creates masters and disciples in nine different ways. The greatness of *Lord Shiva* is that no matter what intensity of his grace is with you, it will carry you to his nature in the end."

"Kundalini shakti is the concealing and revealing energy of *Lord Shiva*. Para (supreme) kundalini is the heart and existence of *Shiva*, in fact it is the life and glory of *Shiva*, it is Shiva himself.

When para kundalini creates the universe *Shiva* conceals his real nature and becomes the universe. Cit kundalini is experienced by great yogins, who through maintenance of awareness, enter the junction and experience the rise of the seven states of turya. Prana kundalini is experienced by those yogins who are attached to spirituality and worldly pleasure side by side."

"There are seven variations in the rise or penetration (vedha) of prana kundalini. These are determined by the inherent desires of the individual aspirant. For example, to achieve recognition of supreme I (aham), to uplift others, to have peace of mind, to become strong and maintain perfect physical condition, to experience kundalini in the form of a serpent (cobra), and to give initiation secretly. The type of rise is however, out of the hands of the individual, as it is automatically determined by ones deepest desires and longings."

"*Kashmir Shaivism* is known as the pure Trika system, which means "the three-fold science of man and his world." It is a system meant for any human being without restriction of cast, creed, color or gender. The four sub-systems of Trika philosophy – known as Pratyabhijana, Kula, Krama and Spanda, form the one thought of Trika. They all accept and are based on the ninety-two scriptures (agamas or tantras) of Shaivism."

"God and the individual are one. To realize this is the essence of Shaivism."

-- Swami Lakshmanjoo

"Trika philosophy is situated in the heart of that supreme energy of God consciousness. It teaches you to realize that this whole objective world, which is already in front of you, is not separate from God consciousness. You do not have to realize God situated in some seventh heaven. God and the individual are one, to realize this is the essence of Shaivism."

Swamiji Lakshmanjoo tells us, "freedom from all our miseries, as Abhinavagupta boldly declares, can neither be obtained through the renunciation of the world, nor by hatred towards this world, but by experiencing the presence of God everywhere."

It is to attain the bliss of samadhi that we should meditate, that we should have our Kundalini awakened by the grace of a master. We do not meditate to attain God, because we have already attained Him. We meditate so that we can become aware of God manifest within us." – Baba Muktananda

Baba Muktananda says, "Chanting the divine name is the most sublime way to develop inner love. The divine lover pursues God through his divine name."

"Chant the mantra with great feeling. Chant with all your heart and the bliss will come. No negativities can withstand the bliss of the Lord's name." OM NAMAH SHIVAYA

"Natural consciousness is the pure embodiment of Consciousness. It is Shiva. All of the thirty-six elements, from Shiva to earth, are created by that natural I-Consciousness. And not only are they created by that Consciousness, they also shine in that Consciousness. His creation is not outside of His nature, it exists in His own Self. He has created this whole universe in the cycle of His Consciousness. So, everything that exists resides in that Consciousness.

This must be your understanding. The creative energy which is attributed to Lord Shiva is not that energy of Lord Shiva that creates the universe outside of His Consciousness as we create outside of our consciousness. His creation is not insentient as our creations are.

This universe, which is created in His Consciousness, is dependent on that Consciousness. It is always dependent on that Consciousness. It cannot move outside of that Consciousness. It exists only when it is residing in His Consciousness. This is the way the creation of His universe takes place.

You must understand that this universe, which is created by the Lord of Consciousness, is one with that Creator Who is wholly self-luminous light with Consciousness.

If this created universe were to remain outside of Consciousness then it would not appear to anyone. It would not exist, just as the son of a barren woman or the milk of a bird do not exist. If we go in the depth of this understanding, we will see that there is a difference between these analogies. If this created universe were to remain outside of Consciousness, it would not appear to anyone because it would not exist at all. Actually only Consciousness exists. In this way, because this universe exists, it is one with Consciousness. In reality, nothing would exist if it were separate from this Consciousness. It is in this sense that we can say that the son of a barren woman or the milk of a bird are existing. They are existing because they are existing in Consciousness as long as they are residing in our thought. When it is in imagination it is existing in Consciousness. Ksemaraja is telling us that this universe is not outside of Consciousness. So, the son of a barren woman or the milk of a bird are not existing outside of Consciousness. We can think of them, so they are also existing inside of Consciousness.

The Consciousness of Lord Shiva is not overshadowed by this created world. The world cannot obscure Consciousness. On the contrary, Consciousness gives rise to the existence of this world.

This world is existing on the surface of Consciousness. So how could this world cover or conceal the nature of Consciousness? The truth is this world gets its life from Consciousness. It is filled with the light of Consciousness. The universe cannot conceal its life, which is Consciousness. If this universe could conceal the Consciousness of Lord Shiva, how would it exist? It would not – it would disappear." – Swami Lakshmanjoo

Source: *Self Realization in Kashmir Shaivism* by Swami Lakshmanjoo, p.57-58
NOTE: *Kashmir Shaivism is not a religion*. It is a philosophy open to those who have the desire to understand it; hence, for its study there are no restrictions of caste, creed, color or gender.

Cannabis and Acupuncture: Two-In-One Boost For Your Endocannabinoid System

Traditional Chinese medicine has been using cannabis and acupuncture together as part of their wellness and healing modalities for thousands of years. While this concept is still fairly new to the Western world, holistic medical practice in the East has long been highly advanced. Eastern civilizations, primarily the Chinese, were well-versed in the use of herbs, tinctures, and knowledge of the human body.

It's no surprise that cannabis and acupuncture has long been used in traditional Chinese medicine; these two, when used together, have shown to have synergistic effects for strengthening the immune system and addressing several different health ailments. In ancient Chinese literature, herbal historians used cannabis to treat more than 100 conditions including hemorrhages, digestive problems, rheumatism, parasitic infections, reproductive disorders in women, cognitive issues caused by age, pain, and much more.

Acupuncture is the ancient technique of inserting needles in key energy points, known as meridians, throughout the body. The objective of inserting needles below the surface of the skin is to remove obstructions in energy, referred to as "qi". These buildups are believed to contribute to disease, pain, sluggishness, and imbalance manifested through many different symptoms.

Cannabis and Acupuncture In Chinese History

In Chinese, cannabis is called "ma", which translates to "help, cannabis, and numbness". It's possible that Chinese refer to cannabis as such because it has been used historically to develop analgesics for surgeries and other intensive procedures.

Cannabis has been referenced several times in Chinese traditional medicine literature. As early as 2737 BC, Emperor Shen Nung, who might have been the first cannabis doctor in history, wrote about various traditional Chinese medicine modalities and discussed the benefits of cannabis for the human body. By 2698-2205 BC, Huang Ti, who was called the "Yellow Emperor", was said to have lived up to 400 years of age. Historians say that he invented the acupuncture needle, among many other things (ships, armor, wheels, etc). One of Huang Ti's most prolific accomplishments was writing the Nei Ching, or the Chinese Canon of Medicine where he outlines different uses of cannabis as well as other herbs used in various Chinese traditional medicine modalities. Many acupuncture students today still read parts of the canon.

In 2350 BC, the Book of Odes, also known as the She King, was produced. The book is a collection of Chinese poetry that had several references to industrial hemp. It's said that the use and cultivation of hemp as a crop originated during this period. In 1 AD, Pen Ts'ao Ching wrote a book which we know today as the oldest herbal book which was also based on Emperor Shen Nung's work. It detailed several therapeutic benefits of cannabis. By 140-208 AD, Hua Tuo became the first person recorded to use cannabis as a pain killer. It's thought that he used a tincture made with a strong CBD-rich strain containing both ground flower and leaf parts combined with wine; he apparently used this with acupuncture to numb his pain before undergoing surgery.

In a 2008 report from the Journal of Experimental Beauty, researchers from the Chinese Academy of Sciences found what might be the oldest cannabis found that was cultivated for psychoactive use, in a remote location in China. The cannabis stash was kept inside a tomb of a shaman.

Using Cannabis and Acupuncture Together

Research shows that acupuncture, just like cannabis, works to help heal and regulate the endocannabinoid system and many of the body's other systems. Not much has been thought about the possible links between acupuncture and cannabis until some researchers from Shanghai Jiao Tong University discovered it. The findings, which were published by the National Institutes of Health, revealed how electro-acupuncture (an electric form of traditional acupuncture) can increase the cannabinoid activity in the body, thereby making pain more tolerable.

In animal models of arthritis, the researchers discovered that repeated treatment using electro-acupuncture increased cannabinoid receptors in the striatum of the brain which is loaded with dopamine cells. The rat subjects showed signs of less pain after being treated with acupuncture. If cannabinoids are the reason why acupuncture works so well in dulling pain, then combining cannabis and acupuncture can be a possible cost-effective, safe, and natural solution for pain and other ailments.

Source: Cannabis and Acupuncture: Two-In-One Boost For Your Endocannabinoid System
https://cannabis.net/blog/medical/cannabis-and-acupuncture-twoinone-boost-for-your-endocannabinoid-system

A Healer's Oath

On reviewing my Traditional Chinese Medical books, I came across an excerpt from the diary of Dr. Chang Teh Hway taken from the back page of the Journal of American College of Traditional Chinese Medicine, 3, 1983 which seems a very fitting summary of all we should remember in practicing Oriental Medicine or whatever form of healing philosophy we practice whether western or eastern.

The following guidelines are very similar to the western Hippocratic Oath which most western physicians have taken as M.D.s during graduation ceremony. I have written the following guidelines especially for my TCM colleagues for their information and review:

The Physician takes care of people's life.

He is placed at the head of the hundred arts and crafts, sitting with equal footing of Premier and Minister.

It is the art of humanity.

One should not look down on the Physician as practicing the Little Tao, only integrated with no false character, tranquil and serene, can a person discuss the subject of medicine.

Those who enter my gate should know that the distress of others is also mine.

No delay should be allowed on a call from a patient.

Do not ask if the patient is noble or poor.

Always keep in heart the saving of life.

The mouth should not cease reciting medical texts; the hands continuously fiddling the hundreds of herbs.

Do not be jealous of the knowledge of others.

Do not comment on the attitude of other physicians.

Do not slander the physician who has cared for the patient previously.

Do not slander the prescriptions of other physicians.

Do not cultivate fame.

Do not be greedy of money.

Do not boast of your knowledge and ability.

Do not flatter the powerful and wealthy person; you would rather have your arm broken than bend your back.

To save life is your sole aim, idea, purpose, and concern.

If the course of disease is baffling without sign of improvement; you must with trembling caution wholeheartedly review your diagnosis and treatment.

If you are visited by monks or Taoists who wish to pay you, accept not a cent.

Zhong Shan's Medical Teachings

March 10, 1933 From the diary of Dr. Chang Teh Hway (1895 - 1971) Oriental Hospital, Teng-Chong, Yunnan.

These are my Traditional Chinese Medicine practice guidelines which I follow and which my Chinese teachers of Traditional Chinese Medicine have also been following for the past century. I always read these guidelines to remind me of my purpose or goal as a TCM practitioner and also to remind me of how I should deal with other health practitioners and my clients.

A medical doctor's quotes on allopathic medicine

"As a retired physician, I can honestly say that unless you are in a serious accident, your best chance of living to a ripe old age is to avoid doctors and hospitals and learn about nutrition, herbal medicine and other forms of natural medicine unless you are fortunate enough to have a naturopathic physician available. Almost all drugs are toxic and are designed only to treat symptoms and not to cure anyone. Vaccines are highly dangerous, have never been adequately studied or proven to be effective, and have a poor risk/reward ratio. Most surgery is unnecessary and most textbooks of medicine are inaccurate and deceptive. Almost every disease is said to be idiopathic (without known cause) or genetic - although this is untrue. In short, our mainstream medical system is hopelessly inept and/or corrupt. The treatment of cancer and degenerative diseases is a national scandal. The sooner you learn this, the better off you will be." - Dr. Alan Greenberg, MD (December 24, 2002) First, do no harm. – Hippocratic Oath

NOTE by Ricardo B Serrano, R.Ac.: I find Dr. Alan Greenberg's quotes above that prescription drugs have toxic side-effects is true, however, I would prefer non-toxic Chinese medicine - herbs, acupuncture, tuina and Qigong that includes medical cannabis instead for treating addiction, depression, PTSD, anxiety, acute and chronic pain.

The WHO has declared medical cannabis is beneficial for cancer, epilepsy, Alzheimer's, Parkinson's and other diseases, and does not carry an addiction risk.(December 13, 2017)

Read Cannabis and Acupuncture: Two-In-One Boost For Your Endocannabinoid System, page 100

For more information on medical cannabis, read "The Cure & Cause of Cancer" by Ricardo B Serrano, R.Ac.

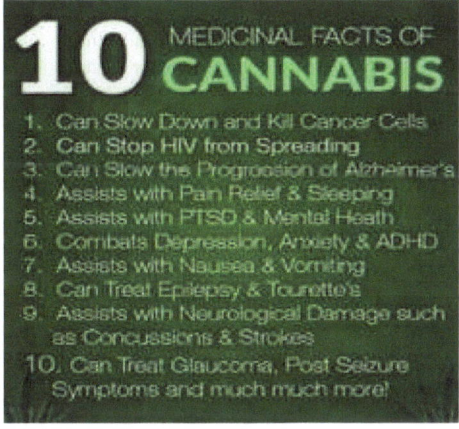

Twelve Steps of Recovery

When I contemplated the Alcoholics Anonymous Twelve Steps of Recovery, several questions and answers appeared in my enquiring mind. Why does twelve steps work for people recovering from addictions? What similarities do the twelve steps have with the eastern psychology, and meditation and Qigong principles and practices? Could these 12 steps of recovery the same 12 steps to enlightenment? What is the implication of the twelve steps to people other than alcoholics and addicts toward recovery from our egos?

Let me quote the following Alcoholics Anonymous Twelve Steps of Recovery with my interpretation from the Oriental psychology perspective:

1. **Admitted we were powerless over alcohol - that our lives had become unmanageable.** Changing from a losing attitude to a winning attitude. Because people are sick and tired of being sick and tired, out of desperation, people will try anything positive to take a leap of faith.
2. **Came to believe that a power greater than ourselves could restore us to sanity.** Positive self-dimension is at work here where a belief that we are all connected to a Greater Healer which represents Mother Earth, Holy Spirit, Heavenly Qi or the One.
3. **Made a decision to turn our will and our lives over to the care of God as we understood Him.** Surrender to a Higher Power which loosens the hold of our negative egos, and frees us from its selfish attachments and desires which is a path to freedom from the eastern philosophical perspective.
4. **Made a searching and fearless moral inventory of ourselves.** Total cleansing of our vessel (mind) has to be done before it can be filled up with the Holy Spirit or Qi.
5. **Admitted to God, to ourselves, and to another human being the exact nature of our wrongs.** This admittance of our wrongs is the opposite of denial which opens or lets go of our negative addictions hold on us.
6. **Were entirely ready to have God remove all these defects of character.** Again, surrender to a Higher Power is a necessary act to open our mind to its cleansing power before positive transformation of character becomes a reality.
7. **Humbly asked Him to remove our shortcomings.** A positive Self-talk with our soul affirming its power to connect with our Great Healer from above and below where healing originates and the healing source for addictions of the ego.
8. **Made a list of all persons we had harmed, and became willing to make amends to them all.** Forgiveness from the people we had harmed is a necessary act to neutralize negative karma before recovery happens.
9. **Made direct amends to such people wherever possible, except when to do so would injure them or others.** We have to use discrimination to avoid more harm than good.
10. **Continued to take personal inventory and when we were wrong promptly admitted it.** No time to lose to ask for forgiveness right away now instead of procrastinating it for some other time that might never come.
11. **Sought through prayer and meditation to improve our conscious contact with God as we understood Him, praying only for knowledge of His will for us and the power to carry that out.** The meditation and Qigong practices which connect the practitioner to the Great Healer from above and below to experience inner love which heals all addictions completely.
12. **Having had a spiritual awakening as the result of these steps, we tried to carry this message to alcoholics, and to practice these principles in all our affairs.** After the spiritual enlightenment or self-realization which results from meditation and Qigong practices, the enlightened ones become messengers of Truth to share what they had experienced for the good of the whole.

What is your personal understanding of the 12 steps of recovery or enlightenment?

I believe that the 12 steps of recovery is applicable not only to people with addictions (who hasn't?) but also is another way to self-fulfillment (enlightenment) and another set of guidelines to become winners in life's challenges.

Another way to enlightenment is through the practice of Ashtanga Yoga by Baba Hari Dass:

- Yoga literally means "union". Through stilling the mind, union with our divine source is achieved. (Yoga is the cessation of thought-waves in the mind.) - Yoga Sutras 1:2
- "Kundalini is the greatest energy in the human body. If kundalini is awakened it entirely changes the person, who then dwells in complete peace and clarity of mind."
- "Path of devotion is the best. By surrendering to God, by chanting God's name and glory, and by meditating on God's form, one can row one's boat in the ocean of the world without getting hit by the mighty waves of desires, attachment and ego."
- "There is an unspoken language. It comes from the silence and can't be heard by the ears, only by the heart."
- "The main thing is selfless service. It sounds easy but it is very hard. Our mind is so selfish that in anything we do it always seeks for its own benefit."
- "No one can please everyone. Your mental peace is more important. If you are in peace then others around you will feel peace. So your best effort should be to work on yourself."
- Identification with the mind is the cause of all suffering. - Aphorism No. 28
- If the mind is not filled with divine light, bliss, and peace, then all the efforts of yoga are useless. - Aphorism No. 53
- Silencing the mind is meditation. - Aphorism No. 66
- The chitta (mind), like fire without fuel, calms down when objects disappear. - Aphorism No. 68
- Sitting in silence will not go to waste; some day you will reap the harvest of peace. - Aphorism No. 73
- That is love when the mind is established in its pure form. - Aphorism No. 112
- A realized being is one whose presence creates a feeling of peace. - Aphorism No. 123

The Eight Limbs of Ashtanga Yoga

- ❖ Self-restraint (*yama*)
  - Non-violence (*ahimsa*)
  - Truthfulness (*satya*)
  - Non-stealing (*asteya*)
  - Sexual continence (*brahmacharya*)
  - Non-possessiveness (*aparigraha*)
- ❖ Fixed observances (*niyama*)
  - Purity or cleanliness (*saucha*)
  - Contentment (*santosha*)
  - Austerity (*tapas*)
  - Self-study; study of scriptures (*swadhyaya*)
  - Surrender to God (*Ishwara pranidhana*)
- ❖ Posture (*asana*)
- ❖ Regulation of breath (*pranayama*)
- ❖ Withdrawal of mind from senses (*pratyahara*)
- ❖ Concentration (*dharana*)
- ❖ Contemplation or meditation (*dhyana*)
- ❖ Superconsciousness (*samadhi*)

Hand mudras are a series of symbolic gestures. They depict the evolution of the universe and the eventual involution of individual consciousness back to its divine source. The essence of hand mudras is devotion, as each mudra is an offering, a gift to the Divine. The hands perform a graceful worship, flowing rhythmically with a slow and steady pattern of breathing. A cycle of 24 movements is offered in preparation for meditation, while another cycle of 8 movements follows meditation.

References: Ashtanga Yoga Primer by Baba Hari Dass, 1981; Fire Without Fuel: Aphorisms of Baba Hari Dass, 1986

Ashtanga Yoga hand mudras, a **Qigong form**, preserve and build the primordial Qi for healing and enlightenment.

Universal Prayer

Starting this new endeavor of writing and sending information through my own book to me is both exciting and challenging from a mental and spiritual point of view because of the new possibilities offered thru this medium which parallels and reminds me of the inherent possibilities from our inner selves which if not tapped remained dormant and disconnected.

This long time yearning of mine to integrate and connect with the inside and outside energy world is finding its expression beautifully thru this book. I believe also that writing and communicating glimpses of what I call soul talk is healthy and necessary.

Because of its timely message let me quote **the Universal Prayer:**

1. May the wicked become good. May the good obtain peace. May the peaceful be freed from bonds. May the freed set others free.

2. Blessings on the subjects of those who are ruling, and may these great lords rule the earth in a just manner. May good always be the lot of cows and Brahmins. May all people be happy.

3. May it rain at the right time. May the earth have storehouses full of grain. May this country be free of disturbances. May Brahmins (and those racially, sexually, and culturally descriminated) be free of persecution.

4. May all be happy. May all be healthy. May all see only auspicious sights. May no one have a share in sorrow.

5. May everyone surmount his difficulties. May everyone see only auspicious sights. May everyone have his desires fulfilled. May everyone everywhere be glad.

6. May blessings fall on our father, blessings on the cows, the fields, the workers. May everything of ours flourish and be an aid to knowledge. And long may we see the sun.

Commentary: In Qigong, the fingers are seen as gateways of Qi and representing organs of the body, emotions and elements. It is recommended that the hand mudras of Ashtanga yoga, a Qigong form, be used by everybody to quiet the mind with its negative emotions, and build and balance the Qi in the 5 elements and the organs associated with each element.

- Littler Finger: This represents the water element, fear and the kidneys.
- Ring finger represents wood, the liver, nervous system, gall bladder and anger.
- Middle finger is fire, the small intestine, respiratory system and circulatory system; haste and impatience.
- Index finger corresponds with the element of metal, the large intestine, lungs and with the emotions of grief and depression.
- Thumb: The thumb is earth, the stomach and anxiety or worry.

I believe that personal peace and universal peace is attainable by opening the heart through the use of Ashtanga Yoga hand mudras with the application of the Gayatri mantra and the 8 limbs of Ashtanga Yoga by Baba Hari Dass. **See What is Raja Yoga?, page 47; 8 Limbs of Ashtanga Yoga, page 104; Epilogue, page 113; Gayatri Mantra, page 138; Hand Mudras, page 139**

Lastly, when ashtanga yoga hand mudras are practiced, the torus also called merkaba, electromagnetic field, aura or energy bubble is activated that facilitates healing and enlightenment. Read **Wei Qi Field in Qigong**, page 62, Oneness with Shiva

Prayer of St. Francis of Assisi

Lord, make me an instrument of peace

Where there is hatred, let me sow love

injury, pardon

error, truth

doubt, faith

despair, hope

discord, unity

sadness, joy

darkness, light.

Divine Master, grant that I might not so much seek

to be consoled, as to console, to be understood, as to understand

to be loved, as to love. For it is in giving that we receive

it is in pardoning that we are pardoned. And it is in dying that we are born to eternal life.

See Awakening your Kundalini, p. 31; Excerpts on Kundalini, p. 121; Shri Yantra Mantras, p. 130; Three Dantiens, p. 133; Bija Mantras, p. 154

Meditation on Twin Hearts

Meditation on Twin hearts is based on the principle that some of the major chakras are entry points or gateways to certain levels or horizons of consciousness. To achieve illumination or Cosmic consciousness, it is necessary to sufficiently activate the Crown chakra. But this can be done only when the Heart chakra is sufficiently activated. The Twin Hearts thus refer to the Heart and Crown chakras.

Since the Meditation is a powerful tool in bringing about world peace, Master Choa Kok Sui has granted permission to disseminate, reprint, copy, and reproduce the Meditation with proper acknowledgement.

WARNING: The following are not allowed to practice the Meditation on Twin Hearts: (1) those below 18 years of age; (2) those with heart trouble, hypertension, glaucoma and severe kidney ailments; and (3) pregnant women. Doing this meditation can have adverse effects to the people with the preceding conditions. People with the above qualifications who insist on practicing the meditation do so at their own risks.

1. Cleansing Exercise. Cleanse the etheric body by doing simple physical exercises for about five to ten minutes. During the exercise, light grayish matter, or used-up prana, is expelled from the etheric body. Physical exercises also minimize possible pranic congestion since the Meditation generates a lot of subtle energies in the body.
2. Invoke for Divine Blessings. The Invocation is important to one's protection, help and guidance. Without the invocation, the practice of any advanced meditational technique can be dangerous.
3. Activating the Heart Chakra. Press the center of your chest (heart area) with your finger for a few seconds. Then concentrate on the front heart chakra and bless the whole world with loving-kindness. The blessing should not be done mechanically. When blessing the entire earth, visualize it as a small ball in front of you, being filled with dazzling bluish pink light. During the blessing with the *Prayer of St. Francis of Assisi*, visualize people smiling and filled with joy, faith, hope, and peace. Visualize enemies reconciling, embracing and forgiving each other. You should also personally feel joy, happiness, and peace filling your entire being while blessing the earth. Do not direct this blessing to infants, children or individuals because they might be overwhelmed by the intense energy generated by this meditation.
4. Activating the Crown Chakra. Press the top of your head for a few seconds. Then bless the planet earth with loving-kindness from the Crown chakra. Feel the same positive energies you evoked in step 3. Visualize brilliant white light from your Crown chakra blessing the entire earth.
5. Blessing with both Crown and Heart Chakras. Bless the earth simultaneously from both the Crown and Heart chakras with golden light. This will align the two chakras and make the blessing more potent. Feel the same positive energies you evoked in step 3 and 4.
6. Achieving Illumination. For illumination (expansion of consciousness), visualize a dazzling point of white light on top of your head (*higher soul*) and simultaneously chant mentally the word AUM (Ah-omm), or Amen (Ah-menn). Concentrate on the intervals or gaps (moments of silence) between the AUMs or Amens, while maintaining your concentration on the point of light. Do this for about 10-15 minutes. When you can fully concentrate simultaneously on the point of light and on the intervals between the AUMs, you will experience an inner explosion of light.
7. Releasing Excess Energy. After meditation, it is important to release all excess energy by blessing the earth through your hands, with light, loving-kindness, peace, and prosperity for several minutes until you feel your body has normalized. Continue blessing if you still feel congested, otherwise the excess energy may cause headaches and chest pains. The physical body may also deteriorate in the long run if there is too much energy in the etheric body.

I used to practice Meditation on Twin Hearts years ago, and now practice Meditation on Three Hearts instead for the following reasons:

The main elements of Three Hearts meditation are:

- Three Hearts refer to navel, heart and crown chakras.
- Three Hearts also refer to three-force energy fields, three dantiens, which is based on the trinity model.
- Three Hearts meditation has no contraindications when combined with Qigong and Kundalini meditation (Shiva and Shakti meditation). See **Awakening your Kundalini, p. 31; Excerpts on Kundalini, p. 121; Three Dantiens, p. 133; Bija Mantras, p. 154**
- Three Hearts meditation is grounded to the center of mother earth which has a calming and nourishing experience that brings one a sense of peace and connection.

The main elements of Twin Hearts meditation are:

- Twin Hearts refer to heart and crown chakras.
- Twin Hearts meditation is not grounded to mother earth.
- Twin Hearts meditation has contraindications such as heart disease, hypertension, glaucoma, severe kidney problems. Please refer to **Meditation on Three Hearts in my book Oneness with Shiva.**

Triangles Work

Much of the material contained herein have been lifted from the "Triangles of Fire," written by Torkom Saraydarian with permission from The Creative Trust, All Rights Reserved. The work is financed by the voluntary donations of Triangles workers to the Lucis Trust, and by the voluntary work of other organizations committed to carrying out the work of the Hierarchy.

A triangle is composed of three people who say *The Great Invocation* daily to invoke light, love and power, in order to create peace, understanding, cooperation, abundance and freedom. The pure energy released by the practice of the triangles work will eventually transmute the substance in which humanity lives, thus providing a pure sphere of love and light in which the function of the forces of Light will be possible with all its power and wisdom.

Triangles was founded by the Lucis Trust in 1937 to stimulate the growth of right human relations by uniting like-minded men and women of good will in a spiritual service.

Triangles is an activity of the mind, using the power of thought and prayer to invoke light and goodwill for all humanity. The work is done by units of three people linked in a worldwide Network.

Benefits of Triangles Work

- Triangle work links various types of people and puts them in subjective communication.
- Triangle work not only brings people closer together, but it opens channels of inflowing energy from the Great Ones to humanity.
- Triangle work literally provides increased inspiration to those who have any artistic talent.
- Working to communicate with Higher Sources brings moral upliftment to those who work in our political, social, economic, religious, medical, and legal fields, gradually eliminating dishonesty, bribery, exploitation, and selfish interest.
- The healing of nations will come from Higher Sources.
- Building triangles of light leads to understanding the value of economy.
- Triangle work will bring in the Aquarian Age.
- Triangle work paves the way for the externalization of the Hierarchy and the reappearance of Christ.

How to Form a Triangle of Light

At a set appointed time everyday, especially during the Full Moon every month, all three participants begin saying *The Great Invocation*. The power of the Invocation increases as one puts real interest, attention, pure visualization and creative thinking into it. Your mind must concentrate upon the words you are saying. The words must be said slowly, with solemnity, and you must not waver over your problems, worries or plans as you repeat it. At the time you say the *Great Invocation*, you must raise your consciousness as high as possible, detaching your mind from personal problems and interests, focusing it on those great concepts and visions found in the *Great Invocation*.

In repeating the *Great Invocation*:

First, visualize the other two triangle participants sitting in the room with you, sitting quietly together in Nature, or in any pleasant setting. Lift your consciousness as high as possible, detaching yourself from all physical, emotional and mental concerns.

Then visualize a golden thread linking all of you, thus forming a living, fiery triangle.

(a). See a beam of light projecting from the middle of your forehead, reaching the first person.

(b). Then see another beam of light reaching the second person. Make your visualization as clear as possible, without strain or stress.

(c). See the beam of light uniting all three triangle participants.

(d). Visualize the energies of Light, Love and Power circulating through the beam of light.

(e). Visualize Christ, shining as pure light in the center of the triangle.

3. Then focus your mind as high as possible, and solemnly begin to repeat the *Great Invocation* word for word, with great concentration. At the same time, invoke the energies of Light, Love and Power into the center of the Triangle, spreading through that center along the beam of light forming the triangle and circulating through the three points of the triangle.

4. Between stanzas, pause and visualize the triangle participants anew, before going on to the next stanza.

5. The next step is to radiate out the accumulated energy within the triangle to the entire world.

6. After you have completed the *Great Invocation*, sit relaxed for a moment, and then silently go about your work.

7. During the day, register any ideas that occur to your mind regarding the triangle work. Share them with the other "points" if you think that your recordings will deepen their knowledge and create greater interest in them toward the triangle work.

After the first triangles is firmly established, you can start other triangles to be repeated at different times, proceeding in the same way. If any participant cannot continue in his task for any reason, then he must be kind enough to inform the other two so that they can choose another person for their triangle.

Men and women of goodwill throughout the world are using the *Great Invocation* in their own language. Will you join them in using the Invocation everyday -- with thought and dedication to the service of humanity? Read the *Great Invocation* on pages 125 and 141

Lalitha Tripura Sundari (the Goddess of the three cities/worlds), **Raja Rajeshwari** (The Devi of the Nabhi as Kundalini comes up**), Sahasraakshi** (she of the thousand-petalled lotus at the **Sahasrara Chakra**)…..the supreme mother at the entry point of consciousness into our body. This is the Devi of Devipuram in South India – very very powerful energy. "I personally have experienced the bliss of samadhi through successfully awakening my kundalini and seven chakras returning to oneness with Divine Mother's (Lalitha Tripura Sundari) grace under the guidance by my kundalini teacher Raja Choudhury." – Ricardo B Serrano **See Awakening your Kundalini, p. 31; Becoming a Beacon of Love, p. 92; Sahasrara Mudra, p. 110; Excerpts on Kundalini, p. 121; Sri Vidya Mantras, p. 126; Bija Mantras, p. 154; Techniques of a Master, p. 159**

Summary of Bio-energetic (Pranic) Chakras Healing Techniques

Basic/Hand Chakras Technique

In the basic/hand chakras technique, the basic chakra is used as the source chakra, and the hand chakra as the projecting chakra. Earth and air prana are drawn by the basic chakra and projected out through the hand chakra. The healer has to visualize light-red pranic energy coming out of his hand. Light-red pranic energy is used to activate the lower chakras - the basic chakra, the sex chakra, the meng mein chakra, and the solar plexus chakra.

Throat/Hand Chakras Technique

In the throat/hand chakras technique, the throat chakra is used as the source chakra, and the hand chakra as the projecting chakra. The throat/hand chakras technique is used to project blue pranic energy. Air prana is drawn by the throat chakra and projected through the hand chakra. Light whitish greenish-blue is used to treat fresh burns, infections, inflammations, food poisoning, and also stop bleeding.

Crown/Hand Chakras Technique

With the crown/hand chakras technique, the crown chakra is used as the receiving chakra and the hand chakra as the projecting chakra.

Divine healing energy from your "higher self" or your higher soul and air prana are drawn and absorbed by the crown chakra and projected out through your hand chakra. The soul pranic energy is electric violet or electric white, and golden yellow in color. Electric violet pranic energy appears as dazzling white or electric white with very light violet or bluish violet. How much soul pranic energy can be drawn depends upon the spiritual development of the practitioner. The more developed the practitioner, the bigger the crown chakra and the thicker the *spiritual cord* that connects the crown and the Higher Self. In an ordinary person, the spiritual cord is hardly visible. The spiritual cord is called the *pillar of light* in the Kabalah, and *antakharana* in Sanskrit (which means a spiritual bridge of light). For powerful healers, it is better to use the forehead/hand chakras technique touching the heart chakra with one hand. Both techniques are used to activate the higher chakras - heart chakra, crown chakra, forehead chakra, or ajna chakra. See *Major Chakras of the Human Body* on page 150

Sri Vidya Sahasrara Chakra Mudra
(See Sri Vidya Mantras, page 176)

Basic Techniques in Bio-energetic (Pranic) Healing

In basic and advanced bio-energetic (pranic) healing, there are seven healing techniques:

1. Sensitizing the hands;
2. Scanning the inner aura;
3. Sweeping (cleansing): general and localized (counterclockwise) using salt water disposal unit;
4. Increasing the receptivity of the patient;
5. Energizing with prana (clockwise);
6. Stabilizing the projected pranic energy (light blue energy);
7. Releasing the projected pranic energy or detaching,

In pranic psychotherapy, there are four additional healing techniques:

1. Removing and disintegrating traumatic psychic energy, negative thought entities, negative psychic entities, and negative elementals with violet pranic energy or violet light.
2. Disintegrating negative elementals and sealing the cracks or holes in the etheric or protective webs using violet light.
3. Activating and inhibiting the chakras.
4. Creating a positive image of the patient or a positive thought entity for the patient.

Source: Master Choa Kok Sui's Advanced Pranic Healing and Pranic Psychotherapy books

Inner Smile

"What sunshine is to flowers, smiles are to humanity." – Joseph Addison

As I pondered on my blissful experience during the meditative state, I have asked myself *"How can I maintain this loving state in my daily 3rd dimensional life with all of its day to day challenges, physical and emotional tensions, and personal and business relationship dealings?"*

"Through the Inner Smile which resonates with your smiling inner heart of your energy body."

The Inner Smile is very useful in dissolving Qi blockages, restoring everyday health and Qi flow in an infinite number of profound applications that come from unconditional self-acceptance. The Inner Smile exercises our ability to love, starting with our own bodies. As we learn to love and accept ourselves, it becomes natural and easy for us to extend this love outward and begin to love and accept other people and nature. As one of the best exercises for stress management and self-healing, the Inner Smile induces a state of deep relaxation. Deep relaxation dissolves physical and mental tensions that cause energy blockages and unhealthy Qi. Its greatest virtue, though, is that the Inner Smile can also be a path to whole body Enlightenment.

By smiling into each of the five internal organs according to the Five Elements of Classical Chinese Medicine – heart, kidneys, lungs, liver and spleen – with its related corresponding emotions of joy, fear, grief, anger, and worry - negative emotions are transformed into positive ones, therefore, changing the general internal emotional state of the whole body, mind and spirit that is aligned with your smiling inner heart of your energy body.

Surya Namaskar (Sun Salutation) and Solar Plexus

There will be no life on earth, without the sun. Surya Namaskar or 'Sun Salutation' is a very ancient technique of paying respect or expressing gratitude to the sun that is the source of all forms of life on the planet. Symbolically, the sun becomes our source of energy as well. About the history of this technique, it has been said by the ancient rishis of India that the different parts of the body are governed by different devas (divine impulses or divine light). The solar plexus (located behind the navel, which is the central point of the human body), also known as the second brain, is said to be connected to the sun. This is the main reason why the ancient rishis recommended the practice of Surya Namaskar, because the regular practice of this technique enhances the solar plexus, which increases one's creativity and intuitive abilities. It is also important to understand the science behind this very ancient technique, because a deeper understanding will bring forth the right outlook and approach towards this very sacred and powerful yogic technique. All our emotions get stored in the solar plexus, and it is also the point from where one's gut feelings arise. The size of the solar plexus is said to like the size of a small gooseberry. However, for those who do yoga, it becomes much bigger - almost three to four times bigger than the normal size. The more expanded your solar plexus, the greater is your mental stability and your intuition. This could be your mantra to stay fit, happy and peaceful. A mantra whose effect lasts through the day. **Source**: Surya Namaskar (Sun Salutation) by International Journal of Advanced Educational Research. **See Surya Namaskar, page 16; Koshas – The Five Sheaths that Wrap Your Soul, page 135; Solar Plexus Chakra, page 151; Healing and Returning to Oneness, p. 157; Techniques of a Master, page 159**

Poem called "Smile" by Barbara Hauck, age 13

She smiled at a sorrowful stranger. The smile seemed to make him feel better.

He remembered past kindness of a friend and wrote him a thank you letter.

The friend was so pleased with the thank you that he left a large tip after lunch.

The waitress, surprised by the size of the tip, bet the whole thing on a hunch.

The next day she picked up her winnings, and gave part to a man on the street.

The man on the street was grateful; for two days he'd had nothing to eat.

After he finished his dinner, he left for his small dingy room.

He didn't know at that moment that he might be facing his doom.

On the way he picked up a shivering puppy and took him home to get warm.

The puppy was very grateful to be in out of the storm.

That night the house caught on fire. The puppy barked the alarm.

He barked till he woke the whole household and saved everybody from harm.

One of the boys that he rescued grew up to be President.

All this because of a simple smile that hadn't cost a cent.

- from Chicken Soup for the Teenage Soul

by Jack Canfield, Mark Victor Hansen and Kimberly Kirgerger

Lalita Tripurasundari (See Sri Vidya Mantras, p. 126)
Return to Oneness with Shiva

God consciousness is not achieved by means of the scriptures nor is it achieved by the grace of your master, God consciousness is only achieved by your own subtle awareness. – Yoga Vasistha

EPILOGUE:

Master Choa Kok Sui's *Meditation for Soul Realization tells us*, "We are all children of God. In each person, there is a divine essence or a divine spark. In Buddhism, there is a *Buddha* in each person. In Christian religion, there is a *Christ* in each person. In Hinduism, there is a *Shiva* or a *Krishna* in each person.

What is the name of this divine essence? When Moses saw the burning bush, he asked, "If the people ask me what is your name, what shall I tell them?" From within the burning bush God answered, "I AM THAT I AM." (Exodus 3:13-14) In Hebrew, this is called *Eieh*. In Sanskrit, this is known as *So Ham* or *Tatwamasi*. There is a universal or planetary I AM. There is a micro I AM in every person.

Jesus says in John 14:6, "I AM the way and the truth and the life. No one comes to the Father except through me." Does Jesus literally mean that he is the way, the truth and the life, or does he mean that the I AM or higher soul within you is the way, the truth and the life? Does Jesus mean himself as the way to the Father or is this a reference to the I AM or higher soul within every person? "The Divine Father" here refers to the divine spark in every person.

The divine spark in every person is a part of God. It is made in the essence of God. The divine spark is one with God and one with all. The divine spark extends a portion of itself "downward", manifesting as the higher soul. The higher soul extends a portion of itself "downward", manifesting as the incarnated soul. In Hindu teachings, the incarnated soul is called *Jivatma*. It literally means "embodied soul." The higher soul is called *Atma*. The divine spark is called *Paramatma*. This is why St. Paul said that you have a body, soul, and spirit (1 Thessalonians 5:23). Here, "*spirit*" refers to the divine spark in each person. To achieve union with the divine spark or the Divine Father within you, you must first pass through the I AM or the higher soul."

The *Self Realization* teachings of *Kashmir Shaivism* taught by Swami Lakshmanjoo say the same message as told by Master Choa Kok Sui when Swami says, "The nature of the universe is the existence of *Lord Siva*. *Lord Siva*'s existence is naturally everyone's nature. Lord Siva is found in rocks; Lord Siva is found everywhere. Lord Siva is even found in the absence of Lord Siva. Even there He is not absent, He is existing.

There He resides, alone in His kingdom. No one else is found there.

In the two cycles of bondage and liberation, the cycle of bondage is concerned with the not-knowing cycle. When you do not know what you are doing, then you do not know where you are established. That is the cycle of bondage. What is the cycle of knowledge? It is liberation! What is liberation? Liberation exists when you come to understand that it is only a trick, that it is the play of *Lord Siva* and nothing else. At that point you understand that nothing has happened, nothing is lost, and nothing is gained.

In brief and exact words, these two cycles, bondage and liberation, are not separate from *Lord Siva*. Why? Because differentiated states have not risen at all. It is only a trick that you are ignorant and somebody else is elevated. But the question arises – whose trick is it? Is it your trick or *Lord Siva*'s trick? It is your trick. Why? Because if it were not your trick then you could not be liberated. It is your own trick that has made you ignorant. You fool yourself. And when that supreme force enters you it will shatter this ignorance into pieces. You do not need anybody's help in shattering it. You have enslaved yourself; you can free yourself and become a king.

You must understand that, in reality, nothing has happened to *Lord Siva*. He is never ignorant. He is never elevated. From which point would He be elevated? Was He not elevated before? Why even use this word "elevation"? Elevation is meant for those who are sunk or who are sinking. If He is never sunk down, and you are one with Him, then why talk of elevating yourself? You are already elevated, you are divine.

This is *Kashmir Shaivism*. This theory of *Shaivism* is misunderstood by many people. You must first come to understand this theory and then you begin to become *Lord Siva*. According to the theory of *Shaivism*, you are *Siva*, and will eventually come to the conclusion that you are *Siva*. And yet, you are not actually *Siva*, because you have not achieved that state.

Even though you have not actually realized that you are *Siva*, it is not a mistake to think that you are *Siva*. You should go on thinking that you are *Siva*. You should always elevate yourself with the thought that you are *Lord Siva* – but do not boast of this. If you tell someone that you are Siva it means that you are not Lord Siva. You must actually understand that if you are *Lord Siva*, then this whole creation is all a joke, an expression of your play.

One might ask, "How do you know whether or not you are fooling yourself thinking that you are *Siva*, or whether you really are *Lord Siva*? How do you know?" The answer is that you will always be blissful. When you are in that state and when something bad happens to you, you will not get worried; and when something good happens to you, you will not get excited. While experiencing pain you will be peaceful.

You must come to know and see in yourself situated in this way. If you are not situated in this way and boast, saying, "I am *Lord Siva*, I am *Lord Siva*", you will be slapped and made to understand that you are not *Lord Siva*.

To actually know who you are is a big problem. You have to find out yourself where you are situated. It happens by the grace of *Lord Siva*, or by the grace of a master, or by the grace of the scriptures (*sastras*).

When, because the grace of Lord Siva is showered upon you, or due to the teachings or vibrating force of your Master, or through understanding the scriptures concerned with Supreme Siva, you attain the real knowledge of reality, that is the existent state of Lord Siva, and that is final liberation. This fullness is achieved by elevated souls and is called liberation in this life. (jivanmukti). – 12 & 13Verses of Wisdom by Abhinavagupta

I, Abhinavagupta, have written and revealed these verses for some of my dear disciples who have very little understanding. For those disciples, who are deeply devoted to me, I have composed these fifteen verses just to elevate them instantaneously.

Both Master Choa Kok Sui and Swami Lakshmanjoo said that one will be able to achieve expansion of consciousness – oneness with *Shiva* – by practicing meditation on the gap, junction or stillness.

> "Be still and know that I am God." – Psalm 46:10

By practicing meditation on the gap, junction or stillness, one becomes aware of the Divine Presence not only within one's self; one also becomes aware of the all-pervasive presence of the Divine everywhere.

There is a saying that if the water is rough, you cannot see through it. If the water is calm, you will be able to see through it. In the same way, when your mind and emotions are still, you can see your true nature. You can achieve oneness with your higher soul. You can realize your Buddha nature.

You do not achieve stillness by stopping the thinking process, but by being aware of the inner stillness. Where is this inner stillness located? It is in the gap, or junction between inhalation and exhalation, between two thoughts, between two mantras, between night and day, between sleeping and waking, between body movements, between nature sounds, and space around human body, trees and nature.

Master Choa Kok Sui said that you cannot achieve soul realization by simply trying to still the mind. It is important to purify and disintegrate the grayish clouds of noisy thoughts and emotions inside your aura. This can be done by using the spiritual flushing-out technique – *Meditation on Twin Hearts*. When a person does *Meditation on Twin Hearts*, the heart chakra and the crown chakra are used to bless the entire earth, every person and every being with loving kindness. The meditator becomes a channel for this spiritual energy. Another effective flushing-out technique that I practice besides *Twin Hearts Meditation* is the combination of *Maitreya (Shiva) Shen Gong* and *Omkabah Heart Lightbody Activation*.

As the spiritual energy comes down through the spiritual cord into the crown center and into the heart center, it radiates out into the aura, causing turbulent, noisy thoughts and emotions to be flushed out.

Through the regular practice of *Meditation on Twin Hearts*, the aura or energy bubble becomes relatively clean within a short period. You will experience inner calmness. Once inner calmness has been achieved, the meditator is ready to practice meditation the gap, junction or inner stillness.

Gayatri Mantra

The beautiful and soothing ancient sounds, the flowing rhythmic patterns, and the powerful intent make the Gayatri Mantra a wonderful part of one's daily spiritual practice. Because it is an earnest and heartfelt appeal to the Supreme Being for enlightenment, it can be universally applied. It really doesn't matter what your religion, your color or your ethnicity is – what matters is your intent, and your authenticity, and your willingness to be moved.

The Gayatri Mantra inspires wisdom in us. In very basic but beautiful language, it says "May the divine light of the Supreme Being illuminate our intellect, to lead us along a path of righteousness".

The Vedas say: To chant the Gayatri Mantra purifies the chanter. To listen to the Gayatri Mantra purifies the listener.

But the mantra does much more, It opens up your heart. And how well we know, when both our minds and our hearts open, we open ourselves up for new possibilities.

One interpretation is that the word Gayatri is derived from the words: gaya, meaning "vital energies" and trâyate, meaning "preserves, protects, gives deliverance, grants liberation".

So, the two words "Gayatri Mantra" might be translated as "a prayer of praise that awakens the vital energies and gives liberation and deliverance from ignorance".

The shorter form of the Gayatri is practiced far more commonly:

OM BUHR BHUVA SWAHA TAT SAVITUR VARENYAM

BHARGO DEVASYA DHEEMAHI DHIYO YONA PRACHODAYAT

We meditate on the glory of the Creator;Who has created the Universe; Who is worthy of Worship;Who is the embodiment of Knowledge and Light;Who is the remover of Sin and Ignorance;May He open our hearts and enlighten our Intellect.

According to the Vedas, there are seven realms or spheres or planes of existence, each more spiritually advanced than the previous one. It is written that through spiritual awareness and development, we can progressively move through these realms and ultimately merge with the Supreme Being. Many Buddhist teachings have also referred to these seven realms.

By chanting this mantra, Divine spiritual light and power is infused in each of our seven chakras and connects them to these seven great spiritual realms of existence.

The sages of ancient times selected the words of the Gayatri carefully and arranged them so that they not only convey meaning but also create very specific vibrations and powers of righteous wisdom through their utterance. Hindu Vedic scriptures describe how many of these sages accumulated tremendous spiritual powers through years of deep meditation and the chanting of the Gayatri – these spiritual powers are called Siddhi.

It is said that these Gayatri Sadhaka (spiritual seeker) begin to feel the presence of divine power in the inner self which induces immense strength and peace of mind.

If you intend to chant the Gayatri mantra, it is quite important that you chant it with the correct pronunciation and with the deepest integrity of intent. This of course, means that one needs to know the meaning of the words behind the mantra. The Sanskrit words of the Gayatri carry tremendous power when chanted correctly and with the purest of hearts.

Put together, we could say:

"We meditate on that most adorable, desirable and enchanting luster and brilliance of our Supreme Being, our Source Energy, our Collective Consciousness….who is our creator, inspirer and source of eternal Joy. May this warm and loving Light inspire and guide our mind and open our hearts."

See Raja Yoga, page 47; 8 Limbs of Ashtanga Yoga, page 104; Universal Prayer, page 105; Gayatri Mantra, page 138; Hand Mudras, page 139

May you apply the Gayatri Mantra with Ashtanga Yoga Hand Mudras, Kundalini Yoga, Hanuman Qigong and mantras, Meditation on Three Hearts with Triangles Work and the Great Invocation, Merkaba Meditation, Invocation to the Unified Chakra, Meditation on the Gap, Five Agreements, and healing codes for healing, quieting the ego-mind and spiritual awakening(ascension). Who and what you meditate on, you become. **Om Shreem Hreem Shreem Kamle Kamlalaye Praseeda Praseeda Shreem Hreem Shreem Om Maha Lakshmiye Namah** *(see p. 130)*

With thanks and acknowledgements to my Kundalini teacher Raja Choudhury, Sheng Zhen Gong teacher *Li Junfeng*, Siddha teachers Baba Hari Dass, *Swami Lakshmanjoo, Baba Muktananda, Bhagawan Nityananda, Master Djwhal Khul, Master Choa Kok Sui* and Mang Mike Nator for their grace, books and contributions to my spiritual awakening (*ascension*) and to the completion of this book. – *Ricardo B Serrano, R.Ac.*

BOOK REFERENCES:

The Hathor Material by Tom Kenyon & Virginia Essene, 1996.

Vibrational Medicine: New Choices for Healing Ourselves by Dr. Richard Gerber, 1988.

Hara: the Vital Center of Man by Karlfried Graf Durckheim, 2004.

The Fifth Agreement by Don Miguel Ruiz and Don Jose Ruiz, 2010.

Advanced Pranic Healing by Master Choa Kok Sui, 1992.

Living in the Heart by Drunvalo Melchizedek,

2003. Shiva Sutras by Swami Lakshmanjoo, 2007.

Self Realization in Kashmir Shaivism by Swami Lakshmanjoo, 1994.

Power of Now by Eckhart Tolle, 1999.

Where are You Going? By Swami Muktananda, 1981

Play of Consciousness by Swami Muktananda, 1978

Empty Force: the Power of Chi for Self-Defense and Energy Healing by Paul Dong, 2006

Qi Dao – Tibetan Shamanic Qigong by Lama Somananda Tantrapa, 2007

Keys of Enoch: The Book of Knowledge by JJ Hurtak, 1977

Tibetan Book of the Dead by Karma Lingpa, 1927

Melchizedek Method Level 1 by Alton Kamadon, 1998

Meditations for Soul Realization by Master Choa Kok Sui, 2000.

An Ascension Handbook by Tony Stubbs, 1999.

What is Lightbody? Archangel Ariel, channeled by Tashira Tachi-ren, New Leaf, 1999.

Fire Without Fuel: The Aphorisms of Baba Hari Dass, 1986; Ashtanga Yoga Primer by Baba Hari Dass, 1981

Mang Mike Nator

MCKS meeting with Mang Mike

Mang Mike was introduced to Master Choa Kok Sui by Samuel in about 1975. MCKS visited Mang Mike a few times in Cebu City prior to Mang Mike's departure for Iran to work as a master baker. He was kind and very accommodating person. He was a gentle soul, full of love for others and a good clairvoyant.

Mang Mike was from a super rich family. His sisters were sent abroad to study in Spain. Mang Mike's mother forced him to study engineering against his will. He was not good in mathematics and science so he shifted his study to liberal arts. He graduated with a Bachelor of Liberal Arts degree with honors. His major study was in English. His parents and family were very happy with him. Mang Mike became a good concert pianist and was also a wonderful singer. He was compared to the famous Mario Lanza.

Unfortunately, most of his brothers and sisters were not interested in the family business. When his parents died, their family lost almost everything. This crisis was actually a great blessing in disguise for Mang Mike, as it drove him to search for spiritual truth. It drove him into the spiritual path. Mang Mike was also very generous and supportive of his immediate family.

Mang Mike spent many years spreading the Baha'i teachings. In spite of being overweight, he walked into the mountains to teach the Baha'i faith. He was indeed a good evangelist. He also taught the Baha'i faith in the national penitentiary. The conditions there were rather dangerous, yet he persisted in teaching the Baha'i faith. All of these qualities are very praiseworthy.

In 1981, Mang Mike was paralyzed due to a stroke. He was hospitalized, given proper medication and physical therapy while in the hospital and after being discharged from the hospital.

Later, MCKS visited him in his house in Cebu City where he was still bedridden and unable to walk. MCKS gave him two or three healing treatments using divine energy. After that, Mang Mike recovered rapidly and was able to walk and travel. In about August of that year, Mang Mike traveled from Cebu City to Cubao, Quezon City, where he stayed with his sister.

Both Mang Nenet Ranudo and Mang Mike later played important roles in Pranic Healing and Arhatic Yoga. Mang Dabon also played a very important role in the inner world through guided transferred clairvoyance during the experiments and provided assistance in healing.

The name of Mang Mike's Spiritual Teacher was Holy Master Gammaliel.

Mang Mike left his body permanently on 15 February 2003.

Samuel's First Meeting with Mang Mike

The first time I met Mang Mike was through Maning in 1971. He introduced me to a group of interesting people which included Mang Nenet and Mang Mike.

During my interactions with Mang Mike in Cebu, he did not do healing as he was a practicing clairvoyant reader who gave psychic readings.

In the later part of 1971, an interesting event occurred during an afternoon at Mang Mike's residence and bakery store. I saw him go into his bedroom. Later, I also went into the room but I could not find him. I noticed that there were subdued sparks of light in the room. I came out of the room, sat outside and continued my conversation with two of his bakers. I told the bakers that it would have been impossible for Mang Mike to leave the room without us noticing him because we were sitting just outside the door. They all agreed that it would have been impossible for him to leave the room unnoticed.

Later, during our lively conversation, Mang Mike shouted from inside the room, "Hey, you guys are very noisy". When I went into his room, I was surprised to see him and asked him where he had gone. He replied that he had been teleported by his Master to a room in a hotel in Argentina, to attend a meeting with his Master and the rest of his Master's disciples. He claimed that he did not teleport himself, but that he was teleported through the power of his Teacher.

Pranic Healing Experiments

MCKS visited Mang Mike regularly and would ask him to clairvoyantly monitor His healing experiments. In order to validate the findings, MCKS traveled every month to Cebu City to clairvoyantly cross-check the experiments with Mang Nenet. These two clairvoyants were not aware that their findings were being cross-checked against each other. Healing experiments were also done on many patients.

Nine Years of Hard Work

MCKS established a Pranic Healing Center in Kamuning Street. He was healing about 10 to 20 patients almost every afternoon from Monday through Saturday. Mang Mike was also healing other patients. This was done to further validate the Pranic Healing techniques for MCKs' Advanced Pranic Healing book. This continued for about two years.

Source: The Origin of Pranic Healing and Arhatic Yoga by Master Choa Kok Sui, 2006.

On April 9, 1933, Miguel C. Nator was born in Cebu with the special gift of clairvoyance.

There is no better tribute to a man than his works and the lives that he has touched. The acronym U.N.I.C.O.R.N. encapsulates Mang Mike – who he is and what his mission stands for. The Union for National Involvement Concerning Operations to Regenerate the Nation is a movement he founded to rally the Filipino people towards spiritual regeneration and transformation. It rallies everyone to the task of raising their country's spiritual consciousness.

Mang Mike teaches us that there are seven steps to this process:

1. Development of harmlessness or non-injury in thoughts, words, feelings, and actions.
2. Development of inclusiveness by regarding every man a child of God.
3. Development of self-forgetfulness and selflessness in the service of God.
4. Demonstration of good thoughts and ideas translated into practical deeds through positive goodwill.
5. Donate intelligently and wisely with loving kindness - time, effort and money to the Great Plan of God.
6. Meditate and Study regularly and conscientiously.
7. Desire nothing for the separative self but desire all for the good of the other Self.

Mang Mike was a living testimony of his teachings. He showed us by example the virtues of harmlessness, selflessness, all-inclusiveness and the need for study, meditation and service. He personified unconditional love. He demonstrated his discomfort whenever he is addressed as Master. Not once did he ever claim to be one. The honorific title of *Mang* was sufficient.

The vehicle for spearheading the U.N.I.C.O.R.N. movement is Serve the U.N.I.C.O.R.N Fellowship Inc. (S.U.F.I.) and its educational arm I.S.I.S. SUFI-ISIS is the vehicle for service and for spreading wisdom. It is Mang Mike's wish that everyone becomes a light worker not only for the Philippines but for the whole world. Together with Master Choa Kok Sui, he was instrumental in the reintroduction of *Pranic Healing* and *Meditation on Twin Hearts* to the world and in the completion of Master Choa Kok Sui's books.

Origin of SUFI-ISIS by Mang Mike Nator

Sometime in 1971, I was operating a bakery business in Cebu. A part of this bakery was devoted to some sort of an ashram where I would teach students and disciples along the spiritual path. One day while baking, something unusual happened to me. It was around 2 o'clock in the afternoon when I fell unconscious. I heard what was like the buzzing sound of a bee followed by a big bang. Then there was this brilliant light, and the next thing I knew I was in a hotel room somewhere in Argentina with four other disciples of the Master.

During what seemed to be a short audience with the Master, we were given assignments. Each one of us was to establish a school and to form a group that would spread the teachings of the Masters. The only one among the students that I met because he was sitting next to me was a man named Mario Luis Rodrigues Cobos. This gentleman's teachings eventually became known as Siloism. I did not take this encounter as anything significant until my disciple, Butch Castañeto, related to me what transpired during that interval.

A student at the San Carlos University, Butch recounted that he was looking for me at that exact time. As I usually lie down when I meditate, he went to my room, but could not find me. He conducted a long search, but I was not to be found. Two to three hours later, he looked inside my room again, and this time found me there. It was only after his story that I believed that I must have been truly in Argentina during that short two to three hour interval.

Four years later, Butch introduced to me his chemical engineering classmate who was looking for a psychic. I read his classmate's aura, and his future. This classmate is now known as Choa Kok Sui, the Master Pranic Healer. I was not to see him again until 1981. Meanwhile I went to Iran the following year 1976 and returned in 1979. It was in 1981 that I suffered a stroke. When he heard of my stroke, Master Choa came to see me. It was our second encounter. He gave me some form of healing and advised me to exercise and to undertake physical therapy. I followed his advice. After that I was able to walk and move.

I eventually moved to Manila to help my sister in her bakery business. By this time, Master Choa was based in Manila because of his business. When he heard that I was in Manila, he looked for me and eventually found me. And that's when we started seeing each other regularly. He would come to the house to do some experiments after lunch at about 12 noon and leave at 12 midnight.

While meditating during one of those experiments, Master Mei Ling appeared because he wanted to communicate with Master Choa. I told him that his teacher, the Lord Mei Ling, wanted to tell him something. Master Mei Ling overshadowed me and told me to tell Master Choa to write books. He was to first write the book on the teachings of pranic healing. We were being watched and our experiments were being observed by Master Mei Ling. If we had any questions regarding pranic healing, we were just to tune in and contact him. So the experiments with Master Mei Ling's inputs started in 1983. In 1986, Master Choa started writing. He finished and published the book in 1987. He compiled all his data and put them in the form of a book.

All this time, I was being haunted by a voice reminding me of my personal mission and urging me to form a group. I would intuit suggestions and I would write them down in notes. I wrote a list of names to form a group to start with. Jess Española was among the first people who were interested. We met for the first time in Master Choa's house. At that time, there were about two or three psychics in the group, students from University of the Philippines, and those who were well versed in theosophy. We would meet almost every afternoon, and talk about theosophy and other schools of thought. That's how we started. Other people joined us. Gerarld Victoria's mother. Followed by Gerarld. The group kept growing and growing. As I look at the group now, it is very well established. I have fulfilled what I have been told to do.

There were certain principles and laws that I have always been reminded to teach. One is that I will accept students who come from different schools of thought. The group should be seekers of synthesis, and that harmlessness, selflessness, meditation, study and service are very much emphasized. There were Rosicrucians. Masons. But some of them could not stay long in the group. Others come and go. But Gerald, his mother, his father, Mang Leo, and the people from the Theosophical Society were attracted to the group.

At first, the Master indicated to me that Self unfoldment would be the focus of the group to make ourselves better persons – spiritually and materially balanced with the spirit of fellowship. So we called ourselves the Self Unfoldment Fellowship. The unicorn came later after several encounters with them. I immediately tied up the unicorn to the idea of regeneration, and a regeneration program came into being. I have been guided to give my full thrust to the idea of regeneration, but this time not from one school of thought. This should come from different schools of thought. What should be emphasized is Self Unfoldment through Harmlessness, Synthesis, Meditation and Selflessness.

Master Djwhal Khul

At that time, I was very much involved in Master *Djwhal Khul*'s work. I became a fellow of the Arcane School and I have been in contact with Lucis Trust. I was able to fortify myself with knowledge channeled to me by Master *Djwhal Khul*, Master *Mei Ling*, and Master *Om*. I interacted with Master Om for a short while. That was some time in 1983 and 1984. But after that, only Master *Mei Ling* and Master *Djwhal Khul* would enter into my consciousness and dictate some things to be taught to students.

The group observed meditation and fellowship every full moon of the month. We established the school, ISIS, when I was already at the Maria Clara apartment. There was a time, I stayed at Gerarld's place from Cubao. I moved to Maria Clara after that.

The group was finally formed. SUFI is independent from the Institute and the Pranic Healing Foundation. Master Choa cannot interfere with the decisions and workings of SUFI.

I emphasized that to him as that is the wish of Master *Djwhal Khul*. At that time, I did not talk about the other Master. My real teacher is Master Gammaliel...Master G. It was like I was being borrowed by Master *Djwhal Khul*.

Master G is the founder of this school. But to be able to understand him requires a different level of consciousness. It is through Master *Djwhal Khul* that Master G will be understood by the people at the present time. Master G is the inspirer or giver of energy, but Master *Djwhal Khul* is the one who defines all the things that are necessary as far as understanding human evolution is concerned. As you all know, Master *Djwhal Khul* inspired *Madame Blavatsky* to found the Theosophical Society, and then the *Alice Bailey* books, but those are not the only ones. He is responsible for many other books in the world today whose spiritual teachings center on humanity's evolution as intended by the Plan. I am merely following whatever suggestions and impressions I receive from the Masters.

Now Master G only comes once in a while if there is great urgency. The revelation of the *Unicorn Disk* is part of his work. It is a tool used in the preparation and the development of the molecular structure not only of the human being, but of all things that are evolving. He is responsible for that and it is part of his dharma to emphasize the rapid development of mankind. We are told to practice with the disk so that with the use of light and vibration, we can gain accelerated improvement of certain faculties. As you know, man uses only 1/10 of his brain. The rapid changes at this present time will allow us the full use of consciousness and the development of the continuity of consciousness or immortality.

This comes down to rarefying the molecular structure of our etheric bodies. As the etheric vibrates at higher and higher frequencies, the higher teachings that would be needed in the future are revealed to the practitioner. So man is now guided to develop certain powers. Images that have not even been tapped. What we will become familiar with may be a hundred times, a thousand times more that our brain will have to expand ... a very complicated matter. And if man is to stay on earth and still have a body, his body will be of a higher kind. By then, it will be mostly etheric and may probably be existing on the fourth dimension. The lower kingdom will also be raised to a higher degree; becoming more likely human. And so it goes on all levels of existence one after the other. What we are trying to do now is to experiment on ourselves individually and as a group in order to fulfill what we were meant to be as demanded by the times. But right now only very few are aware and conscious of what's happening. Others are still asleep. So it's our duty to awaken them but not forcibly. It's our dharma to make them aware of the needs of the times.

The vehicle for service and for spreading wisdom is in SUFI-ISIS. It is my wish that everyone in the group will be able to continue the work. That is how it is supposed to be. Continue specially at this time because the years ahead are going to be rough. So I would like to ask your cooperation and understanding with the desire that you dedicate yourself as a light worker not only for the Philippines but for the whole world.

The preceding is an edited transcription of Mang Mike's sharing during the 1997 SUFI retreat.

Excerpts on Kundalini from *Kundalini, the Secret of Yoga by Gopi Krishna (1972)*

The Bija-Mantras are no less inexplicable. The very nature of the sounds emitted by the mantras, Ham, Vam, Yam, Lam, etc., are a clear indication of the fact that they are fabricated and are as imaginary as the presiding shaktis and the letters of the alphabet. It is evident that when repeated interminably in a state of intense concentration, with diminished breathing heart action, they can serve effectively, with their nasal intonation and monotonous sonority, to induce a state of quiescence preceding the state of trance. Monotonous sounds have been used from prehistoric times and are even now employed by hypnotists and teachers of the occult to induce somnambulistic conditions. In primitive societies, in all periods of history down to times, monotonous chanting and weird music have always used to induce abnormal mental conditions and trancelike states in sensitive persons, susceptible to occult influences. The recitation of the Bijas or other Mantras, prescribed by the Guru, causes the same somnolent effect in the Sadhakas with a largely enhanced effect in combination with the other mental and physical exercises enjoined. It is easy to see that the Mantras of the class Aim, Krom, Srim Svaha, or Hrim, Srim, Krim, Parameshvari (Mahanirvana Tantra vi. 72-74 and 82) or others used in Tantric Sadhna are definitely of the hypnotic type. p. 54

If we accept as true even a tithe of what the ancient masters claim for Kundalini-Yoga — superconsciousness, psychic powers, longevity, radiant health, genius, and a host of other gifts and talents — this points to a hidden source of energy and strength in the body, so marvellous, so potent, and so precious for the peace and happiness of mankind that no price paid for it and no sacrifice made to acquire the secret would be too great. p. 66

It has already been explained that kundalini is the spiritual as well as the biological base of all the phenomena connected with religion, the occult, and the supernatural. Whenever during the whole course of human history some man or woman exhibited uncanny powers which fell in the province of magic, witchcraft, augury, sorcery or mediumship and furnished conclusive evidence that the manifestations were genuine, in every case without exception, it signified the veiled activity of a slightly awake kundalini. In the same way, whenever any man or woman laid claim to prophethood, to direct communion with God or an Almighty Source of Intelligence and furnished irrefutable proof of supernormal faculties, higher moral standards, and mystical insights, it also, in every case, indicated a fully active kundalini that found access to sahasrara, the highest centre in the brain. Just as all variations, perversions, and distortions observed in the sexual behaviour of individuals can only be attributed to the expression of the sex instinct, rooted in the reproductive mechanism, in the same way all the varied manifestations connected with religion and the supernatural have their origin in the dynamic spiritual power reservoir of kundalini. p. 180

Yoga and kundalini are interchangeable terms, for there is no Yoga and no union of the individual with Cosmic Consciousness unless kundalini is activated. p. 181

Kundalini bestows both Yoga (union with the Divine) and Bhoga (enjoyment). But not the unwholesome enjoyment of a libertine nor the morbid sensuous delight of a hedonist, nor the unholy pleasure of one thirsty for power, nor the hectic acquisition of one hungry for wealth, but the incomparable Bliss that wells up from the Fount of Eternal Life within, invulnerable and perennial, and the happiness that comes from an honourable, well-spent, and consecrated life, de-voted to noble pursuits, partaking with great moderation and in a most judicious manner of all the ecstasies and joys of life provided by heaven for the delectation of man. p. 202

Kundalini is the Divine Power, both individually and collectively, which as the controller of evolution, raising man from the position of a speck of protoplasm, is slowly moulding him into a Man-god, amid all the uproar and unrest that characterizes our age, in order to endow him with inner attributes and to crown him with a glory in the millennia to come which are beyond our loftiest dreams. p. 203

Appendix:

In the Sat-Cakra-Nirupan, embodied by Arthur Avalon in "The Serpent Power," there are in all 55 verses out of which no less than ten in clear, unequivocal terms refer to the development of surpassing intellectual powers and literary talents in the Yogi who successfully awakens Kundalini. As this issue is of utmost importance, nine of these verses are reproduced here:

Verse 3. "She is beautiful like a chain of lightning and fine like a (lotus) fibre, and shines in the minds of the sages. She is extremely subtle; the awakener of pure knowledge; the embodiment of all bliss, whose true nature is pure Consciousness. The Brahma-dvara shines in her mouth. This place is the entrance to the region sprinkled by ambrosia, and is called the Knot, as also the mouth of Susumna." Verse 7. "Here dwells the Devi Dakini by name; her four arms shine with beauty, and her eyes are brilliant red. She is resplendent like the lustre of many suns rising at one and the same time. She is the carrier of the revelation of the ever-pure intelligence." Verses 10 and 11. "Over it shines the sleeping Kundalini, fine as the fibre of lotus-stalk. She is the world-bewilderer, gently covering the mouth of Brahmna-dvara by Her own. Like the spiral of the conch-shell, Her shining snake-like form goes three and a half times round Siva, and Her lustre is as that of a strong flash of young strong lightning. Her sweet murmur is like the indistinct hum of swarms of love-mad bees. She produces melodious poetry and Bandha and all other compositions in prose or verse in sequence or otherwise in Samskrta, Prakrta and other languages. It is She who maintains all the beings of the world by means of inspiration and expiration, and shines in the cavity of the root (Mula) Lotus like a chain of brilliant lights." Verse 13. "By meditating thus on Her who shines within the Mula-Cakra, with the lustre of ten millions Suns, a man becomes Lord of speech and king among men, and an Adept in all kinds of learning. He becomes ever free from all diseases, and his inmost Spirit becomes full of great gladness. Pure of disposition by his deep and musical words, he serves the foremost of the Devas."

Verse 18. "He who meditates upon this stainless Lotus, which is named Svadhisthana, is freed immediately from all his enemies, such as the fault of Ahamkara and so forth. He becomes a Lord among Yogis, and is like the Sun illumining the dense darkness of ignorance. The wealth of his nectar-like words flows in prose and verse in well-reasoned discourse." Verse 21. "Here abides Lakini, the benefactress of all. She is four armed, of radiant body, is dark (of complexion), clothed in yellow raiment and decked with various ornaments, and exalted with the drinking of ambrosia. By meditating on this Navel Lotus the power to destroy and create (the world) is acquired. Vani (goddess of speech) with all the wealth of knowledge ever abides in the lotus of His face." Verse 27. "Foremost among Yogis, he ever is dearer than the dearest to women. He is preeminently wise and full of noble deeds. His senses are completely under control. His mind in its intense concentration is engrossed in thoughts of the Brahman.

His inspired speech flows like a stream of (clear) water. He is like the Devata who is the beloved of Laksmi and he is able at will to enter another's body." Verse 31. "He who has attained complete knowledge of the Atma (Brahman) becomes by constantly concentrating his mind (Citta) on this Lotus a great Sage, eloquent and wise, and enjoys uninterrupted peace of mind. He sees the three periods, and becomes the benefactor of all, free from disease and sorrow and long-lived, and, like Hamsa, the destroyer of endless dangers." **See Awakening your Kundalini, p. 31; Becoming a Beacon of Love, p. 92; Shiva and Shakti Meditation, p. 106; Sri Yantra Mantras, p. 130; Three Dantiens, p. 133; Microcosmic Orbit, p. 153; Bija Mantras of Seven Chakras, p. 154**

An Introduction to Winged Unicorn Meditation

I would like to add that practicing the *Winged Unicorn Meditation Technique* not only strengthens the head chakras in preparation for clairvoyance but also balances, regenerates and harmonizes all the chakral energies and subtle bodies of the spiritual aspirant cushioning radical reactions (such as post-*kundalini syndrome*) associated with other advanced meditational practices making it excellent for meditation, thought projection, dreaming, akashic records investigation, channeling and so forth.

When one is successful in treading the Way through the *Winged Unicorn Meditation* Technique and other similar advanced meditation techniques such as *Meditation on Twin Hearts*, *Merkaba Meditation* and *Triangles Work*, he becomes a super person, a higher being, a saint, a mystic, an immortal, a Highlander, and a Master.

He controls time and space, he touches great beauties, colors, music, perfumes, forms, that surpass everything in this world. He will be given keys to enter the locked rooms of the Holy of Holies in his own nature, unveil secrets of the Laws of God to bring down to ordinary life for the spiritualization of humanity. The further he penetrates the higher planes, the closer he comes to the real source of beauty, goodness, truth and proportionally the spirit of bliss, the spirit of understanding. The spirit of power dawns upon his daily life and makes his relationships magnetic, radioactive and blossoming.

My beloved Arhat Yoga Master and Master Pranic Healer teacher Choa Kok Sui commented in his March 4-5, 1995 Clairvoyance workshop I attended about my beloved *Unicorn Meditation* Master Miguel Nator and his *Winged Unicorn Meditation Technique as an awesome Path* with the benefits in learning to open Clairvoyant Vision (All Seeing Eye), "*By learning and understanding the basic required knowledge, skills and practices, clairvoyance can be learned and practiced, just as pranic healing is learned. The ability to see subtle energies in the auras and chakras as well as to see into the organs and cells themselves is both fascinating and very practical in healing.*"

Clairvoyance is another awesome *Path (Winged Unicorn Meditation Technique)* into the world of subtle energy. There seems to be no limit to the learning and skill development possibilities as is evidenced by Mike Nator in Manila. Mike is able to see the colour and spin of the chakras as well as incredible details in the physical, etheric and other energy bodies. As with Pranic Healing, the chakras are very important in the clairvoyance teaching.

"If you are wondering how much difference it could make to your healing abilities, the answer is . . . lots! And it's fun to do. Expand your Wisdom and Ability." My unforgettable experience seeing *auras* of the clairvoyance participants and seeing *Master Choa Kok Sui*'s spiritual heart and crown chakras brought tears in my eyes realizing that *we are spiritual beings*.

Just as your two physical eyes working together give three dimensional vision, so your two non-physical eyes – the 4th eye located high on your forehead directly above the 3rd eye – combine to give you 4th and 5th dimensional vision. The goal of the *Unicorn Meditation* is not only to sharpen intuition and clairvoyance, but most importantly, like the ultimate goal of the other advanced meditation techniques is to experience *inner stillness* that leads to *spiritual oneness* – incarnated soul is achieving a higher degree of oneness with the higher soul, and a certain degree of oneness with God and oneness with all.

Integral Studies of Inner Sciences, a non-sectarian inner way school for inner mastery in Canada and affiliate of ISIS - Integral Studies of Inner Sciences, Philippines , is administered and taught by Ricardo B Serrano, R.Ac., registered acupuncturist, meditation and Qigong teacher/healer. http://innerway.ca

Pancha Kosha (Five Sheaths that wrap your Soul)

Read Awakening your Kundalini, p.31; Pancha Kosha, p. 43; Raja Yoga, p. 47; 8 Limbs of Ashtanga Yoga, p. 104 - 105; Excerpts on Kundalini, p. 121; Incarnated Soul, p. 152; Healing and Returning to Oneness, p. 157; Techniques of a Master, p. 159

Integral Studies of Inner Sciences was founded in honor of my late *Unicorn Meditation* teacher Master Mike Nator, founder of Integral Studies of Inner Sciences, Philippines.

Unfortunately, the Integral Studies of Inner Sciences is not suitable for everybody. So one must not be offended if one is not taught the deeper esoteric practices such as *Unicorn Meditation* after a pre-screening process. This is only because certain applicants may not be healthy enough to withstand the physical, emotional and mental stresses and changes they will be subjected to.

Prerequisites

1. To be initiated into any deeper esoteric training like the Integral Studies of Inner Sciences, it is necessary to have the following qualities already present in the person for a safe and sequential unfolding:
2. Character – Briefly, a student undergoing esoteric training must have more or less built a character of which he is mentally, emotionally, and physically integrated and balanced as a personality, and also spiritually awakened.
3. Physical Health – A student must be a person who is more or less a vegetarian by personal choice; thereby possessed of a refined physical body.
4. Esoteric Background – A student has been on the path for sometime and is well acquainted with Basic Esoteric Teachings provided by Theosophy or other ancient esoteric schools of thought.
5. Will to Persist – Treading the Way of the Spirit is not an easy task. The student in search for the truth meets obstacles and difficulties along the way. Many of which could pin the searcher down so hard that at times one gives up the challenge because progress is not apparent. The student's greatest enemy is usually himself - the man of the world. So having developed the will to persist, a harmless, inclusive and selfless character will guarantee his progress and success in achieving his goal.

It must be borne in mind that once taught, the student is not allowed to divulge or share the deeper esoteric techniques of Integral Studies of Inner Sciences such as *Unicorn Meditation* with anyone who is not an approved and recognized member of the group. The *Unicorn Meditation* at the present time are for only a few who are "ready"; for a shift in consciousness and are of no use for the unprepared and may even prove disastrous for them. The student must keep the techniques to himself, and practice persistently and regularly in order to test effectiveness and achieve results. The student's efforts will be rewarded one day.

Raja Choudhury, Ricardo's second clairvoyance and kundalini teacher

"Our entire system is one vast cosmos of energy centres that are navigated through nodes we call Goddesses or Devis who live along our spine and throughout our whole body. To open your third eye you need to unlock each of the major centres and each has its own key, code, vision, sound and most importantly application of breath. Once released, the energy coiled up at the base of your spine rises up like a serpent climbing through these centres and eventually opens your third eye and links you to a super conscious mind state. Allowing this sacred feminine energy into your life will open up not only the doors of perception to other cosmic realities but unleash a dormant energy that will transform every aspect of your consciousness and life and transform you forever." ~ Raja Choudhury

In 2006 Raja Choudhury had a major Third Eye awakening accompanied by great illumination and inner experiences that transformed his life and set him on his current journey into consciousness research and practice. He now teaches anyone inluding me (Ricardo Serrano, author of this book) who is keen to learn what he has discovered so far. I learned about the secrets behind breath, sounds, mantras, mudras, yantras and how we can use them to activate our inner sacred feminine kundalini energy that will open up the universal consciousness to us. As far as he is concerned, we are all travelers on a journey of enlightenment and some of us are just a little further along or have experienced or perceived a little bit more. His personal mantra is "Be Your Own Guru" and "Awaken the Light" within yourself and he believes everyone can and should experience this awakening. **Read Awakening your Kundalini, p. 31; Becoming a Beacon of Love, p. 92; Excerpts on Kundalini, p. 121**

"My Shaktipat experience with Raja which opened my heart and kundalini is the reason why I know he is an awakened kundalini teacher." - Ricardo B Serrano

"I experience the bliss of samadhi when my heart and third eye open by the process of kundalini awakening." - Acharya Ricardo B Serrano

That is why it is essential to awaken the inner Kundalini Shakti. According to Shaivism, when one acquires the strength of Kundalini, one expands infinitely, and one assimilates this whole universe; one is able to see the whole universe within one's Self. One no longer remains a limited, bound creature; one achieves total union with God. One merges with Shiva and becomes Shiva.

A kundalini teacher essentially guides the path of kundalini through the upward journey in the seven chakras which start from muladhara chakra and eventually culminate in the sahasrara chakra along the spine that include the activation of the subtle energy system (ida, pingala and sushumna nadis) with sounds, mantras, mudras and breath. The session always include shaktipat (shakti transmission) to activate a student's three hearts (three suns - third eye/tongue/neck, heart and lower three chakras). The sahasrara is activated through the thousand suns lotus above the head. The journey's goal should result in the purification of karma with the eventual experience of samadhi. **AEEM-KLEEM-SAUH SAUH-KLEEM-AEEM See Meditation on Three Hearts, p. 107; Sri Vidya Mantras, p. 126; Three Dantiens, p. 133; Incarnated Soul, p. 152**

If the radiance of a thousand suns were to burst forth in the sky, that would be like the splendor of the ultimate reality. ~ Bhaghavad Gita

1. Invocation to the unified chakra
2. Divine light invocation
3. Hologram of Love Merkaba activation
4. Triangles work
5. Meditation on Three Hearts
6. Unicorn Meditation (Third eye awakening via kundalini awakening)
7. Bio-energetic (Pranic) Qi-healing
8. Full Moon Meditation

My personal mantra is "Awaken your inner Guru" within yourself by kundalini awakening. Supplementary Enlightenment Qigong forms are included to root or ground the Kundalini Shakti to Mother Earth, build Yuan Qi and Wei Qi field, expand consciousness and avoid Kundalini syndromes. Sri Vidya kundalini meditation powerfully boosts Qi-healing and Qigong practices when integrated together.

The Great Invocation by *Alice Bailey and Djwhal Khul*

From the point of Light within the Mind of God

Let light stream forth into the minds of men. Let Light descend on Earth.

From the point of Love within the Heart of God Let love stream forth into the hearts of men. May Christ return to Earth.

From the center where the Will of God is known Let purpose guide the little wills of men

The purpose which the Masters know and serve.

From the center which we call the race of men Let the Plan of Love and Light work out

And may it seal the door where evil dwells. Let Light and Love and Power restore the Plan on Earth.

People of goodwill throughout the world are using this invocation daily in their own language. Join them in using the *Great Invocation* every day – with righteous intent, thought and dedication. Use the *Triangles Work* with the *Great Invocation* by Holy Master *Djwhal Khul* and encourage others to use it. No particular group or organisation is sponsored. It belongs to all humanity.

The *Great Invocation* is a powerful means for creating right human relationships – between individuals, groups and nations – for it expresses certain central truths that are widely accepted: the truth of the existence of a basic Intelligence to Whom we give the name God; the truth that behind all outer seeming. the motivating power of the universe is Love; the truth that a great Individuality, called by the Christians the *Christ*, came to earth and embodied that Love so that we could understand; the truth that both love and intelligence are effects of what is called the Will of God; and finally the self-evident truth that only through humanity can the Divine Plan work out.

For fifty years the *Great Invocation* has been used by people of all religions and cultures, living on every continent and in many countries of the world. It has now been translated into more than 75 languages and dialects and is said daily throughout the world.

The idea of the return of the World Teacher has its place in the teaching of the majority of the world faiths, and in some translations of the *Great Invocation* the coming One is known by such names as the *Lord Maitreya*, the *Imam Madhi*, the *Messiah* and *Bodhisattva*.

The *Great Invocation* speaks not to the desires of the personality but to the indwelling soul – to the "thinking entity" within all men and women of good will – for the Sanskrit origin of "man" means "to think." It is this reasoning, thinking aspect which, when awakened in sufficient numbers of human beings, will enable humanity to take its rightful place in helping the Plan of God to find full expression on Earth.

NOTE: According to Tony Stubbs' *An Ascension Handbook*, "The *Great Invocation's* three levels operate in the realms of Light, Love, and Will. It is a series of coded invocations. In the first paragraph, The Light of Truth opens the mind to its own God-self. The "descent of light" results in each person's alignment with his or her Higher Self. The second paragraph invokes the opening of the heart for compassion and understanding. The stream of Love into your heart results in alignment with the *Christ Oversoul*. "May Christ return to Earth" invokes the opening of each of us to the *Unity Band*, or *Christ Consciousness*. The third paragraph opens you to being a *Divine Servant*. When your will is aligned with Divine Will, you become a Divine Instrument. Becoming a Divine instrument is the "purpose which the Masters know and serve." Coming into your mastery aligns you with your *I AM Presence*. "The Plan of Love and Light" refers to *ascension*. "Sealing the door where evil dwells" refers to the dissolution of the veil of separation. When each one of us has dissolved our veil of separation, the illusion will be banished and the Plan will work out. The last statement is a final invocation to Truth, Love, and Power in the *ascension* process."

"The *Great Invocation* is best used with the *Triangles Work* and *Meditation on Twin Hearts*." – Master Djwhal Khul

Sri Vidya Mantras by Sri Amritananda

Sri Vidya is the name of a Hindu religious system devoted to the goddess Lalita Tripurasundari or simply Tripurasundari ('Beautiful Goddess of the Three Cities'). The Sanskrit word vidya means knowledge or lore; so the literal translation of Sri Vidya is Knowledge of the Goddess Sri.

In the theology of the Sri Vidya the goddess is supreme, transcending the cosmos which is a manifestion of her. The goddess is worshiped in the form of a mystical diagram (Sanskrit: yantra) of nine intersecting triangles, called the sricakra that is the central icon of the tradition. The underlying principle of the whole practice is to realize the ultimate unity of the Devata, the mantra, the teacher and the practitioner.
http://en.wikipedia.org/wiki/Shri_Vidya and https://youtu.be/1GYI0VDd4h0

Read Awakening your Kundalini, p. 31; Sri Vidya Mantras, p. 76; Becoming a Beacon of Love, p. 92; Excerpts on Kundalini, p. 121; Raja Choudhury, p. 124; Techniques of a Master, p. 159; Bija Mantras, p. 154

Death, Dying and Spiritual Liberation

"Life's most awesome event is death, and death comes to all without regard to wealth, beauty, intelligence or fame. Death is inevitable, but how you die — terrified and confused, or with confidence and spiritual mastery — is within your control." – Buddhism as an Education

To summarize this very important topic on death, dying and spiritual liberation, Ricardo has a true confession to make: the other main reason why he started his spiritual path besides soul mastery was the uncertainty of what happens after death which is usually accompanied by the feeling of fear of the unknown. Now that he understands the death process and is familiar with it through the actual experience relating to soul realization by his students and himself, his fear at the time of death is removed.

The mystical experiences he had during the passing of his mother (1994) and the passing into mahasamadhi of his late beloved great spiritual teacher Master Choa Kok Sui (2007) made a huge impact to his convictions in the truth of the technology of the soul teachings and spiritual findings (see *Meditation on Twin Hearts*) taught by Master Choa Kok Sui, and the powerful impact of the Guru Yoga of his spiritual mentor Tibetan Buddhist Mahaguruji Bodhisattva Padmasambahva (who embodies a cosmic, timeless principle; the universal master) especially at the moment of death, spiritual liberation and soul realization.

In the west, the only spiritual attention that the majority pay to the dying is to go to their funeral. When someone dies, one of the deepest sources of anguish for those left behind to mourn is their conviction that there is nothing they can now do to help their loved one who has gone, a conviction that only aggravates their grief which is not true. There are many ways we can help the dying and the dead, as shown in the spiritual help for the dying and the dead in this article such as invoking the buddhas, praying and saying the mantras OM MANI PADME HUM and OM AH HUM VAJRA GURU PADMA SIDDHI HUM, doing Guru yoga practices, and reading the "Tibetan Book of the Dead", and so help ourselves to survive their absence.

Just as it is the nature of fire to burn and of water to quench thirst, the nature of the buddhas is to be present as soon as anyone invokes them, so infinite is their compassionate desire to help all sentient beings. For spiritual help for the living, dying and the dead, and especially for healing, the masters have assured us: Call out to them, and the buddhas *will* answer you. As Bodhisattva Padmasambhava says: "*Complete devotion brings complete blessing; absence of doubts brings complete success*." For if you can unite your mind confidently with the wisdom mind of the master at the moment of death and die in that peace, then all will be well.

All we need to do to receive direct help is to ask. Didn't Christ also say: "Ask, and it shall be given you: seek and ye shall find; knock and it shall be opened unto you. Everyone that asketh receiveth; and he that seeketh findeth?"

The Buddha says in one of the Tantras: "*Of all the buddhas who have ever attained enlightenment, not a single one accomplished this without relying upon a master, and of all the thousand buddhas that will appear in this eon, none of them will attain enlightenment without relying on a master.*"

This one verse by *Guru Padmasambhava* from the cycle of the "*Tibetan Book of the Dead*" sums up the whole Buddhist attitude toward the moment of death:

Now when the bardo of dying dawns upon me,

I will abandon all grasping, yearning, and attachment,

Enter undistracted into clear awareness of the teaching,

And eject my consciousness into the space of unborn Rigpa;

As I leave this compound body of flesh and blood

I will know it to be a transitory illusion.

May this article enlighten your mind on death and spiritual liberation, from both the Arhatic Yoga and Tibetan Buddhist point of view, that it will initiate your interest in the same or similar spiritual path that Ricardo has taken for three main reasons: (1) the only thing that can help us at the time of death is our mental/spiritual development, (2) physical death can be transformed into spiritual liberation. It is a priceless, spiritual opportunity to achieve illumination and oneness with one's higher soul, and (3) to be a truly effective health care professional, an understanding of the truth about death, and how to care spiritually with loving-kindness and compassion for your dying patient are as inseparable and are as necessary in the practice of holistic healing -- healing the body, mind and spirit.

Lastly, an important Tibetan Bon Buddhist practice called Dream Yoga's lucid dreaming is a vital complementary spiritual teaching of Guru Yoga which prepares one's awareness in the bardo after death.

According to Tenzin Wangyal Rinpoche, "The Mother Tantra says that if one is not aware in vision, it is unlikely that one will be aware in behavior. If one is not aware in behavior, one is unlikely to be aware in dream. And if one is not aware in dream, then one is unlikely to be aware in the bardo after death."

"If we cannot remain present during sleep, if we lose ourselves every night, what chance do we have to be aware when death comes? If we enter our dreams and interact with the mind's images as if they are real, we should not expect to be free in the state after death. Look to your experience in dreams to know how you will fare in death. Look to your experience of sleep to discover whether or not you are truly awake."

Doing regularly the *Invocation to the Unified Chakra* with the *Merkaba Meditation* is also an important *ascension* practice to prepare your *lightbody* to experience liberation before death of the physical body.

Let this article be dedicated to all beings, living, dying or dead especially to Ricardo's late parents, siblings and friends. For all those who are at this moment going through the process of dying, may their deaths be peaceful and free of pain or fear. This is Ricardo's prayer.

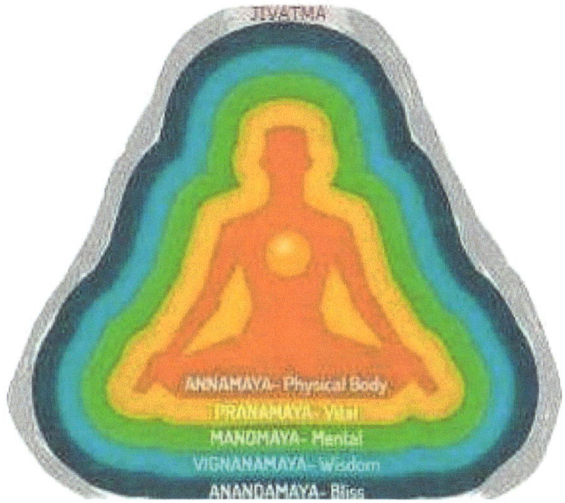

Pancha Kosha (Five Sheaths that wrap your Soul)

Read Pancha Kosha, p. 43; Raja Yoga, p. 47; 8 Limbs of Ashtanga Yoga, p. 104 - 105; Incarnated Soul, p. 152; Techniques of a Master, p. 159

What is Pranic Healing?

"Since the students of Grandmaster Choa Kok Sui's version of external medical chi kung do not have to learn thousands of acupuncture points but, rather, only a few major and semi-major acupuncture points, they can learn and apply his system faster and easier."

In ancient Chinese Medical Science, there are five levels of healing skills. The first and simplest of these healing levels is "*tuina*," or acupressure, in which the healer uses his hands to massage the body. At the second level, the healer uses *herbs*, minerals and sometimes animal products to heal. At the third level, which is more sophisticated and complex than the previous two levels, the healer employs *acupuncture* and *moxibustion*, which is placing a burning stick of moxa herbs in close proximity to the body. At the fourth level, the healer begins to actively manipulate the healing energy or "*chi*," of the patient by using acupuncture with the projection of chi through the needles into the meridians and internal organs. The fifth level, which requires the highest healing skill and the most extensive training, is the projection of chi energy without the use of needles or physical contact. The chi energy can be projected from close range or at a great distance -- even from one continent to another. In ancient China and India, the technique of projecting chi in the manner of a fifth level healer has been a closely guarded secret down through the ages, with the most hidden aspect being the ability to project chi without the healer getting drained of his own energy.

This projection of chi energy without physical contact is called "*medical chi kung*," and it is divided into two schools, the "*internal school*" and the "*external school*." The internal medical chi kung school is by far the more well-known and more popular school. However, internal medical chi kung is also quite difficult to master, for it requires that the healer practice for many years in order to develop sufficient internal chi so that the healer can project his surplus into another person for healing. The use of one's own chi energy for healing also has another drawback: It is quite exhausting, which is why Chinese medical doctors who use this technique typically heal only two to three patients per day.

The external medical chi kung school is less popular and much less known to the public. Practitioners of this school learn to draw in chi energy from the air and the earth, and then direct it to the patient for healing. The external medical chi kung school is superior to the internal school, primarily because it does not drain the healer. In fact, a good external medical chi kung master can heal as many as 20-30 patients per day. It is also easier to learn and apply.

Developing Strong Internal Chi

The internal medical chi kung school and the external medical chi kung school are actually very much related, for in order to become a good healer using external chi, one must have a certain amount of internal power. The greater one's internal chi power, the greater one's capacity to absorb chi from outside the body and then use it to heal another. There are numerous ways that can be used to increase one's internal chi. Yogic physical exercises and breathing exercises, particularly ARHATIC YOGA physical and breathing exercises, are very helpful in developing internal chi. But internal chi is developed most effectively through meditation, primarily those meditations that open and activate the crown chakra or bai hui. When the crown chakra is open, it permits great quantities of *tian chi*, or *spiritual energy*, to enter the body, which helps develop strong internal chi. The quickest and safest way to open the crown chakra is through regular practice of **Meditation on Twin Hearts**.

The external medical chi kung as taught by *Grandmaster Choa Kok Sui* is revolutionary in its simplicity and effectiveness. It uses acupuncture points, but not those from customarily known acupuncture. Rather, it uses 11 major acupuncture points called "*zhu xue lun*," as well as semi-major acupuncture points called "*xiao xue lun*." Since the students of *Grandmaster Choa Kok Sui*'s version of external medical chi kung do not have to learn thousands of acupuncture points but, rather, only a few major and semi-major acupuncture points, they can learn and apply his system faster and easier. See *Major Chakras of the Human Body* on page150

Four Levels of PRANIC HEALING

PRANIC HEALING is divided into different levels. In Level 1, the students learn the basics of the PRANIC HEALING system:

1. how to absorb air prana or chi energy, and how to project it into their patients;
2. how to sensitize their hands and how to "*scan*," or feel the energy body of the patient;
3. how to clean, energize and stabilize the projected chi energy;

4. how to release the projected energy, and how to cut the energy cord between themselves and the patient to prevent contamination; and
5. how to make the patient more receptive in order to accelerate the healing process.

Other lessons include self-healing, divine healing, and distant healing, especially how to project prana or chi at a great distance. Read *What is Distance healing and Its Healing Benefits?*

The next three levels of PRANIC HEALING build on this base students learn in Level 1.

In Level 2, *Advanced Pranic Healing*, students are taught how to use more powerful color pranas to cleanse and energize the patient.

In Level 3, *Pranic Psychotherapy*, students are taught how to use color pranas on psychological ailments. Treating psychological ailments require more time and effort, and greater skill.

In Level 4, *Pranic Crystal Healing*, students are taught how to use crystals to more powerfully focus prana to the patient.

Master Choa Kok Sui's books: The Ancient Science and Art of Pranic Healing (1987), The Ancient Science and Art of Pranic Psychotherapy (1989), Advanced Pranic Healing (1992) and The Ancient Science and Art of Pranic Crystal Healing (1996)

EDITOR's NOTE: Ricardo B. Serrano's *Integral Studies of Inner Studies* includes all the 4 levels of Pranic healing as taught by his late great Filipino Chinese teacher Master Choa Kok Sui since 1994. As a pranic crystal healer, he also practices and teaches regularly all the Meditation Techniques that are invaluable for safe and rapid spiritual development as a Qigong master healer.

Shri Yantra Mantras

AEEM HREEM SHREEM AEEM KLEEM SAUH

Om Shreem Hreem Shreem Kamle Kamlalaye Praseeda Praseeda Shreem Hreem Shreem Om Maha Lakshmiye Namah

See Awakening Kundalini, p. 31; Shiva & Shakti Meditation, p. 106; Excerpts on Kundalini, p. 121; 3 Dantiens, p. 133; Bija Mantras, p. 154

What is Distance Healing and Its Healing Benefits?

Distance healing is basically healing spiritually someone at a distance or remotely in another location (city, country) by a spiritually developed healer. The date and time for distance healing is synchronized between a client and a healer, so that a client or patient is receptive to a distance healer's Qi-healing. Picture of a patient is helpful to establish a stronger etheric link with a patient.

Why does it work?

The following principles are based on the principles of pranic healing:

Principle of Transmittability. Life force or vital energy can be transmitted from one person to another person.

Principle of Receptivity. A patient has to be receptive or at least neutral to receive the projected pranic energy. Being relaxed also helps increase the degree of receptivity. Without receptivity, the projected pranic energy will not be absorbed, or only a minimal amount of it will be absorbed. Patients may not be receptive because: they are biased towards this type of healing, they do not like the healer personally, they do not want to get well, or they are in general not receptive about anything.

Principle of Interconnectedness. The body of the patient and the body of the healer are interconnected with each other since they are part of the earth's energy body. On a more subtle level, it means that we are part of the solar system. We are interconnected with the whole cosmos. The principle of interconnectedness is also called the Principle of Oneness.

Principle of Directability. Life force can be directed. It follows where attention is focused; it follows thought. Distant pranic healing is based on the principle of directability and the principle of interconnectedness.

Healing Benefits of Distance Healing

The same physical, psychological and emotional healing benefits are obtained in distance healing as in a regular one-on-one Qi-healing session. Most clients have noted that their spirits have lifted with an overall experience of tingling all over the body, inner peace, psychological and emotional healing. Some clients have noted that they felt lightness, revitalized, energized and joyful.

Conclusion: Regular one-on-one pranic or Qi-healing session is generally a preferable mode of healing, however, because of distance and time restraints between a healer and a patient, distance healing is another viable option to those who prefer remote distance healing.

Ricardo's principal healing Spiritual guides are *Bodhisattva Padmasambhava* and *Bodhisattva Avalokiteshvara* (*Kuan Yin*) who assist his distance healing work and mission. Other ascended healing masters (*Hathors*) also are at hand assisting during the distance healing session. Divine spiritual (God's) energy or *Tian qi* through the higher soul is directed by a spiritual healer to heal a patient's disease at a distance. Distance healing (holographic sound healing) by Qigong healer Ricardo B Serrano may also assist in the recipient's *Merkaba activation* which initiates the holistic healing and enlightenment process.

Guruji Amritananda Natha Saraswati, Ricardo's Sri Vidya teacher

"The experience of the Shiva linga in yogic meditation is an experience of a pillar of light, energy, peace and eternity." - Guruji Amritananda Natha Saraswati

Chinese Tonic Herbs to Cultivate Jing, Qi and Shen

There needs to be a balance and integration between the heavenly *yang* therapies such as Qi-healing, Qigong and acupuncture with the earthly *yin* aspect such as diet and tonic superior herbs which together create harmony, healing wholeness of yin and yang and spiritual oneness with the universe to truely envision what Taoist master Chuang Tzu said, "*There is nothing which heaven does not cover, yet nothing that earth does not sustain*."

Tonic herbs are herbs which promote a long, healthy, vibrant, happy life without any unwanted side effects even when taken over a long period of time. The tonic or Superior Herbs, essentially, are empowering and healthful "*super-foods*" which benefit our well-being in ways that more common foods cannot. And they have a protective, balancing, vitalizing quality beyond that of any other herbs. They are generally consumed as a herbal supplement to a well-balanced healthy diet for the purpose of optimizing our nutritional needs.

Applying the principle of the *Three Treasures* is the highest form of great herbalism. In the Orient it is called "*the Superior Herbalism*." Six tonic or superior herbs revered by the great sages as the quintessential substances to cultivate the Three Treasures (Qi, Shen, and Jing) are *Reishi* mushrooms, *Ginseng*, *Schizandra fruit* (Wu Wei Zi), *Asparagus Root* (Tian Men Dong), *Gynostemma Pentaphyllum* (Jiao Gu Lan), and *Rhodiola* (Hong Jing Tian). *Shen Nong Ben Cao* (Divine Farmer's Materia Medica) and *Huang Di Neijing* (Yellow Emperor's Classic of Medicine) described them as superior or immortal foods as opposed to the medicinal and radical herbs:

Huang Di asked, "Can you tell me about the three grades of herbs that were recorded in the *Shen Nong Ben Cao* (Shen Nong's Materia Medica)?"

Qi Bo replied, "In ancient times the art of *herbology* was practiced by categorizing all herbs into three classifications. The first category of herbs was called superior, or immortal foods because of their lack of side effects and strengthening qualities. These were often incorporated into one's diet and were used as preventive measures. The second category of herbs was called medium or medicinal and were used to rectifying imbalances in the human body. These were used until the patient recovered from their illness and then withdrawn. The third category of herbs was called inferior or radical herbs, so named because they are strong in action and not without side effects; sometimes they are toxic. Therefore these were used often in small amounts and once the desired action took place they were discontinued immediately.

"The paramount mission in healing is to dispel the pathogen and strengthen the patient."

Quotations on the Three Treasures

The great teacher, Taoist Master Sung Jin Park, used to describe the Three Treasures by comparing them to a burning candle. *Jing* is like the wax and wick, which are the substantial parts of the candle. They are made of material, which is essentially condensed energy. The flame of the lit candle is likened to *Qi*, for this is the energetic activity of the candle, which eventually results in the burning out of the candle. The radiance given off by the flaming candle is *Shen*. The larger the candle and the better the quality of the wax and wick, the steadier will be its flame and the longer the candle will last. The greater and steadier the flame, the steadier the light given off and the greater the light. Master Park described the Three Treasures in some detail:

There are three treasures in the human body. These are known as *Jing, Qi* and *Shen*. Of these three, only Qi has received some recognition in the West so far. Qi is but one of the Three Treasures – the other two are equally wondrous.

Jing has been called the "superior ultimate" treasure, even though even in a healthy, radiant body, the quantity is small. *Jing* existed before the body existed, and this *Jing* enters the body tissues and becomes the root of our body. When we keep *Jing* within our body, our body can be vigorous. If a person cares for the Cavity of *Jing* [a space within the lower abdomen], and does not hurt it recklessly, it is very easy to enjoy a life of great longevity. Without *Jing* energy, we cannot live.

Qi is the invisible life force which enables the body to think and perform voluntary movement. The power of *Qi* can be seen in the power that enables a person to move and live. It can be seen in the movement of energy in the cosmos and in all other movements and changes. Coming from heaven into the body through the nose (Yang Gate), it circulates through the twelve meridians [the energy circuitry of the body] to nourish and preserve the inner organs. **See Sri Vidya Mantras, page 126; Subtle System and Kundalini Path & Chakras, page 133; Bija Mantras, page 154; Techniques of a Master, page 159**

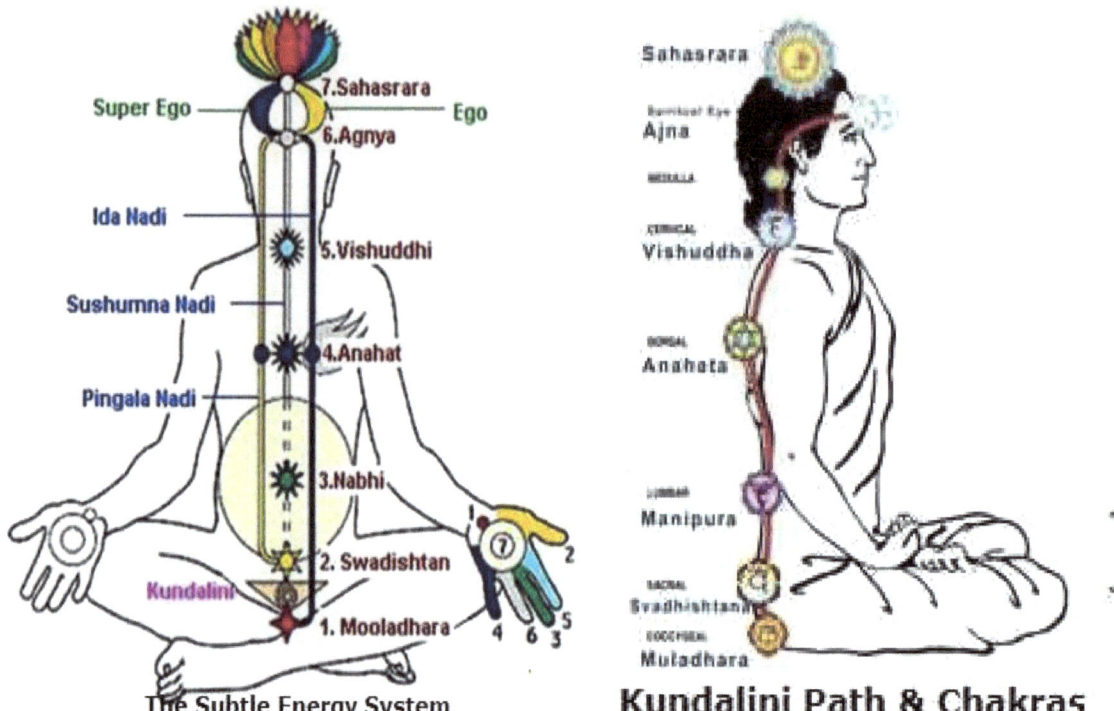

Shen energy is similar to the English meaning of the words "mind" and "spirit." It is developed by the combination of *Jing* and *Qi* energy. When these two treasures are in balance, the mind is strong, the spirit is great, the emotions are under control, and the body is strong and healthy. But it is very difficult to expect a sound mind to be cultivated without sound *Jing* and *Qi*. An old proverb says that a sound mind lives in a sound body. When cultivated, *Shen* will bring peace of mind.

When we develop *Jing*, we get a large amount of *Qi* automatically. When we have a large amount of *Qi*, we will also have strong *Shen*, and we will become bright and glowing as a holy man.

NOTE: The *Three Treasures* are strengthened through the practice of Emotional Freedom Technique (EFT), Qi-healing, Traditional Chinese acupuncture, Chinese Tonic Herbs, Meditation and Qigong (**Three Dantians**). To have and maintain a powerful rooting and grounding like a tree, the *middle* (heart center) and *upper dantians* (ni-wuan) are aligned with the Hara (*lower dantian*). The three dantians are all important because without alignment and activation of the three dantians, the power and stability of the *Tai Ji* pole in the center of the body cannot be manifested and maintained.

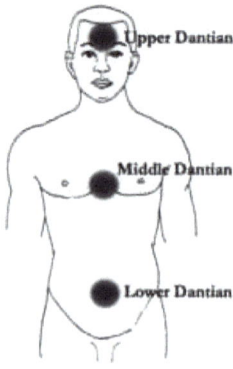

Three Dantians

To energetically align yourself with the universal Qi or become one with universal Qi of heaven and earth – experience Qigong state, *lower dantien* breathing with awareness of the three dantians aligned must be integrated with the postures or movements of Tai Chi, Qigong or eastern martial arts because when our practice harmonizes breath, postures or movements and hara (*lower dantian*) meditation we become Self-realized beings at one with the Dao. Read the *Three Treasures Jing, Qi and Shen*

The Three Dantians:

There are three major energy centers in the human body along the *Taiji Pole* (center channel) that store and emit energy. These Three energy centers in Ancient Daoist Energetic Anatomy and Physiology are called the *three dantians*. Located in the *lower abdomen, chest, and head*, each dantian has its own function and properties.

The Lower Dantian

The *Lower Dantian* is the center of physical strength and stamina and is located in the center of a triangle formed in your pelvic bowel by drawing a line from your perineum, navel, and mingmen (lower back). The lower dantian is also responsible for kinesthetic feeling, awareness, and communication. Expert martial artists learn to become familiar with this important energy center to feel and anticipate an opponent's attack. This energy center houses the mind that gets subconscious feelings or "gut feelings" that the logical mind cannot process.

All Qigong training begins with focusing on the *Lower Dantian* in order to develop familiarity with remaining rooted by gathering the body's Qi and strengthening the foundation of the body's energy.

The *Lower Dantian* is considered the most yin energy center of the three dantians. This Dantian is closest to the Earth (yin) and is associated with the *Jing* (essence) and the physical energy of the body. Because the *lower dantian* is closest to the Earth it naturally gathers and stores the Earth's yin energy which counter balances the great yang energy cultivated during Qigong practice.

The first *Wei Qi field* (energy field) is associated with the *lower dantian* and is the closest to the physical tissue. Because the *Lower Dantian* represents Jing (essence) and matter, it is only natural that the first *Wei Qi* field only extends a few inches past the physical tissue.

The Middle Dantian

The *Middle Dantian* is the center of emotional energies in the human body and is located in the chest area. This Dantian is capable of emotional communication through the empathy of the heart, which means that one can read the emotions of another.

Often times Qigong practitioners will focus on training the *Middle Dantian* to release psycho-emotional patterns. If enough emotions are brought to surface suppressed memories of traumas, which created certain daily behavior and emotional patterns, will manifest. In doing this a Qigong Practitioner will choose to address these issues by intercepting karma, taking responsibility, and projecting no blame. Then the healing occurs in the main organ related to the *Middle Dantian*, the heart. The heart is responsible for forgiveness and is the final stage of healing after addressing all emotions and boundaries created by traumas. This type of practice will often times bring about ego or spiritual deaths where a practitioner will completely change their life, change their energetic resonance and change friends, and increase energetic potential for it takes energy to suppress emotions.

The *Second Wei Qi* field is associated with the *Middle Dantian* and manifests roughly two to three feet distance from the physical tissue. For people who see Auras, this is the Wei Qi field in which the colors of emotions are seen within.

The Upper Dantian

The *Upper Dantian* is the center for intuitive awareness, psychic abilities, and spiritual Communications. Daoist Mystics and Alchemists have interest in the *Upper Dantian* for the Crystal Chamber in which is where psychic perceptions take place. Even though psychic abilities take place here, it is necessary to have all *Three Dantians* balanced for a more proper and effective perceptions.

When peaceful, tranquil, and not disrupted by emotional troubles of the subconscious mind, a Qigong student can intuitively process information taken in by the universe. This ability is to "know without knowing" and is useful for observing the subconscious patterns of the practitioner and others.

Because the *Upper Dantian* is related to the *Shen* (spirit) as well as the 6th, 7th, and 8th chakras, it is used to spirit travel.

The *Third Wei qi* Field is associated with the *Upper Dantian* and manifests from six feet to infinite space. The Upper Dantian is related to *Shen* (spirit) and thought.

Caution: Do not practice *Shen Gong* exercises to open psychic abilities and intuitive awareness without first training the *Lower Dantian* to root to avoid self- induced energetic psychosis.

Sources: Johnson, Jerry Alan. Chinese Medical Qigong Therapy. vol 1. Pacific Grove: The International Institute of Medical Qigong, 2005. 211-33. Print.

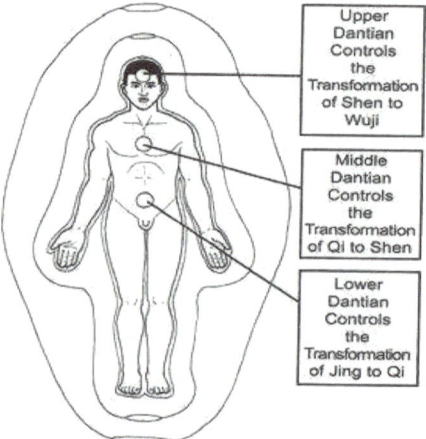

Koshas – The Five Sheaths that Wrap Your Soul

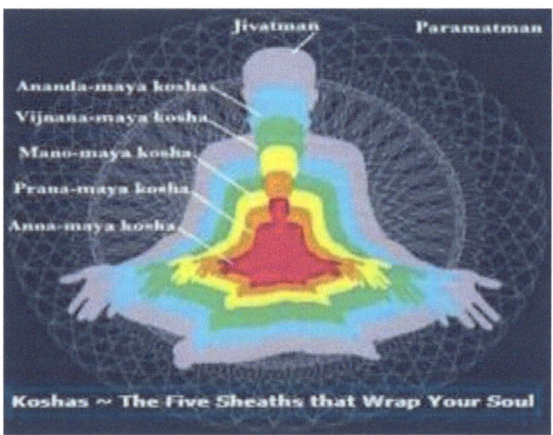

Performing the Mudras such as Hand Mudras and Surya Namaskar cleanse and energise all the five Koshas or layers (sheaths) of Soul consciousness – Annamaya Kosha (body), pranamaya kosha (energy), manomaya kosha (emotion), vijnanamaya kosha (wisdom) and anandamaya kosha (bliss). See **Surya Namaskar, page 16; Surya Namaskar and Solar Plexus, page 111; Gayatri Mantra and Hand Mudras, pages 138-139; Solar Plexus Chakra, page 151; Healing and Returning to Oneness, page 157; Techniques of a Master, page 159**

Qigong is the Pillar of Classical Chinese Medicine

Qi is the basis of Traditional Chinese Medicine (TCM) which includes acupuncture, herbology, massage and Qigong as taught by my classical Chinese medicine teacher Dr. Kok Yuen Leung and practiced clinically at the Hangzhou Hospital of Traditional Chinese Medicine, China where I had my TCM internship in 1993. Historically, Qigong is both the Mother/Father of the later branches of oriental medicine and as a pillar of Classical Chinese Medicine. Drawings depicting Qigong movements have been found in Chinese tombs at least 3500 years old, with other references going back 5000 years or more. This makes it the grandparent of many eastern energy-based healing modalities such as acupuncture and acupressure, tui-na (meridian) massage, chi nei tsang (deep organ massage). It probably guided the development of the internal martial arts such as Tai Chi Chuan and Ba Gua Chuan, and the many derivative Japanese/Korean healing arts such as shiatsu, Do-in, as well as the numerous martial spinoffs of Aikido, Judo, etc. Some historians speculate that Qigong even travelled into India where it became part of the repetoire of yoga and sacred temple dance training. *Thus, Qigong is what Chinese medicine since prehistoric times is based on!*

The Yellow Emperor and the Han Dynasty

The earliest written record of Qigong as a healing technique is found in *The Yellow Emperor's Classic of Medicine*, or Huang Di Neijing Suwen, written during the Han Dynasty (240 B.C.). It shows that classical Chinese medicine is a quasi-religious system relying heavily on ancient Taoist doctrines and a small number of ancient texts that offer a philosophy of balance and harmony between human beings and the environment. It describes the fundamental natural principles that lead to good health, implying that all phenomena of the world stimulate, tonify, subdue, or depress one's natural life force, and that humans are the offspring of the universe and therefore are subject to its laws:

"In the past, people practiced the Tao, the Way of Life. They understood the principle of balance, of yin and yang, as represented by the transformations of the energies of the universe. Thus, they formulated practices such as Dao-in (Qigong), an exercise combining stretching, massaging, and breathing to promote energy flow, and meditation to help maintain and harmonize themselves with the universe.

"They ate a balanced diet at regular times, arose and retired at regular hours, avoided overstressing their bodies and minds, and refrained from overindulgence of all kinds. They maintained well-being of body and mind; thus, it is not surprising that they lived over one hundred years."

"Health and well-being can be achieved only by remaining centered in spirit, guarding against the squandering of energy, promoting the constant flow of qi and blood, maintaining harmonious balance of yin and yang, adapting to the changing seasonal and yearly macrocosmic influences, and nourishing one's self preventively. This is the way to a long and happy life."

Conclusion:

As a seeker of truth, holistic healing and enlightenment (*oneness with Shiva*) since I was in my 20's, I have been fortunate and grateful to have studied under classical Chinese medicine and Qigong teachers and have read the classical references of TCM with Tao Master Lao Tzu's Tao Te Ching, Huang Di Neijing, Shen Nong Ben Cao, and the other classical teachings of my Qigong teachers which assisted me greatly to the eventual realization that with no understanding, application and mastery of Qi through the practice of classical Qigong, and without the wisdom of the fundamental correct doctrines of the classics, deeper and faster healing of clients or the fullfilment of the goal in becoming a self-realized Qi-healer will be just a pipe dream. Read Three Treasures (*Shen, Qi, Jing*) and *Three Dantians*

"The teaching focuses essentially on the purification of Jing-Chi-Shen into its final product: the elixir of pure-person." - Door to All Wonders, *Tao Te Ching*

"For clinicians, it shifts our focus from a battle with disease to a cultivation of health."

"For practitioners of Qigong, it gives us an experiential understanding of greater balance within ourselves and the cultivation of our individual physical, mental and spiritual potential." – Kenneth Sancier, PhD

NOTE by Ricardo B Serrano, R.Ac: I have chosen the following article by Dr Kenneth Sancier as the source of this **Book's Manifesto** because the *Qigong biological benefits* stated below I find are true through the years of my meditation, Qigong and Qi-healing clinical practice. With my thanks and acknowledgement to Dr. Kenneth Sancier for his article.

One of the authors has discussed the *medical benefits of Qigong*. (Sancier KM 1994; Sancier KM 1996a; Sancier KM 1996b; Sancier KM 1999; Sancier KM Weintraub 2000) Wang and Xu, two western-trained doctors in China explored some of the multiple health benefits of self-practice as summarized in the table (Wang CX 1991; Wang CX 1993; Wang CX 1995):

- Activities of two messenger cyclic nucleotides
- Anti-aging
- Antithrombin III
- Asthma
- Blood flow to the brain for subjects with cerebral arteriosclerosis
- Blood pressure
- Blood viscosity
- Bone density
- Cerebral functions impaired by senility
- Endocrine gland functions
- Erythrocyte deformation index
- Factor VIII-related antigen
- Hypertension
- Immune system
- Longevity, 50% greater; after Qigong 30 min/twice daily, 20 years
- Plasminogen activator inhibitor
- Serum estradiol levels in hypertensive men and women
- Serum lipid levels
- Sexual function
- Strokes, 50% fewer after Qigong 30 min/twice daily, 20 years

One of the prime benefits of Qigong is *stress reduction*, and a main ingredient of practice is *intention* (i.e., Yi) that uses the mind to guide the Qi. While Qi itself has not been measured, multiple types of measurements demonstrate the effects of Qi on the body. For example, simultaneous measurements of the interaction between a Qigong master and receiver included respiration, EEG, vibrations, blood pressure, skin conductivity, and heart rate variability. (Yamamoto M 1997)

Different physiological measurements have sought information about the effects of Qigong on the brain and emotions. These include measurements by high-resolution electroencephalography (EEG), functional MRI (fMRI), neurometer measurements, and applied kinesiology. Neuroimaging methods were used to study regional brain functions, emotions and disorders of emotions. Differences were found on the effects on the brain during meditation by Qigong and by Zen meditation.(Kawano K 1996)

The effects of emitted Qi (*waiqi*) has also been extended to cell cultures, growth of plants, seed germination, and reduction of tumor size in animals. (Sancier KM 1991) Spiritual healing, which involves the mind, has been the subject of two volumes by Benor.(Benor DJ 2001; Benor DJ 2002) His discussions also include scientific studies describing the beneficial effects of prayer on subjects' health.

The work of Richard Davidson and Paul Ekman, researchers of the Mind and Life Institute, may go along way to illustrate the role of intention alone on the brain and body.(Davidson JD 1999) In current studies underway at University of California at San Francisco Medical School and University of Wisconsin, they are observing the electrical mechanisms in the brains of highly trained Buddhist lamas during various states of focused intention. Using functional, fMRI, high-resolution EEG and state-of-the-art reflex monitoring, their early results illustrate that electrical activity and blood flow in the brain can be directed by conscious intention.

Through systematic and repeated practice of intention, well-practiced lamas have succeeded in training the brain to direct electrical activity away from areas associated with the biochemistry of stress, tension and disturbing emotional or physical states (i.e., the amygdala and right prefrontal cortex) and increase activity in the area associated with the biochemistry of healthful emotional and physical states (i.e., the left prefrontal cortex).

Moreover, they have observed that the state of conscious intention on compassion engages a state of relaxation and well-being which surpasses even that achieved during a state of rest. The early results of this research suggests that parts of the brain thought previously to be fixed in function, such as the stress reflexes of the reptilian brain, may in fact be plastic in nature, able to be changed, shaped and developed through ongoing practice of conscious intention.(Lama Dalai 2003)

Cost containment of healthcare is a subject of vital contemporary interest. For example, in the treatment of asthma self-applied Qigong led to significant cost decreases, such as reduction in days unfit for work, hospitalization days, emergency consultation, respiratory tract infections, and number of drugs and drug costs. (Reuther I 1998)

Recommendations: The vast research of medical benefits of Qigong offers a rich source of information for benefiting mankind. Medical cost containment is an attractive benefit of Qigong practice and should be further explored to provide healing potential without side effects.

The science and art of Qigong may open a window into new thinking about health, medicine, psychology and spirituality. It is a physical, mental and spiritual practice that continuously supports our natural tendency toward homeostasis.

If that tendency is supported with regularity, allowing one to hover more closely to that point of balance, then the entire being can experience a tremendous evolutionary advantage.

Innate abilities have an opportunity to develop; the senses more keen, organ function more consistent and strong, the sympathetic nervous system relaxed, parasympathetic nervous system efficient, the mind relaxed, alert, clear, freely channeling messages in a multitude of new and diverse directions.

From a scientific point of view, the promise of Qigong practices provides new avenues for understanding some of the subtle aspects of human life and its natural inclination to strive for balance.

For clinicians, it shifts our focus from a battle with disease to a cultivation of health.

For practitioners of Qigong, it gives us an experiential understanding of greater balance within ourselves and the cultivation of our individual physical, mental and spiritual potential. – *Kenneth Sancier, PhD*

Biography: Dr Sancier is the founder and Chairman of the Board of Directors of the Qigong Institute. He is a professor at the American College of Traditional Medicine in San Francisco. He received a Ph.D. from Johns Hopkins University and has carried out basic and applied chemistry research. As a research chemist he published 70 articles in scientific journals and holds 12 patents.

He is an editor of the Journal of the International Society of Life Information Science (JISLIS), Director of the California Information Center of ISLIS, on the Advisory Board of the Journal Of Alternative Therapies, and is on the Council of the World Academic Society Medical Qigong.

Since 1986, he applied his scientific background to study and evaluate reports on Qigong that claimed health and healing benefits. This evaluation depended on a series of activities including participating in international Qigong conferences in China, Japan, Canada and USA and sponsoring the First World Congress of Qigong in San Francisco.

Ashtanga Yoga Hand Mudras (page 139), a Qigong form, preserve and build the primordial Qi for healing and enlightenment.

When ashtanga yoga hand mudras are practiced, the torus also called merkaba, electromagnetic field, aura or energy bubble is activated that facilitates healing and enlightenment. **See What is Raja Yoga?, page 47; 8 Limbs of Ashtanga Yoga, page 104**

The practice of Ashtanga Yoga Hand Mudras is supplemented with the Gayatri Mantra, meditation and Qigong for healing and enlightenment. See **Enlightenment Qigong Forms, page 66**; **Universal Prayer, page 105; Epilogue, page 113**

Gayatri Mantra: OM Bhur Bhuva Svaha Tat Savitur Varenyam, Bhargo Devasya Dhimahi Dhiyo Yonah Prachodayat

O God, The Giver of Life, Remover of pains and sorrows, Bestower of happiness and Creator of the universe; Thou art most luminous, pure and adorable; We meditate on Thee; May Thou inspire and guide our intellect in the right direction.

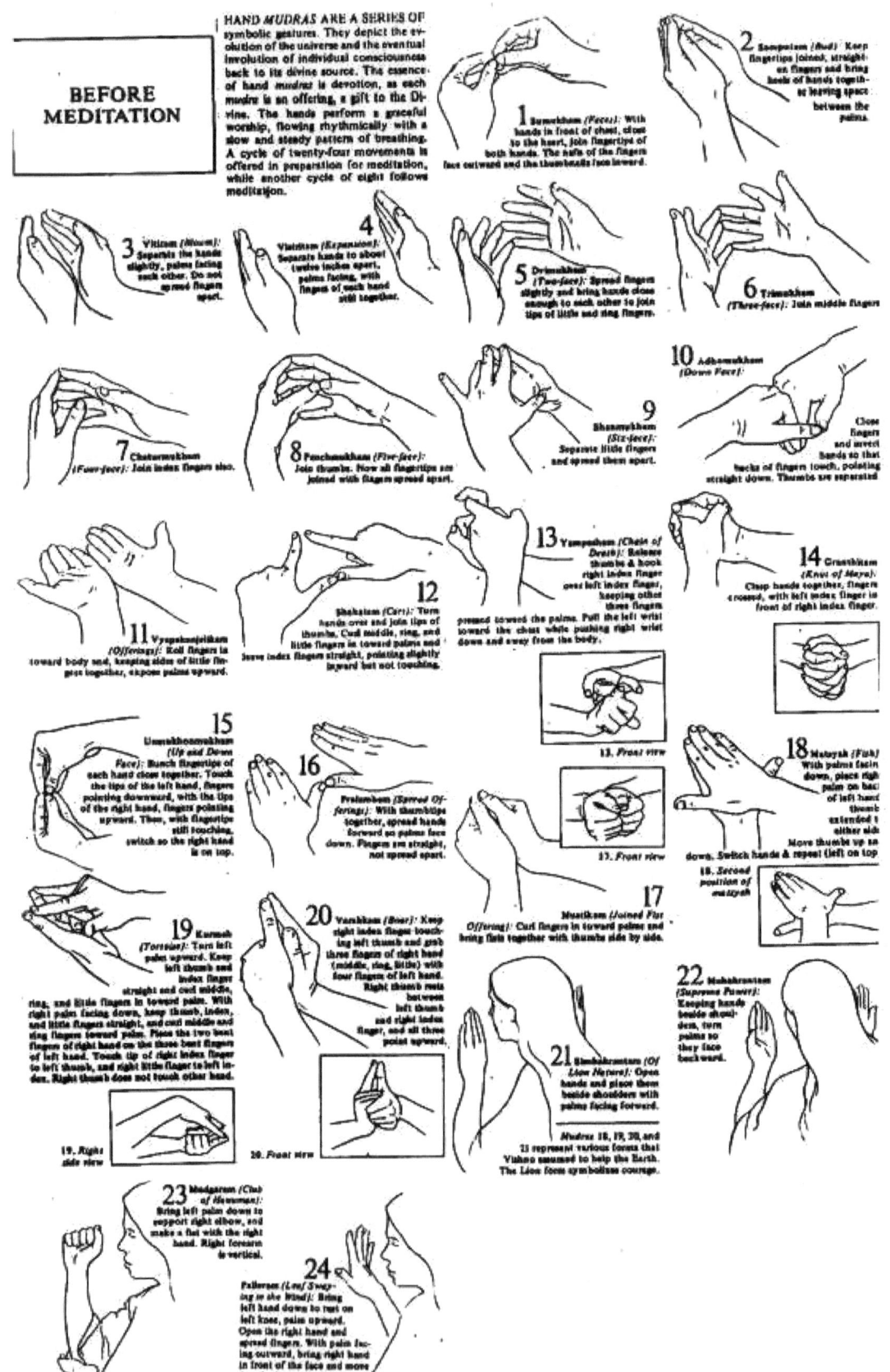

What is Ascension?" you asked.

According to Master Enoch, *"Ascension is basically a change in frequency and a change in focus of consciousness. Because the energy you are has frequency, you can change it. That's all ascension is. As you raise the rate of the lowest frequency energy in your physical body, it becomes less dense and incorporates energy of ever higher frequency. As it does, you will see things and think things that were not possible before. You will literally become a 5th-dimensional being, operating on the 5th dimension, working with other 5th-dimensional beings. The low-frequency stuff of fear and limitation will fall away and you will live in a state of what you would today call ecstasy, at one with your spirit and with the spirit of everyone else. That's ascension."*

The *divine vehicle* for *ascension* is the *Hologram of Love Merkaba*. The higher your vibration of Cosmic Christ Consciousness embraced in Unconditional love, the stronger is your *Merkaba* field. The *Merkaba* is the chosen interdimensional vehicle of the Masters. To truly extend ourselves into their conscious realms we must raise the vibration of Love within our personal *Merkaba*. The Hologram of Love is the ever continuous pattern of God's mind and thought because God only thinks and manifests in unconditional Love. The *Hologram of Love Merkaba meditation* accesses the unified field of consciousness through the galactic timing of the universe (13:20:33).

The following is a condensed record of my spiritual experiences during the October 24-26, 2003 Level 5 *Merkaba Meditation* workshop with Alton Kamadon in Banff, Alberta:

During the Introduction to Zenith Merkabah meditation, Master Enoch stated that I am one of them which I acknowledged by saying Thank you! While I was in my Zenith lightbody I saw the Orion nebulae while I felt at the same time the expansion of my heart chakra to infinity. I had also the sensation of surfing the Zuvuya (intergalactic memory circuit connected to everything and everyone). I continuously saw clairvoyantly the auric field of Master Enoch behind Alton while Alton was speaking and sharing the teachings in front of us.

During the Sun Meditation, I felt bliss and love with the opening of my heart which put lots of tears in my eyes. I also felt a strong connection to Lord Melchizedek with a message that "What you give is what you receive". During the Orionis Galactic Council meditation, I felt a tremendous intense light and love pouring in my heart opening it to a greater degree from the Ascended Masters inside the Orionis Galactic Council. I felt being healed from behind. I received acknowledgement from the Council for a great job I was doing for the Order of Melchizedek and they stated that they will assist with their presence when called for.

I had a Self-realization illumination experience where Light and Love poured down from above which brought unceasing tears to my eyes during the DNA Meditation. Finally, I find the Metatronic Zenith Orionis Healing awesome where I felt clearing, unblocking sensations and shaking around my spine, vibration around my solar plexus and energy flow sensations moving down my arms and legs. I had the overall sensation of inner calm, quiet mind and heat sensation around the lower back of my spine.

Footnotes: Melchizedek Eternal Lord of Light. Sovereign of Light in charge of organizing the levels of the heavenly worlds of YHWH for transit into new creation. Co-equal with Metatron and Michael in the *"rescue, regenesis and reeducation of worlds"* going through the purification of the Living Light. (Gen. 14:18; Heb. 5:7-10)

Spirituality is the personal path of soul consciousness, the "one destination, with many paths," which each of us are free and empowered to consciously choose.

Enoch "One who initiates into Light." **Metatron** "The Garment of Shaddai."

Orionis Code word for Orion in terms of the many thrones and dominions of the spiritual-angelic hierarchies serving the Brotherhoods. **Read the *Invocation to the Unified Chakra,* page 69 and *Merkaba Meditation,* page 92**

Shamballa Temple of Love

The *Shamballa Temple of Love* is not a place but rather a dimensional realm of light that has a high frequency of *Unity Band* or Christ Consciousness with the single intent to serve humanity within its quest for *ascension* expressed by *the Great Invocation*.

> From the point of Light within the mind of God Let Light stream forth into the minds of men. Let Light descend on Earth.
>
> From the point of Love within the heart of God Let Love stream forth into the hearts of men. May Christ return to earth.
>
> From the center where the Will of God is known Let purpose guide the little wills of men – The purpose which the Masters know and serve.
>
> From the center which we call the race of men Let the Plan of Love and Light work out and may it seal the door where evil dwells. Let Light, Love and Power restore the Plan on Earth.

According to Tony Stubbs' *An Ascension Handbook*, *Serapis* states, "Spirit creates the illusion of separation up to the seventh dimension; at higher frequencies, distinctions become completely meaningless and all is Spirit. A definite frequency band exists in all levels which acts as a unifying medium, a common frequency – like the public channel on CB radio, except that you don't just talk on it but you are part of it. If you match your consciousness to the frequency of this *Unity Band*, you experience complete unity with all that is. It is also known as the *Christed Band* and emanates from the Christed level. It throws off subharmonics into all the lower frequency planes. The energy in the Christed level is your energy. It is the level at which you exist as a *Christed Being*, above separateness. For the sake of convenience, we often term this unity function the Office of the Christ, and in Earth's history, this function has manifested directly in human form without intermediate levels of Spirit. You know these beings as *Quetzalcoatl, Hiawatha, Lao Tzu, Krishna, Buddha*, and *Jesus*. They are direct projections of the *Unity Band* and appeared at different points in history to change the course of events by reminding mankind of its unity. We also use the name *Sananda* as the *Christ Collective*.

The *Unity Band* therefore is a frequency and its subharmonics occur in all planes or dimensions. If you attune to that frequency, you know unity – it isn't even an issue. Attuning to the subharmonics is like taking an elevator to the top floor; quick, direct, and effective. The doors open and the wave of love swamps you.

When Spirit enacted the historical *Christ, Buddha*, and *Krishna* functions, for example, it expressed the unity and unconditional love of the Source through these forms – human beings just like you who had cleared the lower fields and unified them sufficiently to handle the high frequency energy of the upper dimensions. This comes automatically when two things happen: first, you love yourself unconditionally, and second, you know that you are in unity with all that is. Then, unconditional love is inevitable. Being one with Spirit, you are made of exactly the same "stuff" as those historical figures, and your spirit-stuff does indeed perform the *Sananda* or *Christ* function."

There are many such multi-dimensional etheric temple structures like *the Shamballa* residing in the higher dimensions of light that one can access which has been designed with the single intent to serve humanity within its quest for *ascension* expressed by the *Great Invocation*. As you raise your frequency it responds, aligning the individual soul with his Higher Self, Christ Consciousness and I AM Presence. The *Shamballa* is the planetary center *where the will of God is known* and relates directly to love, unity and service to restore the Plan of Love and Light that refers to *ascension* with the dissolution of the veil of separation – *sealing the door where evil dwells.* When each one of us has dissolved our veil of separation through *ascension*, the illusion will be banished and the Plan will work out.

The *Shamballa Temple of Love* with its *Ascended Masters* can be experienced through the Merkaba meditation facilitated by Ricardo B Serrano of the *Melchizedek Order of Mastery* (*Shamballa Temple of Love*).

Kodoish, Kodoish, Kodoish Adonai Tsebayoth – Heb. "Holy, Holy, Holy is the Lord God of Hosts / Armies."

Ascended Masters of the Shamballa Temple of Love

Thyroid connection to healing and spiritual ascension

Most people are not aware that their healing and spiritual ascension are essentially associated with the functioning of their thyroid gland or throat chakra.

The two main reasons are:

1. The energy and speed or rate of metabolism of the body depend on the health of the thyroid gland. If there is a physical thyroid problem, either caused by lifestyle (smoking, drugs, overdrinking), nutritional deficiencies or emotional stress, the thyroid gland cannot function optimally to distribute the energy to every organ in the body situated in the triple heater (upper, middle and lower sanjiao). The pituitary, pineal, sex, thymus, pancreas, and adrenal gland functions are also affected when the thyroid gland is not functioning optimally resulting in fatigue, sleep, cognition, immune system and digestion problems.
2. The throat chakra is the intermediary between the heart and head chakras, so if the Qi flow is blocked in the throat chakra because of some physical thyroid disease, the energetic connection between the head and heart chakras is not made possible. Touching the tip of your tongue to your upper palate facilitates the energetic connection between the head chakras, throat, heart and lower chakras during meditation.

How to normalize the physical and etheric function of the thyroid gland:

1. By dealing with the causes of thyroid dysfunction: stopping smoking, drug consumption and alcohol drinking that overtax the adrenal gland and thyroid gland, and supplying the necessary nutrients such as amino acid L-tyrosine, potassium iodide found in supplements and seafoods. I take and recommend *Thyrosmart* to my clients with hypothyroidism. See *Lorna Vanderhaeghe's* www.hormonehelp.com
2. By the practice of lower dantian breathing with Qigong movements and taking Chinese tonic herbs to cultivate the Jing (essence), Qi and Shen. See Enlightenment Qigong forms on page 66
3. By chanting mantras to activate the throat chakra which cleanse and energize it and the other chakras and expand the energy bubble (aura). For balancing chakras and hormones, the regular practice of the *Five Tibetan rites* is necessary accompanied with *pranic healing* by a highly developed *advanced pranic healer*.
4. By practicing the meditation techniques - invocation to unified chakra, merkaba meditation and meditation on twin hearts to cleanse and energize all the chakras and expand the energy bubble.
5. By exercising physically to speed the body's metabolism and cleanse the physical body's impurities.

I have had this low thyroid gland problem (hypothyroidism) since I turned 50 years old and have also observed this thyroid gland problem in my clients with various symptoms such as depression, fatigue, overweight, arthritis, MS, allergies, carpal tunnel syndrome, diabetes, heart and circulatory problems, etc. Most of them have been taking thyroid hormone prescribed by their medical doctors. Because thyroid and endocrine balance is necessary for health maintenance, the above recommendations to normalize the thyroid gland function will assist the client with thyroid gland dysfunction to heal his disease(s) faster and feel better. *It is best to have your TSH, T4 and T3 tested*.

When the thyroid gland (*the body's thermostat*) is functioning normally, spiritual ascension is assured when the meditation and Qigong practitioners practice the meditation and Qigong techniques recommended in this book.

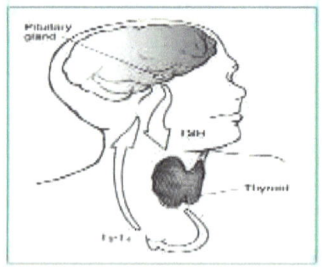

Thyroid Health - It's Not Black and White!

It is estimated that 200 million people in the world have some form of thyroid disease. In Canada there is a staggering number of people affected. Recent studies indicate that 30% - over 10 million people - suffer from a thyroid condition of one type or another! That means one in every three Canadians has a thyroid disorder. Of those, as many as 50% are undiagnosed!

Thyroid health affects all aspects of well-being, both genders, all ages. Until this gland goes awry, very little attention is given to its small, butterfly shaped presence at the base of the neck. The hormones it secretes are essential to all growth and metabolism.

The domino effect. Most people are unaware that cardiac disease, lupus, reproductive difficulties, diabetes, arthritis as well as many other health issues are associated with a poor functioning thyroid gland. Research has shown that early thyroid assessment can, in many cases, reduce the incidence or severity of these high profile diseases.

There are many types of thyroid disease, including:

1. Hypothyroidism (underactive thyroid)
2. Hyperthyroidism (overactive thyroid)
3. Graves' eye disease
4. Thyroiditis (Hashimoto's, Postpartum)
5. Cancer of the thyroid
6. Nodules
   Source: The Thyroid Foundation of Canada http://www.thyroid.ca

Thyroid gland: A gland that makes and stores hormones that help regulate the heart rate, blood pressure, body temperature, and the rate at which food is converted into energy. Thyroid hormones are essential for the function of every cell in the body. They help regulate growth and the rate of chemical reactions (metabolism) in the body. Thyroid hormones also help children grow and develop.

The thyroid gland is located in the lower part of the neck, below the Adam's apple wrapped around the trachea (windpipe). It has the shape of a butterfly: two wings (lobes) attached to one another by a middle part. The thyroid uses iodine, a mineral found in some foods and in iodized salt, to make its hormones. The two most important thyroid hormones are thyroxine (T4) and triiodothyronine (T3). Thyroid stimulating hormone (TSH), which is produced by the pituitary gland, acts to stimulate hormone production by the thyroid gland. The thyroid gland also makes the hormone calcitonin, which is involved in calcium metabolism and stimulating bone cells to add calcium to bone.

Recommended Books on Thyroid Gland to read: *Thyroid Balance* by Dr. Glenn Rothfeld, 2003 and *Solved: The Riddle of Illness* by Dr. Stephen Langer, 2006. These books show how low thyroid function can be the underlying cause of a multitude of ailments and show ways to improve overall health through diet, lifestyle changes, and natural alternatives, as well as a full range of medical options.

Hypothyroid Symptoms

You can gather evidence through the *Barnes Basal Temperature Test*, a careful review of your medical history, and a check of your symptoms against the following telltale physical and emotional signs: (1) weakness; (2) dry, coarse skin; (3) lethargy; (4) slow speech; (5) swelling of face and eyelids; (6) coldness and cold skin; (7) diminished sweating; (8) thick tongue; (9) coarse hair; (10) pale skin; (11) constipation; (12) gain in weight; (13) loss of hair; (14) labored, difficult breathing; (15) swollen feet;

(16) hoarseness; (17) loss of appetite; (18) excessive and/or painful menstruation; (19) nervousness; (20) heart palpitation; (21) brittle nails; (22) slow movement; (23) poor memory; (24) emotional instability; (25) depression; and (26) headaches.

If your temperature, medical history, and symptoms indicate that you are hypothyroid, report to your doctor or health care practitioner with the facts and request treatment. Dr. Gerald S. Levey, MD, states that these conditions can be improved or reversed with natural thyroid hormone replacement.

Natural Desiccated Thyroid Supplement

- **Why natural Armour desiccated thyroid?** This contains physiological amounts of T4/T3, as well as T1 and T2. The latter two play an important role in overall thyroid functioning. *Mad cow disease* known officially as bovine spongiform encephalopathy (BSE), is a brain-wasting infection that affects only cows. But the infection can cause a related disease in humans, called variant Creutzfeldt-Jakob disease (vCJD). Although vCJD is very rare, it is always fatal. People get vCJD by consuming products from cows infected with BSE. There is no way to test for the presence of BSE in bovine products. *Armour*, *Westhroid*, and *Nature-Throid* brands of natural desiccated thyroid are porcine, or from pig sources. This eliminates any risk associated with BSE. All USP thyroid products should be of porcine origin, and sticking to brand-name products is one way of assuring this. If you have any doubts, ask the pharmacist to confirm the products origin.

    Products sold as nutritional supplements could contain bovine thyroid extract. Read labels carefully. If the label says the source is bovine or if the label doesn't list the source, don't buy the product.

- **What are the other brands of desiccated natural thyroid?** A new generic by *Acella* hit the picture by late 2010. Additionally, some patients are using a natural desiccated thyroid called *Thyroid-S* or "Thiroyd" from Thailand, as well as Erfa's *Thyroid* from Canada.
- **What are the units of measure per tablet/capsule?** With the main brands, such as *Naturethroid*, *Westhroid*, *Armour*, *Erfa*, etc, each tablet/capsule is measured in milligrams (mg.). The typical tablet is 60 mg or 65 mg, which is called *one grain*. So, a 1/2 grain tablet is 30/32.5 mg. A 2 grain tablet is 120 mg/130. A 3 grain tablet is 180/195 mgs. A 4 grain tablet is 240/260 mg. A 5 grain tablet is 300/325 mg.
- **Are there any non-prescription desiccated thyroid products?** One more well-known over-the-counter (OTC) natural thyroid supplement is called *Nutri Meds* which is available in either porcine or bovine desiccated thyroid. You may find other fine OTC products on the shelf of your local health food store. *Thyroid-S* or *Thiroyd* from Thailand are non-prescription.
- **What if I'm on T4 or T3?** T3 is significantly more potent than T4, the ingredient in levothyroxine, and rapid-acting. Because of this, doctors tend to consider T3 supplement a less reliable method for managing hypothyroidism. You need to take T3 twice a day (or even three times a day, depending on the dose). It goes straight to the cell, so it has an effect almost immediately. This causes doctors to worry about overdosing.

    T3 supplementation isn't for everyone. If you are stable and feel fine on T4 (natural desiccated or levothyroxine), there's no reason to add T3 (sold as the brand-name product *Cytomel* in the United States) to your treatment regimen. T3 supplementation is most effective for people who have trouble finding balance with T4 supplementation, and also who are willing to take T3 on a fairly rigid schedule. But for the majority of people who use T3, overdosing is a very slight risk. Symptoms of a dose that's too high include jitters, heart palpitations, sweating, and sometimes nausea. They generally pass within six to eight hours. If you experience such symptoms, call your doctor before your next T3 dose.

- **How do patients dose with natural desiccated thyroid?** The strength of natural desiccated thyroid products is measured in milligrams and generally starts at 15 mg. Sometimes you'll see the old fashioned "grain" measurement; 15 mg is roughly equivalent to ¼ grain, and a full 1 grain strength is equivalent to 60 mg. There really isn't a standard starting point for dosing; doctors typically start with a fairly low dose and build up to the dose that relieves your symptoms without causing other problems. Expect regular blood tests until your thyroid levels stabilize, and then blood tests annually.

If your thyroid produces, and your body uses T3, doesn't it make sense to supplement or replace it as well when thyroid function is low? This practical question has a convoluted, and in the end inconclusive, answer. T3 is many times more potent than T4, and affects cells almost immediately. This makes the potential for overdose quite high. Your body accommodates this sensitivity by having just a limited amount of T3 in circulation, even though it's T3 that your cells must have. Your body makes T3 by converting it from T4, a time-consuming process. If the demand for T3 exceeds the rate of conversion, your endocrine matrix can then boost T3 producton in your thyroid gland to get the T3 out there right away. As further proof of the marvelous interconnectedness of body processes, varied factors affect the conversion to T3 including stress; amount of saturated fat in the diet; various nutrients, herbs and medications; and even exercise. In any case, the process is complex enough that when your thyroid is in balance, it's very unlikely that you'll have too much T3 circulating in your system.

How do I take it? One factor that contributes significantly to variations in the effectiveness of thyroid hormone supplements, whether in natural or synthetic forms, is inconsistency in the way they're taken. Variations in timing by as little as an hour, and in the kinds of foods you eat and how much time passes between eating them and taking your thyroid supplement, add up to make big differences in how rapidly the hormone is absorbed into your blood stream and how much of it actually makes it into your body. Be sure to follow these guidelines: (1) Take your thyroid supplement at the same time each day, and take it everyday. (2) Take your thyroid supplement one hour before or two hours after eating, so you take it on an empty stomach. Food can affect how much thyroid hormone gets absorbed in your system. (3) If you are taking thyroid supplement, do not take other medications, prescriptions or over-the-counter, without talking to your doctor or pharmacist. (4) Check refilled prescriptions to make sure you receive the same brand of thyroid hormone that you've been taking. (5) Do not take your thyroid supplement at the same time you take vitamins, iron, calcium, or other dietary supplements. These products interfere with how thyroid hormone gets into your system.

> Consistency is key. Get settled into a routine for taking your thyroid medication, and then stick with it. This makes it easier to evaluate your situation if the hormone supplement doesn't relieve your symptoms, and makes it easier for you to identify any changes or problems as they might arise.

- **How do I know when I'm on enough?** Before labs were developed, doctors treated hypothyroid patients by symptoms successfully. Patients and many wise doctors have found this an ideal way to treat—by symptoms. One important symptom is your temperature. Temperature reflect metabolism, and metabolism is controlled by your thyroid. Find a mercury or liquid oral thermometer, which is more accurate than most digitals. Generally, you want your morning temp (before rising) to be 97.8 to 98.2, and your afternoon temp to be around 98.6. You may find your temperatures correcting before you find your optimal dose. Unfortunately, doctors are trained to put a HUGE reliance on labs over symptoms. But labs only tell PART of the story. Patients have discovered that the free T3 can be the most informative. But you have to figure out where it is great for you, based on symptoms. When patients get their free T3 at the top, (or when all symptoms are eliminated), they will often have a TSH far BELOW range, i.e. below one, and that does NOT necessarily mean you are hyper. Patients have found the TSH is less important once treatment is started, and just because one's TSH can get lower than 1 while getting the free T3 up there, does NOT mean hyper has set in. Many doctors are uninformed about this, so be prepared, and pass along to your doctor what we have learned.

- **Why is desiccated thyroid a better treatment?** People who continue to have symptoms of underactive thyroid after trying levothyroxine for a period of time (six months is a good minimum) sometimes find that switching to a natural desiccated thyroid supplement relieves their symptoms. This is probably because of the trace amounts of T3 and other hormonal substances that natural desiccated products contain, although there is little scientific evidence to support this perception. If natural desiccated thyroid relieves your symptoms when levothyroxine has not, however, scientific evidence means very little! Doctors with a holistic or integrative approach to health and health care often choose a natural desiccated thyroid product when starting new treatment for underactive thyroid.

- **Why is the T3 and T4 in desiccated thyroid so important?** The best way to lose weight is to first restore your thyroid balance. Both underactive and overactive thyroid can leave you feeling lethargic and disinterested – you have little interest in anything except resting or sleeping. This is because thyroid imbalance throws your metabolism out of kilter. Not only do you feel that you have no energy; you actually don't. Your cells are not able to make ATP, your body's long-term energy supply, without adequate thyroid hormone. And even if you have too much thyroid hormone, as with hyperthyroidism, the increased metabolic rate that results burns the ATP in an effort to keep up with your body's intensified demands for energy. The only way to interrupt this cycle is to restore balance to your thyroid.

T3 and T4 play essential roles in cell metabolism. Your cells require two kinds of fuel, glucose (sugar) and oxygen. Insulin regulates how cells use glucose, and thyroid hormones regulate how cells use oxygen. When a T3 or T4 molecule enters a cell, it must "plug in" or bind to a thyroid receptor in the cell. This "opens" the cell to receive oxygen molecules. The cell "burns" the oxygen, which creates chemical interactions that release energy and heat to fuel your body's function.

- **How do I find a doctor who understands desiccated thyroid?** It might seem obvious, but you must be your own advocate when it comes to matters of your thyroid and your health. Practically speaking, it's just not possible for your doctor to keep up with every development in medicine. So doctors choose to keep up with the developments that affect the greatest percentages of their patients. If your doctor treats a lot of people with thyroid imbalance then he or she probably keeps up with research results, gene therapy concepts, and other new treatment approaches. If not …

  Keep a record of how you feel – write notes or write in a journal. This gives you a perspective over time of how well your treatment regimen is working for you. Perhaps you schedule your annual doctor's appointment during vacation time, so you don't have to take off from work or school. But you're also likely to be better rested and more relaxed because you're away from daily details of your life.

  Keeping a record also helps you monitor circumstances and situations that make your thyroid balance better or worse, giving you insights into the kinds of lifestyle changes you might make to better support your thyroid and you endocrine matrix. The more we learn about thyroid function and balance, the more we recognize how integrated and interrelated everything is. Therapeutic balance is really life balance.

- **How high do I raise desiccated thyroid?** As your doctor helps you raise your desiccated thyroid, a certain amount may give you better energy, but may not be quite enough to stop chronic low grade depression, for example. So another raise may be warranted. By observation, it appears that many hypothyroid patients end up in the 3-5 grains, with some lower, and some higher when they find their optimal dose. It's individual.
- **Are there other issues I need to correct?** Often, there are other areas that need assistance when you are being treated with desiccated thyroid products. For one, many patients need to optimize their Ferritin/iron levels, which are low in many thyroid patients. Low Ferritin can cause very similar symptoms as being hypothyroid, or can cause you to have hyper-like symptoms when you try to raise desiccated thyroid. If upon starting desiccated thyroid, you have very strange symptoms, including anxiety, insomnia, shakiness, it's a strong sign that you may need adrenal support. Cortisol is needed to distribute thyroid hormones to your cells, and if you are not making enough cortisol from sluggish adrenals, your blood will be high in thyroid hormones, producing the above symptoms. Adrenal support is used to give back to your body what your adrenals are not, which in turn allows the thyroid hormones to get to your cells. Unless you have *hypopituitary*, adrenal support is not meant to be for life for most, but to allow your adrenals to rest and recover. It is strongly recommended that you do a 24 hour adrenal saliva test – there are labs you can do them. 24 hour saliva tests give you far better information than the one time blood test that doctors will tend to recommend. You don't need a STIM test, by the way, unless there is strong suspicion of *Addisons* or a *pituitary* problem. Work with your doctor on all this.
- **Are there any beneficial supplements that I can take with desiccated thyroid?** Other vitamins, minerals and essential fatty acids (EFA) aid thyroid function. Beta carotene helps your thyroid gland produce thyroid hormone. In return, T3 is necessary for your body to produce vitamin A from beta carotene. Some people develop a yellowish coloration on their palms and the soles of their feet if they are unable to convert the carotenes in their diet to active forms. This can be a subtle sign of thyroid deficiency. Selenium is necessary for the de-iodinase enzyme that produces T3 and T4. Vitamin E protects thyroid hormone from being broken down. Zinc plays a key role in immune function and also cell health. And calcium, even though you need to take it separately from thyroid hormone supplement, is particularly important when thyroid balance is a factor, because thyroid function affects how your body uses and stores calcium. If taken in high doses, L-carnitine, an amino acid used for energy, can suppress thyroid function by blocking T3 production. Alpha lipoic acid, a potent antioxidant, has a similar effect.
- **Any other diet tips to help your thyroid balance?** *For underactive thyroid*: Limit the amount of goitrogenic foods (such as cruciferous vegetables such as cauliflower, broccoli, kale, brussel sprouts) rutabagas, turnips, radishes, carrots, peaches, strawberries, peanuts, spinach, watercress, soybeans and food products high in soy isoflavones; Eat moderate amounts of foods that are high in iodine, such as fish; Eat enough protein to supply your body's tyrosine

needs; Eat foods that supply B vitamins, vitamin C, vitamin E, and beta carotene (a form of vitamin A) and the minerals calcium, selenium and zinc. *For overactive thyroid*: Eat moderate amounts of raw cruciferous vegetables and other goitrogenic foods to help limit your thyroid hormone production. Eat plenty of colorful and flavorful fruits and vegetables; Eat foods that are high in vitamin C; Eat adequate, but not excessive, amounts of foods that supply protein.

- **What is the Traditional Chinese Medicine (TCM) perspective?** Common remedies for underactive thyroid are kidney yang tonic (jin gui hen qi wan) and right restoration formula (tou gui wan). Thyroid problems are also treated with acupuncture in the Triple Warmer and Pericardium meridians. Common remedies for overactive thyroid are kidney yin tonic (liu wei di huang wan), liver cleansing (zhi zi qing gan tang) and heart yin tonic (tian wang bu xin dan), depending on the TCM diagnosis. Acupuncture can be useful in controlling symptoms of hyperthyroidism, particularly the racing heart, anxiety, and heat intolerance. Needles are placed with a "dispersion" technique, meaning that the needles are retained and the patient lies still, allowing energy to disperse or calm down. Treatment of the heart and triple warmer channels. Called "Fire" energy for their heat and activity-stimulating effects, disharmony in these channels can lead to many of the symptoms associated with hyperthyroidism. Also common is strengthening of the Kidney or Water channel, because water will help to cool down fire. Ear acupuncture can assist in symptom control. Qigong and yoga (shoulder stand) are also powerful adjuncts for stress reduction, adrenal energy strengthening and endocrine glands balancing.

Sources: Excerpts from *Thyroid Balance* by Dr. Glenn Rothfeld and *Solved: The Riddle of Illness* by Dr. Stephen Langer.

As a licensed health care practitioner, I sometimes recommend to my clients who are not taking prescription thyroid hormone or thyroid supplement a well-known over-the-counter (OTC) non-drug natural thyroid glandular supplement called *Nutri Meds* (nutri-meds.com) which is available in either porcine (preferable to avoid BSE or mad cows disease) or bovine desiccated thyroid.

Cooking with coconut oil and taking 1 tbsp. of virgin coconut oil with meals 3x a day will boost thyroid health.

Virgin Coconut Oil (VCO) is an oil obtained from the fresh mature kernel of coconut by mechanical or natural means without the use of heat or undergoing chemical refining, bleaching or deodorizing and which does not lead to the alteration of the nature of the oil. It is suitable for consumption without further processing.

The active component of Virgin Coconut Oil is Lauric Acid, a medium chain fatty acid (MCFA) which is converted to monolaurin in the body that helps boost the immune system and fights microorganisms.

Virgin Coconut Oil is called a "functional food" because of the following health benefits:

1. Provides an immediate source of energy.
2. Strengthens and supports immune system function.
3. It is good for thyroid problems, hypertension, diabetes, allergies.
4. Helps prevent bacterial, viral and fungal infections.
5. Reduce risk of cancer.
6. Aids in promoting weight loss.
7. Reduces risk of atherosclerosis and heart disease.
8. Improves digestion and nutrient absorption.
9. Supplies important nutrients necessary for good health.
10. Boosts physical, mental, and emotional wellness.
11. Helps prevent or fade stretch marks, scar tissue, & age spots.
12. Helps moisturize your skin, thus prevent premature aging and wrinkling of the skin.
13. Protects scalp and produce strong silky hair.

Medical Cannabis

Cannabis hemp oil is believed to treat various disorders by acting on the endocannabinoid system. The endocannabinoid system is a system of the body that controls many basic functions. It is made up of natural molecules known as cannabinoids and the pathways that they interact with. Together, these parts work to regulate a number of activities including metabolic disorders, inflammation, mood, memory, sleep and appetite.

For more info on medical cannabis, herbs, ketogenic diet, and Guo Lin Qigong, read "The Cure & Cause of Cancer" by Ricardo B Serrano, R.Ac.

For more info on the Eight Extraordinary Meridians Qigong, Atma (Soul) Yoga of Immortality and medical cannabis, read the supplementary book "Oneness with Shiva" by Ricardo B Serrano, R.Ac.

DISCLAIMER: Consult with your physician or licensed health care practitioner regarding the treatment of any medical condition. The author is not held responsible for any negative effects of the THYROID hormone medications or supplements. This book is for educational purposes only.

Another technique to assist the normalization of thyroid function is by stimulating the Vagus Nerve.

Three Ways to Stimulate the Vagus Nerve

Inflammation is the root cause of most chronic diseases and vagus nerve stimulation can effectively reduce inflammation.

Three clinically proven ways to naturally stimulate the vagus nerve are: intracranial intranasal light therapy, auricular therapy and Qi-healing (prana mudra) with Sri Vidya chanting. **See page 120, Oneness with Shiva and pages 44, 135, The Cure & Cause of Cancer**

Besides high blood pressure, depression, dementia, migraines, fatigue and anxiety, some people with tinnitus, sleep apnea and epilepsy, and much more have been helped with these techniques. Try it! These are life-saving techniques!

The balancing yin yang effect in the body by vagus nerve stimulation activates the Yuan Qi in the central channel not only for healing but also results in samadhi (oneness with Higher Self). See Sri Vidya mantras, page 76 and forms, page 66

Qi is the commander of Blood. Blood is the mother of Qi.Yi (intention) guides Qi. Qi and love are never separate. Hreem Shreem Sauh Hasakaphrem

When Shiva and Shakti are reunited, samadhi is the outcome

"*Nothing has the greatest power to heal, but Self*". The body has the innate power to heal itself, we just need to allow and open up.

To be grounded in the Self, to be at home with the Self, to be established in the Self, then the wisdom of the body awakens and guides you. That is the yogic concept of healing.

When the ida and pingala pathways are rebalanced and reunited, and the kundalini shakti in the sushumna (middle channel) is awakened via the vagus nerve Qi-healing with Sri Vidya chanting, samadhi and healing are the outcome. Thus, it is said in kundalini yoga that when Shiva and Shakti are reunited, samadhi is the resultant outcome. See Subtle Energy System, page 133

The ida and pingala pathways correspond to the vagus nerve that runs in the left and right side of the neck that connect to the points in the organs down to the abdomen. The vagus nerve also corresponds to the thrusting channels of the eight extraordinary meridians which can be stimulated by the eight extraordinary meridians Qigong. See 8 extraordinary meridians Qigong, Oneness with Shiva, page 65 – Ricardo B Serrano, R.Ac., Originator of Vagus Nerve Qi-healing

IMPORTANT NOTATIONS on the MAJOR CHAKRAS OF THE HUMAN BODY

According to Dr. Richard Gerber's book Vibrational Medicine on Chakras, "In reality, the first three centers (root, sacral, and solar plexus chakras) form a lower triad of physiologic and grounding functions. The uppermost three centers (throat, brow, and crown chakras) form the higher spiritual triad. The heart chakra is the bridge between the lower and the higher triads. It is only through the manifesting of one's higher love nature that one can unite the higher and lower energies. The ultimate expression and the unfoldment of the heart chakra is unconditional love and the active demonstration of the Christ consciousness. When one learns to develop and manifest the higher spiritual aspects of the heart chakra, one comes closer to eliminating physical disease not only from heart and associated organs but also from the entire physical body."

Through the *Omkabah Hologram of Love Merkaba* and the other *Soul Realization* meditation techniques and practices in this book *Return to Oneness with Shiva*, the unity of the higher and lower energies of the chakras makes possible the manifesting of one's higher love nature and the demonstration of Christ consciousness.

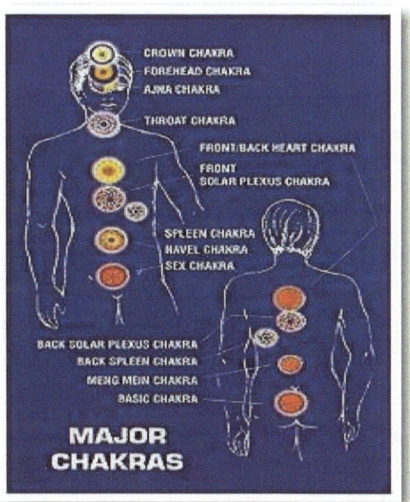

Major chakras are actually major acupuncture points. Energy centers are very important parts of the energy body or light body. Just as the visible physical body has vital and minor organs, the energy body (*light body*) has major, minor and mini energy centers. These chakras control and energize the major and vital organs of the visible physical body. Major energy centers are just like power stations that supply life energy or prana to major and vital organs of the visible physical body. When the power stations (*chakras*) malfunction, the vital organs become sick or diseased because they do not have enough life energy to operate thoroughly. There are **11 major chakras**. See *Pranic Healing* on page 110 and *What is Pranic Healing?* on page 129

Chakra is a Sanskrit word for "wheel". Just like our physical body has organs, our energetic anatomy has energy "organs" that clairvoyantly look like spinning wheels. According to highly-trained clairvoyants, there are **11 Major Chakras** and hundreds of minor ones. The popular **7 chakra model** is good for beginners on the spiritual and healing path. However, to be able to properly access specific organs and heal severe ailments, an accomplished healer works through **11 Major chakras**. Those chakras also directly correspond with the *11 Sepiroth* on the *Kabbalistic Tree of Life*. In addition, each verse of the "Lord's Prayer" directly activates each of the **11 Major chakras**. (**Source**: *Your Hands can Heal You* by Master Stephen Co and Dr. Eric B. Robins, MD, 2003)

1. The **Crown chakra** (Keter) is located at the top of the skull, energizing and controlling the brain and the pineal gland. It is also the major entryway for Divine or Soul Energy.
2. The **Forehead chakra** (Chokmah) is located in the center of the forehead, close to the hairline. It energizes and controls the nervous system and memory. This one is often affected on Alz-heimer patients and Autistic children.
3. The **Ajna chakra** (Binah) is located between the eyebrows and controls the pituitary gland and endocrine system. The ajna is also often mistakenly called the "third eye", the forehead is actually the real third eye, but since many insist on the existence of just seven chakras, the ajna is usually pinned as the "spiritual eye" or "third eye." Cancer and AIDS patients usually have very weak ajna chakras.
4. The **Throat chakra** (Daath) is located at the Adam's apple and controls the throat, trachea, larynx, esophagus, thyroid/ parathyroid glands and lymphatic system. The throat chakra is also connected to the sex chakra, as it is the upper center of creativity, while the sex chakra is the lower center of creativity.
5. The **Heart chakra** (Chesed) is in the center of the chest and has two aspects: a *front* and a *back* heart chakra. The front heart chakra is located directly on the sternum or breastbone. The heart chakra controls the heart, lungs and thymus gland. The heart chakra is also the gateway to our Higher Astral Body. It is the center of love and compassion.
6. The **Spleen chakra** (Netzach) also has both a front and back aspect. The front spleen chakra is located near the left lowermost rib, or what is called the floating rib. This chakra is important because it draws in prana, assimilates it, and distributes it to the other chakras. Healers/health professionals usually get drained by their patients through the spleen chakra. This chakra is often blocked in depressed patients.
7. The **Meng Mein chakra** (Hod), or "gate of life", is located on the back between the kidneys directly opposite the navel chakra. This acts as a pumping station for energy from the basic/root chakra. It affects the kidneys, adrenal glands and upper urinary tract, and directly controls the blood pressure.
8. The **Solar Plexus chakra** (Gevurah), like the heart and spleen chakras, has a front and back aspect. The front solar plexus chakra is located in the soft area just below the sternum or breastbone and controls the stomach, pancreas, intestines and diaphragm. The solar plexus chakra is the seat of lower emotions. This chakra is easily agitated by negative emotions so it constantly has to be cleansed and normalized to prevent a person from having a chaotic life. **See Surya Namaskar (Sun Salutation) and Solar Plexus, page 111**
9. The **Navel chakra** (Tipareth) is located at the belly button area. It controls the large and small intestines and affects the birth process. Below it is our energy reservoir called the "dantien".
10. The **Sex chakra** (Yesod) is located on the pubic bone. The sex chakra energizes the legs, sex organs and also the brain. Working on the sex chakra is critical in healing autistic children, Alzheimer patients and other brain and nervous system-related problems.
11. The **Basic chakra** (Malkuth) is located at the base of the spine, at the tailbone or coccyx. The basic chakra controls the bones, the muscles, the soft tissue and blood production, as well as the adrenal glands. This critical chakra is also directly related to one's ability to make money and be successful. Without a strong basic chakra, spiritual practitioners have a tendency to "space out" and not accomplish success in their life both materially and spiritually.

Ain Soph Aur and the Twelfth Sephirah

In pranic healing and arhatic yoga there are **11 major chakras** within the body, plus the **12th chakra** located outside the body, **12** inches above the head. Therefore, in pranic healing and arhatic yoga there are also **12 chakras.**

Above the *Tree of Life* are *Ain Soph Aur* and the **12th** sephirah. The literal meaning of *Ain* is "no," *Soph* is "limit," and *Aur* is "light." The literal translation is therefore, "no limit light" or "limitless light." *Ain Soph Aur* means "Infinite Light." Where does this Infinite Light come from? Above *Ain Soph Aur* is *Ain Soph*, which means "no limit" or "infinite." The Infinite Light comes from what is called "The Infinite," *Ain Soph*. The Infinite what? Obviously "The Infinite Source." *Ain Soph*, therefore, means not only *The Infinite*, but the *Infinite Source* from which *The Infinite Light* comes from. *Ain Soph* comes from *Ain*, the literal translation for "No" or "Nothing."

The Incarnated Soul

Ain Soph Aur is actually the incarnated soul. The incarnated soul is "located in the **12th chakra** or the **12 sephirah** which is one foot or 30.5 centimeters above the head," as stated in Master Choa Kok Sui's book *Meditations for Soul Realization*. The 12th chakra looks like a golden star. Sometimes it is called the "Soul Star." The Tree of Life – the physical body and the energy body is actually within the incarnated soul, *Ain Soph Aur*.

From the **12th chakra**, the incarnated soul radiates outward, forming the "soul aura." The three silver cords and the three permanent seeds, the different bodies (the physical body, the energy body, the astral body and the mental body) are infused with the essence of the soul. This is also called the "Soul Energy." Just as the etheric body interpenetrates the physical body, and it is inside and outside the physical body, likewise, the essence of the soul interpenetrates the physical body; at the same time, it is beyond the physical body. That is why the physical body is actually within the soul, and not the soul within the physical body. The physical body is like a sponge. If you put the sponge in a bathtub filled with water, the water is inside and outside the sponge. In other words, the sponge is inside the water. The physical body, energy body, astral body and lower mental body are all inside the incarnated soul. Therefore, it would be accurate to define a person as "a soul with a physical body," rather than "a physical body with a soul." To express this more accurately, a person is a soul with a physical body and other subtle bodies. *Why is the incarnated soul called The Infinite Light?* To understand this, it is necessary to have a certain degree of inner experience or spiritual insight. You have to remember who you are. An intellectual comprehension that you are not the body is the first stage in spiritual development. The second stage is experiencing the body "disappearing." In the third stage, the yogi experiences himself as a being of divine flame radiating simultaneously in all directions throughout the inner cosmos. This is why the incarnated soul is called *Ain Soph Aur*, Infinite Light.

In the Christian tradition, the **12th chakra** and the incarnated soul are referred to as the *Pentecostal Fire*. It is called by Saint Paul as the "Holy Spirit." In the Egyptian tradition the incarnated soul is called *Ba*. In the Hindu tradition, it is called *Jivatma*, *Jiv* means "embodied" while *atma* means "self" or "soul." In Tibetan Buddhism, the incarnated soul is called the "Buddha nature." In Taoism, the incarnated soul is called the "spiritual fetus." The *Ain Soph Aur* or *Infinite Light* comes from the *higher soul*. This is why the *higher soul* is called *The Infinite Source*, the *Ain Soph*. The *higher soul* resides in a vehicle that is called in theosophy as the *causal body*. (**Source:** *The Spiritual Essence of Man* by Master Choa Kok Sui, 2003)

In many yoga texts you'll find the five sheaths - Annamaya Kosha (body), Pranamaya Kosha (prana), Manomaya Kosha (emotion), Vijnayanamaya Kosha (wisdom) and Anandamaya Kosha (bliss) - grouped into three. The physical body and vital force are called the sthula sharira, the "gross body." The mental body and intellect are called the sukshma sharira, the "subtle" or "astral body." The bliss sheath is called the karana sharira, the "causal body." The gross body disintegrates at death. The subtle body disintegrates at rebirth, allowing you to develop a new personality in your next life. The causal body reincarnates again and again, carrying your karma with it like luggage. It finally disintegrates at the time of liberation, when the higher Self disengages from the cycle of birth and death.

In the tantric tradition, spirit is often symbolized as Shiva, the transcendent Lord who is ever immersed in divine consciousness. Matter/energy is called Shakti, the Supreme Goddess whose divine body is this entire universe. It's said that they love each other with unspeakable intensity. Their supreme love is experienced in the anandamaya kosha, where spirit and matter passionately embrace. We can awaken our bliss sheath through three practices. The first is seva, selfless service. This opens our heart to our innate unity with other beings. The second is bhakti yoga, devotion to God. This opens our heart to our unity with the all-pervading Divine Being. The third is samadhi, intensely focused meditation, which opens our heart to our own divine being. By getting to know your five bodies and the inner Self (whose awareness illumines them all), you can experience the health and fulfillment of an enlightened life. **See Awakening your Kundalini, p. 31; Pancha Kosha, page 43; Koshas, five sheaths that wrap soul, p. 135**

The Microcosmic Orbit.

This is a classic Taoist Meditation method, with it's roots in India, for circulating and refining Qi via the circuit formed by the 'Governing Channel' from perineum up to head and the Conception Channel from head back down to perineum. Practicing the Microcosmic Orbit is a key step that enables more advanced practices.

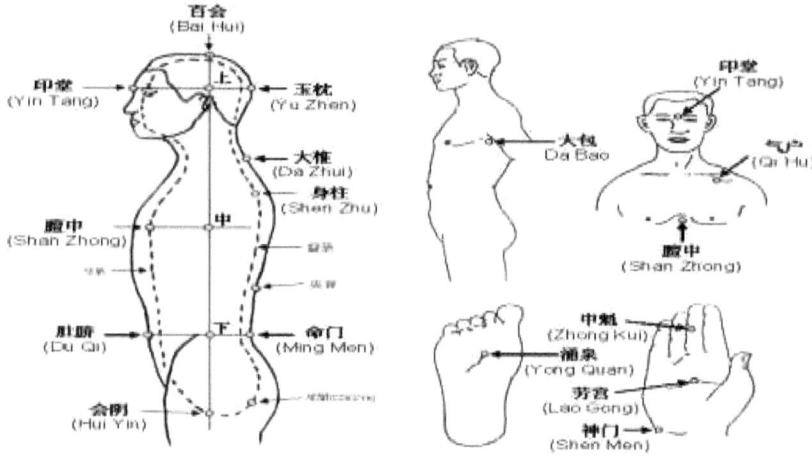

The Practice of the Microcosmic Orbit.

1. The first steps are to still the body, calm the mind, and regulate the breath. Sit, stand in Zhan Zhuang or lay on your back, in a quiet place, eyes closed lightly. If you are sitting, you should be upright, with your feet flat on the floor, sitting forward enough so your genitals are off the chair. Advanced practitioners can use many of the different Zhan Zhuang postures.
2. Focus your attention on your Dan Tien (just below your navel and above the Du Qi), and visualize a small ball of energy, a ball of golden or white light, bright and pure. Maintain the attention on the Dan Tien until you feel the energy of the ball. This could be heat, vibration, warmth or just a sensation of its presence.
3. Begin abdominal breathing. This breathing method starts when you inhale through your nose and your abdomen expands, not your chest. It is the way babies breathe. Exhale through your slightly opened mouth, keeping your tongue lightly touching your palate just behind your upper front teeth. When you exhale your abdominal muscles contract lightly to help expel air.
4. Inhale and visualize or imagine this small ball of Qi passing down from the Dan Tien, past the Hui Yin, up through the coccyx. Then visualize or imagine the Qi ball rising up to the Ming Men and then to where the ribs meet the spine, then going through this area and right on up to the back of the head, where it joins the neck.
5. Then visualize or imagine this Qi ball in the center of your brain, taking in healing energy through the Bai Hui point on the top of your head.
6. Next, focus your attention on the Yin Tang point between and just above the eyebrows and draw energy into the ball of Qi from this point as the ball passes and goes to the roof of your mouth. This may cause a tingling or throbbing sensation there. This ends your inhalation.
7. You may wish to stay and work with this Qi for a few minutes, before letting Qi sink down through the palate and tongue (which you still have lightly pressed onto your palate), into the throat to the heart (Shan Zhong point). Taking a breath or two while the Qi is in your mouth can help you focus on the ball.

8. Exhale and send the Qi down to your heart (Shan Zhong Point). From the heart, draw it down through the middle Dan Tien at your solar plexus, past your navel, and down into the lower Dan Tien, where energy gathers, mixes, and is reserved for internal circulation. Then begin another cycle.

Once the Qi is circulating, your breath will naturally become fine. This means it is smooth, not ragged or irregular. You can do this meditation from one to dozens of times. Qi circulation harmonizes and reforms, so that the vital fluids produced by daily life can produce true vitality.

If you have any physical problems or discomforts in a particular section of your body, while doing the orbit, hold the circulation and focus your Qi at the discomforting point and let it pulse there for a while. This will help heal and rejuvenate and improve the Qi flow.

This meditation may also cause the head to rock or the body to tremble, which, some believe, are signs of progress. If you have high blood pressure and want to use this meditation as part of your treatment, reverse the flow of the orbit, so that your Qi goes up during the inhale and back and down on the exhale.

The Microcosmic Orbit is a good practice for all Qigong students, and can be used before other meditations. You can use a few orbits in both directions during the day, to reduce stress. You can also do this lying down before sleep. Don't do this while driving or operating machinery!

If you have trouble visualizing or imagining the flow, you can think of a golf ball or ping-pong ball. You can even use one hand to trace the flow when you are sitting or standing.

NOTE by Ricardo B Serrano: The Microcosmic Orbit is the key to balancing energies in the body and the basic foundation for other advanced meditative practices such as the *Merkaba activation* and *Holographic Sound Healing* which I also facilitate. The Earth, Cosmic and Heavenly Energies derived from *Merkabah* activations are circulated, stored and grounded in the body's Microcosmic Orbit enhancing the physical, energy and spirit bodies while preventing at the same time Kundalini syndrome (psychosis) and other side effects of ungrounded energy practices. The Microcosmic Orbit Meditation with intention (Yi) will connect you to the Sun, Moon, planets, North Star and Big Dipper constellation (Heavenly Qi), Higher Self (Cosmic Qi) and Earth Qi adding more Qi into the microcosmic orbit (functional and governor channels) of your physical, energy and spirit bodies. These powerful meditation techniques on the human bioenergetic system are enhanced further by the addition of the Inner Smile, Invocation to unified chakra and Soul Realization meditation techniques and practices in this book.

Practical, tangible health benefits result from opening the Microcosmic Orbit. Increased resistance to stress and illness are the most evident. A heightened general level of energy follows from the conservation and recycling of the Life Force. A distinctly more centered and harmonious awareness results from balancing of internal energies through their circulation in the Orbit. Lowered internal tension helps the immune system by promoting the freer flow of lymph fluids.

The above practice of the Microcosmic Orbit is best done with me as your facilitator to safely awaken and regulate your kundalini energy through a special meditation that moves the *Soul Energy* through a series of energy channels called the "microcosmic orbit." Circulating the *Soul Energy* helps extract the "ancient seeds", pent-up emotions and negative crystallized thought patterns. **Read Bija mantras of seven chakras below; Awakening your Kundalini, page 31; Pancha Kosha, page 43**

You will first undertake the purification of the physical, etheric, astral, and mental bodies, then the chakras are substantially activated in a secret sequence to *safely and effectively awaken* and then circulate the Kundalini energy throughout the body. This technique is practiced by very advanced and evolved yogis. It is the foundation for building the much coveted *Sahhu* immortal energy body or "Golden Body"!

Bija Mantras of Seven Chakras

1. "LAM"- chakra 1 (root)
2. "VAM"- chakra 2 (sacral/navel)
3. "RAM"- chakra 3 (solar plexus)
4. "YAM"- chakra 4 (heart)
5. "HAM"- chakra 5 (throat)
6. "OM"- chakra 6 (third eye/brow)
7. "OM" or "AH" - chakra 7 (crown)

The seven chakras including their Bija mantras are activated along the Microcosmic Orbit from the root chakra up to the crown chakra.

CONCLUSION

NOTE by Ricardo B Serrano: I attended the July 20-29, 2012 *Sheng Zhen Teacher Training* in Rosemary Heights Retreat Center, Surrey, B.C. with teacher Li Junfeng and his daughter Li Jing where we practiced Hanuman Qigong, origin of the heart. It was an unforgettable heart opening experience where my heart integrated with spirit and heaven integrated with earth. I strongly felt my mind quieting down merging with the most purest Qi and love in the universe. The practice of Hanuman Qigong, *origin of the heart*, expresses these truths.

Thank you Heavenly Father and Mother for this beautiful world and the gift of Oneness.

"Unconditional love is the fulcrum of this universe, the original point of the universe. In the practice of Hanuman Qigong, efforts must be made to integrate the mind and heart, to feel the interaction between Love and Qi, restoring the experience of harmony in the world, in nature, and the Universe. In starting the day with the practice of Hanuman Qigong, one holds within, the desire to integrate heart and spirit, to arrive at the experience of Oneness. The rest of the day unfolds naturally from this sublime intention. At this moment, this is the highest service a human being can perform to humanity, to the universe, to Heaven.

When one finds true Oneness, there will be no words. Nothing can explain what Oneness truly is. One will only have the experience of Love and a smiling heart. No words can express that happiness and peace. It is beyond words. Oneness is everything. Oneness is the only truth worth seeking. Oneness is a gift from Heaven."

– *Hanuman Qigong, the practice of integrating the Heart and Spirit, a form of Sheng Zhen Gong*

1. What is Sheng Zhen Wuji Yuan Gong?

Sheng Zhen means the highest sacred truth which is unconditional love. Sheng Zhen is all forms of love put together such as kindheartedness, fraternal love, filial love, love for nature, love for oneself. Sheng Zhen is the essence of the universe. It is the spirit that permeates and moves the practice of Wuji Yuan Gong.
Sheng Zhen Wuji Yuan Gong is the original, timeless most basic form of Qigong that has the moving and non-moving forms with the goal of returning to Oneness through the *union of the three hearts* – union of your heart with the heart of the Universe and the heart of Mother Earth.

2. What is my understanding and experience of Sheng Zhen?

From my own experience as a Sheng Zhen practitioner and teacher for six years, I have seen that it is a medical, emotional and spiritual Qigong for myself and my students. As a medical Qigong, it improves the blood circulation and strengthens the physical body. It can remove stress, worries, anger, hatred, and nervousness so that its practitioner remains calm, at ease and balanced – therefore, it is an emotional Qigong. As a spiritual Qigong, it opens and purifies the heart and elevates the spirit. Only when the heart is open can the Qi flow and make you truly happy and free.

3. Why do I want to be a Sheng Zhen teacher?

I want to share the blessings that I have received through the practice of Sheng Zhen practice. As a Sheng Zhen teacher, I want others to experience the physical, emotional and spiritual benefits I have experienced from its practice.

Of all the number of Qigong styles I have practiced in the past, Sheng Zhen Gong is very special because its philosophy and practice has the power to open the heart which rules the Qi. In Chinese medicine, it is the Qi that rules and leads the blood. What rules the Qi? It is the power of an open heart that rules the Qi and makes the practice of Sheng Zhen life-transforming. To conclude, the reason why I want to be a Sheng Zhen teacher is because Sheng Zhen is my path to freedom and happiness, and is a gift from Heaven. Its non-moving and moving Qigong forms unite my heart with the heart of the Universe and the heart of Mother Earth for healing and returning to oneness

Ricardo B Serrano, R.Ac.

Certified Sheng Zhen Gong teacher

Healing and Returning to Oneness

"Let Love light your path, Truth guide your way, and Joy sing from your soul." – Sananda

I am grateful and fortunate to have studied within the span of 30 years with my pranic healing, meditation and Qigong teachers that made me realize my long-time dream of mastering energy healing, and eventually returning to oneness in the process.

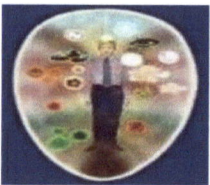

Negative emotions, thought forms in aura (*the problem*)

How is it done? What are the necessary keys to healing stress-related diseases, and self-mastery or soul-realization? These inquiries assisted me to search for the answers to these questions from the ancient eastern yoga, pranic healing and Qigong perspective.

How do I know that I am on the right path? I know I am on the right path because of the blissful and heart opening gift of oneness I am continuously experiencing when I practice the spiritually empowering pranic healing, Surya Namaskar, meditation with Ashtanga Yoga Hand Mudras, Gayatri Mantra and Hanuman Qigong regularly integrating heaven and earth, and integrating my heart with spirit – my soul and the soul of the universe.

The word mudra means "seal" or "lock." Mudras are practiced to awaken and direct the flow of kundalini (Qi), to induce stillness and strength, and to "lock in" the benefits from the healing and returning to oneness practices such as Surya Namaskar, Hand Mudras and Asanas (postures) of Ashtanga Yoga and Qigong.

I have lovingly recorded and written these ancient eastern yoga teachings, meditation and Qigong techniques – *Techniques of a Master* – integrated path on how to become a divine medium through this book and the other six books of the *You Hold the Keys to Healing* to benefit those serious seekers seeking a real ancient, time-proven, safe, grounded and balanced approach to energy healing and soul-realization.

"The most beautiful thing we can experience is the Mysterious. It is the source of all true science." – Albert Einstein

"As long as one is substantially connected to the higher soul, one remains whole and healthy." – Pranic Healing *Grand Master Choa Kok Sui*

"To better the quality of qi, to improve the circulation, human hearts must open. Unconditional love is the key that unleases the power of qi. When the heart is open, immersed in the experience of love, the interflow of qi can take place making the qi work." – Sheng Zhen Gong *Master Li Junfeng*

"*Ishvarapranidhan*a (surrender to God): Recognition that the limited, ego-self is an illusion; channeling of energies toward the realization of truth, or God. One who sees the Self in all beings and who has surrendered the ego of being the "doer" is the true practitioner *of Ishvarapranidhana*. Perfection *of Ishvarapranidhana* brings success in *samadh*i (superconsciousness)." – Baba Hari Dass

Love is. Love will always be. Love is eternity.

Important Quotations on Pranic Healing, Character Building and Soul Realization by Grand Master Choa Kok Sui:

"Pranic Healing is a bridge to spirituality. Healing is Active Meditation. Healing is Meditation in Motion."

"A Healer's attitude is very important. It is only when you are humble that you become a Powerful Healer."

"Character building is very important because it is a way to purify the incarnated soul. As you purify yourself thoroughly, your incarnated soul will be able to function on a higher level of consciousness until it can unite with your higher soul."

"Inner forgiveness is therapeutic. If you do not forgive, you cannot be internally healed. Forgiving heals the soul. Make a list of all your enemies and those who have hurt you. Mentally visualize forgiving each one of them."

"You are a Soul with a body, not a body with a Soul. The Soul is the Gateway to Heaven within you. When you are filled with soul energy you become magnetic."

11 Teachings to help on the journey to Soul Realization: (1) Practice humility; (2) Give up pride and self-delusion; (3) Practice loving kindness; (4) Give up anger, hatred and vindictiveness; (5) Practice generosity; (6) Avoid greed and stealing in its different aspects; (7) Practice honesty; (8) Avoid maliciousness and exploiting lies; (9) Practice moderation; (10) Avoid excessiveness; (11) Do not allow yourself to be enslaved by your lower nature.

"When you get angry with someone and you are about to say or do something nasty, touch your heart, bless the person and silently say: "God's blessings and peace be with me and be with you. I am constantly radiating Goodness; Only Goodness can come to me."

"Whether or not you have a better life depends on you. It depends on your attitude. Forgiveness is not a matter of who is right or wrong. It is a matter of doing the right thing. If you seek revenge, you will not have inner peace. By forgiving and blessing, you stop wallowing in mud and you achieve Inner peace and freedom."

"Spiritual Development is dependant upon Inner Purification or character building. Without inner purification, the meditator may become psychologically imbalanced. It is also important to generate good karma by doing service or tithing."

"Every time you refrain from unwholesome action the connection with your higher Buddha Nature increases."

"When you seek to console, you are filled with light, love and power instead of wallowing in your own mud, in your own selfish misery and pain."

"Loving energy is real! It can be used to neutralize antagonistic energy. The antidote for cruelty is Loving Kindness and Non-Injury. Without love there is only criticism, hatred and anger."

"Do not meditate too much on those who hurt you or aggravate you. What you meditate on, you become! Meditate on the Guru and the Higher Beings and their disciples who are spiritual energy transformers."
"The moon, the earth, the planets, the sun, the galaxy and the universe are spiritual energy transformers."

"Spiritual energy is needed for expansion of consciousness and traveling in the inner worlds. Stillness and awareness are not enough. No spiritual energy, no expansion of consciousness."

"The more you develop the virtues, the stronger your connection to God will become."
"Dirty food dirties only your body, but dirty words dirty your Soul!"

"Every day you take a shower. Practicing the *Meditation on Twin Hearts* is like taking a Spiritual Shower. When your aura is clean, you experience a Higher Level of awareness. When your aura is clean, you see through things more clearly. Even your Good Luck increases."

"Soul-realization is nothing more than the incarnated soul realizing that it is not the body and it is one with the higher soul or the I AM. This is the meaning of yoga or illumination." "The soul, its subtle vehicles and its physical body, must be given very minute dosages of intense spiritual energy, of very minute dosages of oneness with God. The capacity of the soul and its vehicles, and its physical body must be gradually developed. Too much intense divine energy, too much divine oneness may cause the body to become sick, to become permanently damaged or to die." – *Grand Master Choa Kok Sui, Meditations for Soul Realization* and *The Existence of God is Self-Evident*

Techniques of a Master

There are many paths to healing and returning to oneness, however, this is my integrated path that works for me, and as my mission to serve others I'm sharing the ancient Advanced Qigong Meditation Techniques of a Master – integrated path on how to become a divine medium thoroughly covered in this book and the other six books of the *You Hold the Keys to Healing*.

The Advanced Qigong Meditation Techniques included in the seven books:

- Enlightenment Qigong forms – Pan Gu Shen Gong, Primordial Wuji Qigong with Sheng Zhen Gong
- Hanuman Qigong and mantras for healing and returning to oneness
- Qigong for Prevention and Treatment of Post-Kundalini Syndromes
- Kashmir Shaivism Tantric meditation techniques and Tibetan Shamanic Qigong (Qi Dao)
- Merkabah activation technique, Triangles Work and Great Invocation
- **Yogic breathing with mantras**
- Meditation on the Soul, Circulation of Soul energy
- Soul realization – union of the incarnated soul with the higher soul
- Pranic Healing techniques, Chakras and Energy Bubble (Aura)
- Guru Yoga, Gurukripa Yoga or Guru Meditation
- Relationship Healing with the Five Agreements
- Abundance meditation, meditation on three hearts, unified chakra meditation, invocations
- Healing Conscious Mind Encodements with hologram of love Merkabah energy ball of light
- Character building, discipline or inner purification, and Prayer of St Francis of Assisi
- Psychic Self Defense through Merkabah meditation
- Other ancient and modern holographic sound healing techniques and ascension techniques ...
- Acupuncture, Qigong, Herbs, nutrition, EFT for stress, thyroid conditions, drug addiction, chronic diseases!
- Awakening your Kundalini and Attainment of the Sahhu or immortal golden lightbody
- Ashtanga Yoga Hand Mudras with Gayatri Mantra, and Hanuman Gayatri Mantra, Kuan Yin Standing Qigong
- Awakening the Soul Qigong, 8 Extraordinary Meridians Qigong, GuoLin (Anti-Cancer) Qigong and Surya Namaskar

A Note from a Finder of Lost Tech ...

I want to take this opportunity to thank you for taking the time out of your busy schedules to read this book and hopefully my other six books that include *Oneness with Shiva* and *The Cure & Cause of Cancer*. For more than three decades, I have studied and practiced with eastern and western Meditation and Qigong masters to make meditation and spiritual healing as workable and practical as possible for initiates as well as experts. Because of the safety and results of the integrated expanded system I have evolved from my spiritual studies and experiences, I believe that the Advanced Qigong Meditation Techniques can speed up your spiritual quest for healing and Self-Mastership or Soul-Realization in this lifetime.

The Atma (Soul) Yoga meditation and Qigong Forms is an integration of Surya Namaskar, Sri Vidya Kundalini meditation, Ashtanga Yoga Hand Mudras with Gayatri Mantra, Kuan Yin Standing Qigong, Awakening the Soul Qigong, Hanuman Qigong, Eight extraordinary meridians Qigong, and Guo Lin (anti-cancer) Qigong that will heal your disease and return you to oneness with Spirit Soul. Why does it work? By building the Three Treasures – Jing, Qi and Shen, and the body's Wei Qi field, healing and enlightenment have been made possible for centuries in every ancient spiritual tradition.**See Atma (Soul) Yoga Meditation and Qigong Forms** at http://innerway.ca/?p=6454

Rather than experimenting on your own the many spiritual paths for healing and Self-Mastership which is time consuming, downright risky without a guide and sometimes disappointing, why not benefit from a workable SYSTEM (Save Your Self Time Energy and Money) I have compiled from my over 30 years of spiritual studies, experiences and research by attending my healing, meditation, and Qigong workshops through the Integral Studies of Inner Sciences (innerway.ca)?

My blessings to you! Thanks again for your time and interest. May God's grace be with you!

Ricardo B Serrano, R.Ac., Master Pranic Healer

Notable Quotations by Ricardo B Serrano, R.Ac. aka Yogi Sharanananda

"A Master Pranic Healer can transmit Shakti (Shaktipat) to a student at a distance during a healing or kundalini session much the same way as an Arhatic Yoga Master does."

"The Merkabah meditation magnifies Pranic Healing a hundred fold. The Merkabah meditation also magnifies Crystal Healing a hundred fold.

Holographic Sound Healing exponentially amplifies holographic healing. Therefore, an integration of Qigong, Pranic Healing, Crystal Healing, Holographic Sound Healing, and the Merkabah meditation with Acupuncture and Herbs is my method of choice depending on the needs of my client."

"Healing a client from a distance no matter how far is best done with the Merkabah meditation augmented with Holographic Sound and Meditation on Twin Hearts."

"Learning and practicing Qigong by rooting or grounding to Mother Earth is the best remedy and preventive measure for the common illness of meditators which is the Post Kundalini syndrome."

"You become a Master when you practice Merkabah activation, pranic healing and Qigong because every Master uses Merkabah as a vehicle for light body activation, healing and spiritual ascension."

"The Merkabah meditation and Holographic Sound healing have been gifted by the Ascended Masters to provide us again with the tools to regain our birthright and powers as spiritual beings."

"One can become enlightened if one questions one's thoughts and realizes that uninvestigated thoughts and beliefs cause one's suffering."

"God is luminous Light and ever-expanding sea of Qi energy and universal consciousness as experienced and described by yogis and masters in all spiritual traditions as an ecstatic state of unconditional Love."

"Darshan is an experience of overwhelming love, joy and happiness by opening one's heart to God's vibration of unconditional Love through a Master."

"With compassion, one can love unconditionally, With unconditional love, one can heal boundlessly,

With boundless energy, one can ascend spiritually." See **Gayatri Mantra with Ashtanga Yoga Hand Mudras, pages 138-139**

"Become aware of the *five gateways* – Baihui or crown chakra, Laogong of both hands, and Yong Quan (bubbling spring) of both feet – when practicing Qigong, pranic healing and meditation to connect with heaven and earth."

"Inner Forgiveness or law of mercy and character building or inner purification are absolutely necessary for meditators, pranic healers and Qigong practitioners to heal and purify the *incarnated soul* so it can unite with the *higher soul*. Without inner purification, the meditator may become psychologically imbalanced, and soul realization – union of the *incarnated soul* with the *higher soul* or *the I AM* – is not possible."

"Ascension is achievable through God's grace when you unify through your heart center all your chakras into one and balance and purify the threefold flame within your heart where God is through inner forgiveness, inner purification, the Merkabah Hologram of Love activation, pranic healing and Qigong."

"I truly believe that, "Nothing has the greatest power to heal, but Self". The body has the innate power to heal itself, we just need to allow and open up. I like that the word for health in Sanskrit is svastha, meaning to be established in the Self, to be at home. The beauty of the Sanskrit is that these are not just words, but philosophies. The concept of Self and home is missing in the West. To be grounded in the Self, to be at home with the Self, to be established in the Self, then the wisdom of the body awakens and guides you. That is the yogic concept of healing." See **Awakening your Kundalini, page 31**

About the Author: Ricardo B. Serrano, R.Ac., a registered acupuncturist, master pranic healer, author of Meditation and Qigong Mastery book with Omkabah Heart Lightbody Activation, Serpent of Light Omkabah, and Maitreya (Shiva) Shen Gong Procedure videos and other related meditation and healing books, Qi-healer and certified Qigong teacher/ founder of Maitreya (Shiva) Shen Gong and integrative Enlightenment Qigong. He has been trained by Pan Gu Shengong Master Ou Wen Wei, Wuji Qigong Master Michael Winn, Sheng Zhen Qigong Master Li Jun Feng, Master Pranic Healer Choa Kok Sui, Master Mike Nator, Master Nona Castro, Zhan Zhuang Qigong Master Richard Mooney, Merkaba Master Alton Kamadon, Qi Dao Master Lama Somananda Tantrapa, Toltec Master don Miguel Ruiz, Baba Hari Dass, Raja Choudhury and other meditation, Qigong, herbal, nutrition and acupuncture teachers. He has been practicing herbal, Qi-healing or pranic healing (Qigong with acupuncture) for over 30 years.

He specializes in stress and pain management, cancer and chronic diseases, and alcohol and drug rehabilitation through natural healing alternative modalities – *functional medicine* – such as counselling, meditation, nutrition, exercise, holographic sound healing, Qigong, Qi-healing, intranasal light therapy, EFT, acupuncture, herbs, acupressure – *Techniques of a Master*. Mitochondrial dysfunction is the root cause of chronic diseases. For more information on intranasal light therapy, read *Return to Oneness with the Tao*, and *The Cure and Cause of Cancer*.

Ego says: Once everything falls into place, I will find peace. **Spirit** says: Find peace and everything falls into place. Follow your spirit/heart/inner guidance's voice and find your peace. You can find your peace through the regular practice of meditation and Qigong. When you find your peace, the world takes on a new perspective.

He continues to educate his clients and everyone worldwide through his meditation and Qigong workshops, downloadable ebooks, and holistic websites at holisticwebs.com, qiwithoutborders.org, qigonghealer.com, freedomhealthrecovery.com, qigongmastery.ca, acutcmdetox.com, innerway.ca and keystohealing.ca. His seven books are: *Meditation and Qigong Mastery, Return to Oneness with the Tao, Return to Oneness with Spirit through Pan Gu Shen Gong, Keys to Healing and Self-Mastery according to the Hathors, Return to Oneness with Shiva, Oneness with Shiva and The Cure & Cause of Cancer.* His two companion DVDs are *Maitreya (Shiva) Shen Gong* and *Omkabah Heart Lightbody Activation*.

To prevent *Kundalini syndromes,* Enlightenment Qigong forms have to be integrated with meditation by rooting or grounding the *Kundalini Shakti* to Mother Earth.

"Functional Medicine is a true combination of Chinese Medicine, Western Medicine and scientific research. It combines the philosophy of balance and how to restore function from Chinese Medicine and the knowledge of biochemistry and physiology of Western Medicine with the latest scientific research about how our genetics, environment and lifestyle all interact with each other. Functional medicine focuses assessment and intervention at the root levels of metabolic imbalance and is an evolution in the practice of medicine that addresses the healthcare needs of the 21st century by focusing on prevention and uncovering the underlying causes of serious chronic disease. Instead of just suppressing symptoms, it deals with the root causes of disease and is less concerned with making a diagnosis and more concerned with the underlying imbalances, which are the mechanisms of the disease process. As opposed to Western Medicine, Functional medicine treats the patient and not the disease. In addition, it provides a framework for the practice of medicine that uses all the tools of healing, both conventional and alternative, to address the whole person rather than an isolated set of symptoms. I have studied Acupuncture and Chinese Medicine which taught me to see the body from a holistic perspective. Now Functional Medicine gives me a framework to combine this with a Western understanding of the body." – *Dr. Frank Lipman* Whatever the diagnosis of your disease, you do not have to expect the worst. For every problem, there are solutions. You hold the keys to healing. We are not human beings having a spiritual experience, but *spiritual beings* having a human experience.

www.ingramcontent.com/pod-product-compliance
Lightning Source LLC
Chambersburg PA
CBHW041518220426
43667CB00002B/26